CHURCHILL'S FOLLY

ALSO BY CHRISTOPHER CATHERWOOD

Why the Nations Rage: Killing in the Name of God

*Whose Side Is God On?: Nationalism
and Christianity*

*Christians, Muslims and Islamic Rage: What Is
Going On and Why It Happened*

*The Balkans in World War Two: Britain's
Balkan Dilemma*

CHURCHILL'S FOLLY

*How Winston Churchill
Created Modern Iraq*

CHRISTOPHER CATHERWOOD

CARROLL & GRAF PUBLISHERS
NEW YORK

CHURCHILL'S FOLLY
How Winston Churchill Created Modern Iraq

Carroll & Graf Publishers
An Imprint of Avalon Publishing Group Inc.
245 West 17th Street
11th Floor
New York, NY 10011

AVALON
publishing group incorporated

Library of Congress Cataloging-in-Publication Data is available.

ISBN: 0-7867-1351-8

Printed in the United States of America
Distributed by Publishers Group West

To Richard and Sally, two very special friends without whom this book would never have happened. And to Paulette, my wondrous wife and most special friend, who makes all my books possible.

CONTENTS

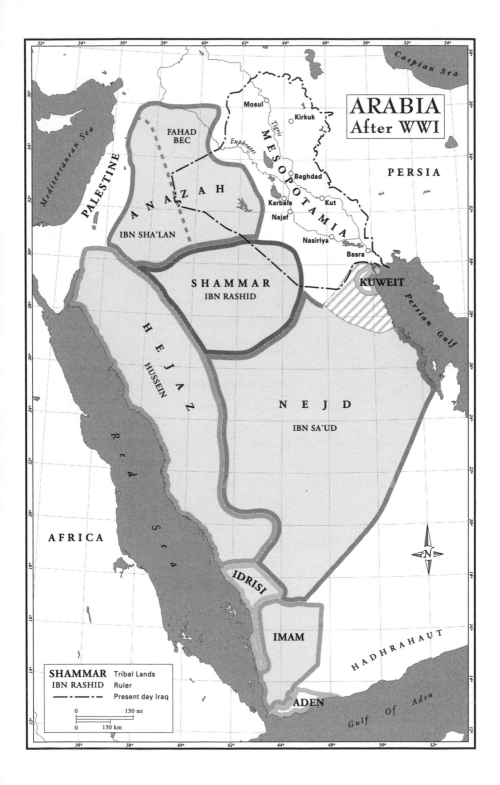

ACKNOWLEDGMENTS

Most authors conclude their acknowledgments by thanking their long-suffering and patient spouse. So let me break with tradition and start by thanking mine—my wife Paulette. She is my constant muse, best critic, inspiration, friend, soul mate, encourager, and far more besides. No thanks to her could ever possibly express the debt of fullest gratitude that I owe to her.

So far as family is concerned, my parents, Fred and Elizabeth Catherwood, most kindly gave me an office in the attic of their home in Balsham, where I can work in beautiful, tranquil, and highly conducive fifteenth-century settings. To them my thanks is also profound.

I was once an editor myself, so I would next like to give warmest possible thanks to my three splendid editors, Philip Turner of Carroll & Graf in New York, and the excellent freelance editor he chose, Doris Cross, also in New York; and in London, Nicola Chalton of Constable & Robinson. I know what a difficult job being an editor can be, and no three people could have done it better. My most heartfelt thanks go to them all.

This book also arose, indirectly, out of conversations with several friends, especially Richard Reynolds, the legendary bookseller at Heffers in Cambridge, and Gene Brissie, the equally revered doyen of publishing in New York. Richard introduced me to another much-loved character of the publishing world, Andy Hayward, of Constable & Robinson. Andy in turn enabled both Gene and me to consolidate a happy link with Carroll & Graf. To all of them I owe profound thanks, and since Richard and Sally Reynolds are two of my and my wife's dearest friends, the dedication of this book to them is thus fully deserved.

Very special thanks must go to the first-class and efficient staff of the Churchill Archives at Churchill College, Cambridge. The vast majority of the documents quoted in this book are to be found in the archive, especially in Chartwell Papers 16 and 17, which deal with the Iraq issues during Churchill's time as Colonial Secretary. These papers are a treasure trove, and their preservation is something for which generations of historians have had cause to be very grateful.

I need to add here that I am also more than grateful to the archives staff and to the copyright holders of the archives (the Churchill family for private correspondence and the British government for Churchill's official correspondence) for their very kind permission in allowing me to quote from the many letters and papers that Churchill wrote back in 1921 and 1922.

I have the pleasure of being attached to several splendid academic bodies, all of which made this a much easier book to write. (Here, as always, I must add that any mistakes or differences in interpretation in this book are my fault and not theirs.)

The first of these is the University of Richmond in Richmond, Virginia. This university has me as a teacher every year in their annual summer school, which enables me to teach a group of highly intelligent, often slightly older, mature students about the subject of whatever book I am writing at the time. Warmest thanks, therefore, to Pat Brown, Cheryl Callahan, David Kitchen, Michele Cox, and Krittika Osanit for making this annual event possible. Not only that, but the History Department makes me a Writer in Residence, with awesome facilities generously given to me—so long as a book appears. The present book is the product of such a recent visit, and I am more than grateful to the legendary John Treadway and his equally delightful colleagues, Hugh West (the Department Chair), John Gordon (his predecessor), Robert Brencher (for lending me so many helpful books), and Bob Kenzer, all of whom have been models of encouragement and kindness. The warmth of everyone toward a visiting Briton and his British ways could not be greater.

Still on the same side of the Atlantic, I am also continually grateful to my friends Professors A. E. Dick Howard and Larry Adams of the University of Virginia. My re-entry into academic life and my rediscovery of the history of the Middle East owe much to both of them, not least for their helping John Treadway get me a much-needed fellowship in 2001 at the Institute on Violence and Survival at the University of Virginia's Virginia Foundation for the Humanities and Public Policy.

My debts of gratitude in Cambridge are almost too many to mention. I will start with Professor Geoffrey Lee Williams and his wife, Janice, who run the American-linked Institute of Economic and Political Studies (INSTEP). It is affiliated with Wake Forest, Tulane, Villanova, and several other well-known American universities; and it is teaching history for them that enables me to spend the rest of my time indulging in that increasingly rare academic luxury—writing books. Major thanks go to them and to the mutual friend who linked us, Dr. Philip Towle, the distinguished former Director of Cambridge University's Centre of International Studies.

I am also more than grateful to St. Edmund's College, Cambridge, for allowing me the pleasure of being part of a collegiate body in Cambridge. St. Edmund's is perhaps unique in the international spread of its student body and for the fact that most of its undergraduates are mature students, over twenty-one years old. It therefore has a very special and cosmopolitan atmosphere that makes membership in it all the more precious. Special thanks go to the retiring Master, Professor Sir Brian Heap, for extending my stay at St. Edmund's, to the Finance Director, Moira Gardner, and her front-office team, for making it so effortless, and to numerous members of the Senior Combination Room, especially Drs. Simon Mitton and Brian Stanley, for making possible so many fascinating and enlightening conversations there over many a cup of coffee.

I also have the pleasure of teaching for Cambridge University's Institute of Continuing Education, which means I am lecturing to older students, all of whom really want to learn. Teaching them, and responding to the incisive questions they ask, is always good for the gray cells, and warmest thanks are due here to those who make it possible: Linda Fisher, Katherine Roddwell, and the soon-to-retire Graham Howes.

Finally, many special thanks are due to those on my e-mail list, some of whom I have thanked already, who give me moral support that is most welcome. In addition, Mark Ashton, Will and Corinna Powell, and James and Camilla Ward in Cambridge, and Frank and Carolyn James and Professor Richard and Mrs. (Shirley) Chewning in the United States have been unstinting in their encouragement. I thank them all.

Christopher Catherwood
Cambridge, England
January 2004

INTRODUCTION

We live in a world that many great people have made, not to mention scores of unsung individuals across the generations. Winston Churchill, surely indisputably, is one of the "great men" of history. The countless ordinary soldiers of World War Two—justly described today as the "greatest generation"—also played their vital roles, men like my wife's Uncle Lacey, who spent his sister's wedding day in 1944 crossing the English Channel, thousands of miles away from the happy ceremony in Virginia, to land and fight on the beaches of Normandy. Winston Churchill, Lacey Foster Paulette, Jr.—they have been, in their own ways, the history-makers of our times.

In calling this book *Churchill's Folly*, I am not necessarily taking sides, either supporting those who ascribe everything that happens to the decisions and whims of a few outstanding individuals (what our nineteenth-century ancestors called the "Great Man Theory of History"), or supporting the Marxists and others who equally vigorously ascribe the course of history to impersonal forces and inevitable economic factors. What I have tried to do in this book is demonstrate that our fate is often a mix of the two: the interaction of someone like Winston Churchill, one of the most dynamic and influential men of recent centuries, with the forces of Arab nationalism that reflect the wish of all oppressed peoples to be free from tyranny. My hope is that this exploration of the interplay of unique individuals and impersonal tidal forces that reordered the landscape of the Middle East in 1922 will shed some light on the world we live in today.

Take just two wars in the immediate past in which British, American, and other troops have fought: Kosovo and Iraq. These wars were the result of decisions made by leaders such as Winston Churchill, Woodrow Wilson, and other statesmen of the period from 1917 to 1922.

Look at a map of Africa. How many straight lines do you see? The answer is that, of the boundaries separating one country from another, *many* are straight lines. But how many straight lines do you see in a map of Europe? Not nearly as many. A great number of Africa's borders were created by European conquerors in the nineteenth-century era of colonial expansion; the sole concern of the officials who drew them was often to apportion how much land would go to each of the competing empires.

But groups of people do not live according to straight lines drawn with a ruler. Ethnic boundaries are very complex things, as the peacemakers at Versailles quickly discovered. Worse still, some ethnic groups live in separated enclaves, surrounded by other groups that hate them. As we know, this was to be a major cause of the Second World War, as Hitler used the fact that German minority groups lived all over parts of Central and Eastern Europe as an excuse to begin his campaigns of conquest.

The ethnic problems that the peacemakers could not solve after the First World War did not end with the Allied victory in the Second. In the twenty-first century, we *still* live in a world created early in the twentieth by Wilson, Lloyd George, Clemenceau, Orlando, and others.

If you look at a map of Europe in, say, 1909, the year after the massive Austro-Hungarian empire formally seized Bosnia, and then at a map of the same region in, say, 1923, you will discover a country that literally did not exist before—Yugoslavia, the land of the Southern Slavs. What we are talking of here some sociologists call *imagined communities,* or artificially created states that have no history *in their present format*—a very important qualifier. What it means is that many ancient regions rich with history did not exist prior to 1919 as the countries they are called on today's map. They were mere provinces of the Ottoman Empire, ruled from Constantinople.

Of course empires themselves are artificial, whether centered around a nation's conquests or the prowess in battle of a particular warrior. The Ottoman Empire, of which present-day Serbia and present-day Iraq were both part, was exactly that—an accumulation of lands, from the Hungarian border in Europe to the Atlantic coast of Morocco, conquered over the course of centuries by a powerful dynasty and its generals.

Up until 1912, both Kosovo and Iraq, now very distinct and geographically distant countries, were an integral part of the empire of the Ottoman Turks, who, as a fairly insignificant Turkish Muslim group in the fourteenth century, began to create an empire in Europe, Asia, and northern Africa that would last right up until 1918, and, as a legal entity, until 1922.

In 1918, following the fatal decision of the Ottomans to ally themselves with Germany against France and Britain in World War One, their once-great empire was defeated and utterly shattered. The same year saw imperial collapse on a previously unimaginable scale, with the downfall of the Austro-Hungarian, Russian, and German empires as well. The end of empires is often the result of great tides of economic fluctuation and of ideological passions—in the case of the empires that fell in 1918, a wave of nationalism and the corresponding desire of subject peoples to rule themselves.

"Impersonal forces"—war, nationalism, declining economies—have the upper hand, it seems, and the wishes of any individual are no match against the tide of inevitability. But the story does not end here. The key thing is that rulers have *choices,* and, as I argue in this book, their reactions, often made on very human grounds, make the crucial difference in the course of history. This is exactly what happened when it came to the key decisions that were made on what to do with the collapse of the centuries-old Ottoman Empire and, in particular, that part of it we now call Iraq.

In another book I wrote, *Why the Nations Rage: Killing in the Name of God,* I show how the choices Woodrow Wilson made about how to divide the European part of the old Ottoman possessions, such as Kosovo, set in motion a chain of events that led right down to that region's war in 1999.

This book looks at some of the other choices that had to be made: in particular, what to do with the Arab-speaking Asian region of the old empire. The decisions made by Winston Churchill, the British Secretary of State first for War and then for the Colonies, included the creation of an entirely new country, Iraq; and his actions had repercussions that led to the war in which British and American troops fought in 2003.

At the start of the twenty-first century, we live in a world that has not yet fully coped with the consequences of the fall of those once-mighty empires back in 1917 and 1918. The wars in the 1990s over Bosnia, Serbia, and Kosovo, the Gulf War in 1991, the conflict over Iraq in 2003, the endless Israeli-Palestinian dispute, and even the crazed dreams of Osama bin Laden and the horrors of September 11, 2001—*all* can be traced directly back to the slow decline of the Turkish Ottoman Empire. This decline stretched from the

year of Napoleon's successful attack on Egypt, 1798, to the defeat of the Turks
in 1918 and the Ottoman Empire's formal abolition in the 1920s.

When it came to the crucial decisions on what to do with the Asian
possessions of the Ottomans, few people played as pivotal a role as Winston
Churchill. He was to favor first one solution and then another; but by the
time he lost office in 1922, he had created a map of the Middle East that,
with a few changes here and there, has lasted until this very day.

Iraq—or Mesopotamia, as it was originally known during Churchill's
tenure of office—was a wholly new state created by the great man himself.
Unlike other artificial nations brought into being at that time, such as the
former Yugoslavia, now broken up into several states after bloody civil wars,
Iraq, for all its artificial borders, still exists. But just as the death of the local
strongman of Yugoslavia, Marshal Tito, led to the violent disintegration of
his country and the bloodbath of the 1990s, so too might Iraq now slide into
chaos as its three very different component cultures seek to coexist without
the glue of tyranny to hold them together. Some ethnically diverse countries,
such as Switzerland, for example, have managed to remain cohesive for centuries. One can only hope that such will be the fate of the Iraqis now that
they are free. If it turns out otherwise, one can only lament that so unlikely
and disparate a nation existed because of Churchill's folly.

A final word should be said about the archives upon which I have
based this book. These are the Chartwell Papers at Churchill College, Cambridge, at their archives center. Since Churchill's official biography was completed some years ago, this archive has been a treasure trove for historians, as
Churchill kept just about everything, even down to restaurant receipts and
railway tickets.

Other historians had, of course, delved into the Chartwell Papers
before I did, not least of whom is Sir Martin Gilbert himself, Churchill's official biographer. But I think that *Churchill's Folly* is the first book to hone in
on the documents that relate specifically to the creation of Iraq and to repro-
duce many of them in its pages.

The official life of a figure of Churchill's stature has two disadvantages.
First, it is almost too detailed, in that it encompasses absolutely everything
Churchill; in our period, for example, his paintings as well as his politics.
Second, Sir Martin is deliberately narrative and nonanalytical. This is fine for

learning precisely what Churchill did on any particular day of his life, but there are no assessments, no critical analysis of, for example, whether a decision was a good one. For those just wanting an old-fashioned story, this is fine; but these days, surely, historians are expected to examine their subjects in a more inquisitive way.

Naturally, many historians have looked at Churchill's role in Palestine and written excellent books, such as those by David Fromkin and by Efraim and Inari Karsh. But they, I think, give us a slightly incomplete picture; the aim of the present book is to include what others have either left out or only skirted over in passing. Not only that; I look at the events of the time specifically through the prism of Churchill himself. While Churchill is pivotal to the authors I have just mentioned, they devote equal attention to the many other key players, whereas Churchill is truly central to this account of the creation of Iraq.

My aim, therefore, was to combine a look at one of the historically most interesting areas of the world, Iraq, with a study of Winston Churchill, perhaps the greatest Briton of all time, at a time before the events occurred that made him so deservedly famous and revered.

CHAPTER ONE

FROM ABRAHAM TO ALLENBY

I
n March 1921, Winston Churchill, the newly appointed Secretary of State for the Colonies, summoned a large team of his advisers to meet together in a luxury hotel in Cairo. Over the course of a few days, the assembled experts, including such luminaries as T. E. Lawrence (Lawrence of Arabia), Gertrude Bell, the eminent archaeologist, and other specialists, created a brand-new country—Iraq. Ever since its creation in 1922, its name has evoked war, intrigue, oppression, and general mayhem. Yet the land Iraq inhabits has a history that is very familiar to us, particularly if we have ever studied ancient history or been taught Bible stories in Sunday School.

The common heritage of biblical history explains the international outrage at the looting of the Baghdad museums in 2003. There are few major museums in the West today that do not count among their possessions artifacts from the major archaeological expeditions to the region early in the twentieth century (which include those made by two of Churchill's key advisers, Gertrude Bell and T. E. Lawrence). Today, certainly in Western Europe, far fewer people read the Bible than was the case in the 1920s for Churchill and his contemporaries, who, even if they were not regular churchgoers later in life, would most likely have learned the Bible stories in childhood.

Because of our childhood memories, many of us think we know the history of the region, but what we remember is often misleading.

Consider the following:

Abraham was an Iraqi exile who moved to Israel. . . .

That, we quickly realize, is an *anachronism,* rather like the famous lines in Shakespeare's *Julius Caesar* when one of the conspirators hears the chiming of a clock, a device that was not invented until more than a millennium after Caesar's death.

History is, unfortunately, full of such anachronisms, with people reading present-day realities and disputes back into the past. Tragically, during the twentieth century, millions of people were massacred purely on the basis of such readings of history—the subject of many recent books and one of the main themes of this book: *Churchill invented Iraq, and the present-day country of that name did not exist before he did so.* To see how anachronistic this statement is, we need only go back to the prehistoric times of the geographic area that is now within the borders of Iraq. To see the dangers of this view of history, we need only look at one of its main practitioners—none other than Saddam Hussein, who misused the past in order to bolster his hold on power.

Abraham, the father of the Jewish nation, indisputably came from Ur, a city now within Iraq; but to call him an Iraqi would, of course, be ridiculous. Saddam Hussein, however, did not hesitate to liken himself to the great Assyrian ruler Nebuchadnezzar. Saddam even spent a large fortune rebuilding the ancient city of Babylon, emblazoning his own name on the façades of replicated buildings, just as the city's ancient rulers had left theirs on the original structures. Saddam's pretensions were as absurd as considering Abraham an Iraqi, but Saddam did not hesitate to appropriate the potent imagery of earlier, mighty regimes to maintain his repressive control of his people right up until he was deposed in 2003.

It is vital to keep this historical perspective in mind as we take a bird's-eye tour of the history of the land between the two rivers—the Tigris and the Euphrates, the cradle of much of the world's civilization.

No histories of Iraq predate Churchill's creation of it, and in the memoranda he issued to Colonial Office officials, he had to remind them to use the name of the new state rather than the ancient, Greek-based name for the region, *Mesopotamia,* which means *land between the rivers.* It is also called the Fertile Crescent, as the land that surrounds the Tigris-Euphrates valley itself is mainly uninhabitable desert.

Bringing together the history of this geographic region could also be called anachronistic, as it is something that people of earlier times would not have done. For example, while much of today's Iraq was at one time among the lands of the great Abbassid Caliphate or the later, equally powerful Ottoman Empire, other areas of the present country spent centuries under various rulers of Persia, whose successor state is today's Iran.

With that in mind, we take a fleeting look at the amazingly rich and complex past of the land between the rivers, the region in which some of the very earliest signs of civilization have been discovered. Although we now know of other places, such as Mohenjo Daro in the Indus Valley, that are as old, we can call the ancient Mesopotamian culture *a* "cradle of civilization" even if "*the* cradle" is no longer appropriate.

Some of the oldest forms of writing (known as *cuneiform*) were discovered on clay tablets in some of the oldest cities in the world in Mesopotamia. Many of our most revered myths, such as the flood story, *Epic of Gilgamesh,* also come from tales told thousands of years ago in cities such as Ur. Certainly, so far as we in the West are concerned, much of what we now call Judeo-Christian civilization originated several millennia ago in the floodplains of the Tigris and Euphrates rivers.

Some of the greatest lawgivers of history began there, too: the laws of Hammurabi may now be thousands of years old, but we recognize in them an ancient attempt to create a system of justice that in its concern for the poor and underprivileged of society as well as for the wealthy, was remarkably progressive in its outlook. Hammurabi, the lawgiver king, was, alas, yet another of the ancients whose name was purloined by Saddam Hussein, who named one of his military divisions after him.

The ruins of Ur, the Chaldean city of Abraham, can be visited in Iraq today, and while it is incorrect to refer to Jews as Iraqi exiles, they are unquestionably of the wider Semitic groups of people of the region.

The signs of the zodiac would have been familiar to Abraham, as would the seven-day week. All this, too, we owe to the original Mesopotamians.

We know from the Bible that Saddam was not the first aggressor to spring up in the region. One of the earliest examples of foreign conquest in the Old Testament is the subjugation of Mesopotamia in the eighth century BCE by the Assyrian ruler Tiglath-Pileser III, whose bloodthirsty methods of capturing cities have a horribly contemporary ring.

The people known today as Assyrians converted to Christianity and, unlike most peoples around them, remained Christians throughout the Islamic era. (The terrified Christian Assyrian refugees became one of Churchill's main concerns at the Cairo Conference in 1921.) Being Christian, many Assyrians were less antagonistic to Christian Western interference, and today, in the twenty-first century, the not-inconsiderable Christian minority in Iraq naturally views the possible arrival of an overtly Islamic state with more than a little fear.

The famous Rembrandt painting *Belshazzar's Feast,* of an anxious Belshazzar reading the warning from God on the wall, reminds us that even the aggressive and warlike Assyrian Empire could not last forever. Nevertheless, since the past of Mesopotamia is part of our cultural heritage, Assyria's history is ours as well.

Throughout recorded history, the land between the rivers was a battleground between empires. In the centuries before Christ, the battles were often between the great Roman Empire and the large Sassanian Empire in the east, based for a long time at Ctesiphon, now a ruined city not far from present-day Baghdad. Mesopotamia was disputed frontier territory, sometimes divided between the two warring empires and at other times principally under the control of one of them. Not for thousands of years was the territory of the present-day Iraq entirely part of one of the warring empires.

In the West, we forget that while the Western Roman Empire fell in the fifth century to barbarian invaders, the Eastern Roman Empire, more commonly known as the Byzantine Empire, lasted, in one form or another, almost continuously until its defeat in 1453. Not only that: the Byzantines, while Greek-speaking, thought of themselves as Romans, even though their link with the original Latin-speaking Roman Empire eventually became tenuous and distant.

Rulers and would-be conquerors swept in and out of the Mesopotamian region for millennia, but there was continuity in one thing: perennial border warfare with the peoples who controlled what is now Iran, a country whose direct political history is one of very few (along with China's) that can be described as continuous over thousands of years. That is not to say that the dynasties ruling Iran did not change or that the rulers were always native to the peoples they ruled. But Iran does have an unbroken cultural history, something that is far less true of the Arabs in the land between the Tigris and the Euphrates.

By the seventh century CE, the millennia-long warfare between the main empire controlling what we now call the Middle East—the Byzantine—and whoever was controlling Iran was, unsurprisingly, exhausting both sides. This meant that, despite their antiquity, both combatants were highly vulnerable to any new power arising in the region.

In 622 CE, exactly such a power arose—Islam.

Muhammad himself came from what we now call Saudi Arabia. It is not within the scope of this book to go into enormous detail about the spectacular Arab conquests of conversion that followed. Suffice it to say that in the course of just a few years, the Arabs created an empire that stretched from the Hindu Kush in the east to the Atlantic coast of Spain in the west. (They also, incidentally, gave Iran the rare experience of being just part of a larger empire for the first time since the conquests of Alexander the Great nine hundred years earlier.)

Since the overwhelming majority of today's Iraqis are Muslims, we need to stop and look at some significant events in Islam's early history, those that created major divisions in Iraqi society and culture.

Muhammad, the founder of Islam, died in 632, having successfully conquered most of the Arabian peninsula. It was under his four chief successors, the Rightly Guided Caliphs, that the real exponential expansion began—of the new faith itself and of the lands over which his followers ruled.

Unfortunately, Muhammad did not bequeath a clear line of succession, and some devout Muslims believed, and believe today, that the post of Caliph (military/political/theological successor) should be elective, that the Caliph should be chosen by the *umma* (the community of the faithful). Others believe that the natural line of succession from Muhammad should be through the family of the Prophet himself. But even here we have difficulties, for some of Muhammad's earliest opponents within his own lifetime were from his own family—the *Quraish* family, or clan. And as Muhammad had no sons, it was a question of which male branch of the Quraishi should be chosen as successors (female descent did not count unless it was also linked to male-line kinship).

All this might seem rather obscure to us in the twenty-first century, but it is the cause of the first major division within Islam—one that is still substantial: the split between *Sunni* and *Shia* Islam. Because the split had a powerful impact on the decisions made in Cairo by the British in 1921 and remains a major issue in contemporary Iraqi politics, we cannot ignore it.

Soon, victorious Arab armies had conquered most of what is now Syria, Iraq, Egypt, and Persia, with most of today's Spain and Portugal also falling to the Islamic armies not long after, early in the eighth century. In one sense, therefore, one could say that Iraq has been part of the Islamic world ever since. But to cut a very complex story short, differences arose among the various Arab clans, and the halcyon days of the early conquests had a strong downside.

While the Islamic armies were highly successful in the battlefield, two of the first three Caliph died violent deaths within fourteen years of the death of the Prophet, one of them murdered by the son of the first Caliph, Abu Bakr. Ali, a close blood relation of the Prophet (a male-line cousin as well as the husband of Muhammad's daughter Fatima), became the fourth Caliph, but his authority was challenged from within his own ranks, and the powerful Umayyad clan refused to recognize him as Caliph. When he was assassinated by members of another clan, his first son Hasan succeeded him but then was bribed by the Umayyads to vacate the post. Mu'awiya of the Umayyads became Caliph, and the Caliphate was moved to Damascus, the ancient city in what we now call Syria, after the Roman province of that name.

Ali's second son, Hussein, was made of sterner material and went to war with the Umayyads. His supporters were called the *Shia't Ali,* or the Party of Ali, and it is from this name that all subsequent followers are named *Shia* or *Shiite* Muslims.

We now associate Shia Islam with Iran, but to do this is to be anachronistic, since the vast majority of the early Shiites were, like Hussein himself, Arabs, unlike the Persians (later, the Iranians). The heartland of Shia Islam is still to be found in what we now call Iraq, and all the most sacred

Shia sites are in that part of the Muslim world. It was not until centuries later that a Shah of Iran made Shia Islam the official religion of that country.

Despite Hussein's impeccable bloodline, the majority of the Muslim *umma* followed the Umayyads. In the Battle of Karbala in 680, Hussein and his forces were defeated, with Hussein losing his life. It is his death— martyrdom, to Shiites—that the Shia of Iraq and Iran commemorate to this day (and in February 2004's commemoration in Iraq, they were the victims of explosions that took many lives). If, by the time you read this, elections have been held in Iraq and a Shiite majority regime follows, it will be one of the few times that Shiites have ever controlled the sacred core territory of Shia Islam.

After the Party of Ali made its stand, most Muslims followed the Umayyads, and today this majority is known as the *Sunni* Muslims, named after the *sunna,* or core teachings and example, of Muhammad. Today, 80 to 85 percent of Muslims worldwide are Sunni, including the Arabs of the central part of modern Iraq (the "Sunni triangle") and the ethnically distinct Kurdish minority in the country's north. The Shia include the vast majority of Iranians, Azerbaijanis, and 60 to 65 percent of ethnically Arab Iraqis who live predominantly in the south of the country.

Most Shiites are what is called "Twelvers," meaning they acknowledge that there were twelve anointed successors (*imams*) to Muhammad, starting with Ali. A minority among Shiites acknowledge a lower figure of imams, the best-known group being the Ismailis, whose spiritual leader today is the Aga Khan, a descendant of Muhammad. The majority of Iraqi Shiites are Twelvers. It is important to remember that for many years in the Middle Ages, Egypt was also controlled by a Shiite dynasty, the Fatimids; this is another reason why it is incorrect to associate Shia Islam uniquely with Iran, since historically that is far from being the case.

The Kurds are an ancient people thought to be of Indo-European descent, ethnically close to the present Iranians, and therefore not Arab. Some people link them to the Hittites of biblical times, but at this distance it is not possible to be precise. They have been an essentially nomadic people for most of their history and have never had a powerful state of their own. The regions they inhabit are the borderlands between the great Roman/Byzantine empires to the west and the Iranian lands to the east that today encompass the border areas of Iran, Iraq, and Turkey (whose governments, one strongly suspects, would like to see them disappear).

Perhaps the most famous Kurd in history is Saladin, the victorious Muslim general and ruler who successfully beat the European crusader armies in the twelfth century. Saddam Hussein always liked to compare himself favorably with heroes of the past, and Saladin was among them—especially appropriate because Saladin beat the forces of the West. Nevertheless, Saddam brutally suppressed the Kurds and in 1987 and 1988 used poison gas to kill thousands of Kurdish villagers—notoriously so in the town of Halabja in March 1988—so it is ironic that he used history's most famous Kurd to bolster his image of power.

Theologically, the Kurds chose Sunni rather than Shia Islam, and it was the desire of Feisal, the first King of Iraq, to balance the Shia Muslim majority in southern Iraq with Sunni Arabs in the center and Sunni Kurds in the north. Feisal's scheme was one of the key factors in Britain's unfortunate decision to absorb Kurdish territory into Iraq in the 1920s rather than give the Kurds their independence; in the twentieth century it was to cost them heavily. In any case, an independent Kurdish state—even if it had included the Kurdish lands in Turkey and Iran—would have been economically rather unviable without the oil wealth of Mosul.

To return to the main story, the history of the Caliphates is long and complicated; but in summary, the early successors of Muhammad, the Umayyad Caliphs, soon established an empire that went all the way from today's Iran to present-day Spain. Were it not for a battle in 732 near the French towns of Tours and Poitiers, they might have conquered the whole of Europe as well. In 749, however, the Umayyads were overthrow and replaced by Caliphs who were from another part of the Prophet's family, those of his uncle, Abbas. The Abbassid Dynasty succeeded the Umayyads, who then fled to Spain, under Muslim rule at that time, where they established one of the most magnificent and highly developed cultures of all the Islamic dynasties.

The new Abbassid Caliphs are significant because they moved the capital (the Caliphate) from Damascus to a new, hitherto rather unremarkable town—Baghdad. We know from history, archaeology, and fairy tales such as the *Thousand and One Nights* that Abbassid rule in Baghdad was the Golden Age of Islam. In a sense, one could say that Islam has not been as great—as learned or as splendid—since the Abbassid period. We in the West should never forget that during this era, the Islamic world was *far* ahead of Western civilization in virtually every respect: in literacy, medicine, technology, the arts, and the sciences. The Caliphate based in Baghdad was one of the great centers of world civilization when the West was no more than a comparative backwater. But, leaving out the many details, the power of the Abbassids, too, soon began to decline.

Abbassid civilization was Arab, with a strong admixture of Persian/Iranian influence, but soon a Central Asiatic Turanian people, the Turks, following their conversion to Islam, began to have an impact on the Abbassid Dynasty. Many Turks were taken in by the Caliphs as elite body-guards in the same way that both Western and Byzantine Roman emperors employed Germanic or Nordic mercenaries such as the Varangian Guard. Those guarding the Caliphs were called *Mamluk,* and in time their influence slowly, imperceptibly, but steadily increased. They eventually became so influential that they were able to seize the reins of real power, rendering their nominal Abbassid overlords impotent and essentially decorative. During some periods, Persian-based dynasties (from present-day Iran) were also able to exercise power over the Caliphate.

The Caliphs were Arabs as well as Muslims. But after the savage Mongol conquest of Baghdad in 1258, Arab civilization would never be the same. In time, the Mongols converted to Islam, and by the fifteenth century a mighty new Islamic empire had arisen—that of the Ottoman Turks. Their Sultans, symbolically centered in what hitherto had been the Christian capital of Constantinople (now Istanbul), adopted the old title of Caliph, though, unlike their predecessors in this post, they were neither Arab nor descended from Muhammad.

The Ottomans proved to be the longest-lasting and by far the most pow-erful of all the great Turkish dynasties. New converts themselves, they not only conquered the heartland of Islam, they got rid of the great Christian Byzantine Empire that had been, for well over seven centuries, the Christian West's bulwark against Islamic invasion from the southeast. Constantinople, a mighty city refounded by Constantine the Great himself in the fourth cen-tury, fell to Ottoman siege in 1453. By then, much of the Balkan territory had also been overrun, and in 1526 even the bulk of Hungary became, for over a century, part of the Ottoman Empire. The attempt by the Ottomans in 1529 to capture Vienna itself, the capital of the Holy Roman Emperors, though a failure, was a very close contest, and one can convincingly argue that for the next 160 years, the Ottomans held the advantage over the armies of Christian Europe. Beyond that, they were equally successful in the east, taking back from the Iranians much territory that had been lost to them by former Turkish dynasties over the preceding centuries.

The Ottomans also proclaimed themselves Caliphs of the Faithful, even though they were Turks, not Arabs, and there were still lawful Arab descendants of the Prophet, notably the Hashemite branch of Muhammad's own Quraishi clan, living in Arabia. But soon, with the rise of Ottoman power and the evident success of the new Muslim superstate, few Muslims questioned the Islamic authority of the new dynasty of Caliphs. It was a Turkish, not an Arab, empire, but *Muslim* pride had been very effectively restored by its supremacy.

The strength of the early years of the Ottoman Empire can clearly be seen in its ability to fight a two-front war—against the Europeans in the west and the Iranians in the east—often at the same time. Again to leave out the details, direct control over the area that is present-day Iraq did not come quickly, and there were times when, for example, the Iranians were able to seize back lost territory, including Baghdad itself. But by the eighteenth century, the present Iraqi/Iranian border, then the Ottoman/Persian border, was more or less the same as it is today.

There is arguably little doubt, though, that from 1689 on, when invading Ottoman armies failed to capture Vienna, the Ottoman Empire was in retreat, losing land to the Europeans rather than conquering it from them. By the nineteenth century, the once-mighty Ottoman Empire became known as the "Sick Man of Europe," and as far as the European portion of the empire went, that was certainly true. Greek territory was increasingly lost from the 1830s onward, and in the 1850s Serbia also began to regain a major degree of independence. After the 1870s, the trickle became a flood, and by 1913, most of the Ottoman possessions in Europe were gone.

Over five hundred years after the first Ottoman conquests of the Balkans had begun, the peripheral Ottoman possessions in northern Africa were also lost. The French were able to conquer increasingly large portions of present-day Algeria beginning in the 1830s; by the early twentieth century, lands such as the countries today called Libya and Tunisia had also fallen to European control.

Perhaps the biggest loss to the Ottomans, though, was Egypt, over which they lost *actual* control as far back as the 1820s. (Here it is important to remember that *theoretical* and *nominal* Ottoman sovereignty over Egypt lasted right up until 1914.) The first loss was to a ruthlessly effective Muslim Albanian, Mehmet Ali. His seizure of power in Egypt in the 1820s was nearly a complete disaster for the Ottomans, since he conquered not just Egypt but also much of what is now Palestine (including Israel), Lebanon, and Syria. This was a step too great for concerned European leaders and, under much pressure, Mehmet had to hand back his non-Egyptian conquests; but never again would Egypt be under direct Ottoman rule.

Then, with the building of the Suez Canal by France and Egypt, many decades of direct European interference in the region began, culminating in Britain's outright annexation of Egypt in 1914 when it found itself at war with the Ottoman Empire.

The importance to the British of the Suez Canal cannot be overestimated: right up until the Suez disaster of 1956, next to India itself—Britain's jewel in the crown—the canal was probably *the* most important strategic holding the empire had to protect and defend. Not until the production of oil began in 1927 in Iraq did the Suez Canal share importance with any other British possession. The reason was that it drastically and most usefully reduced the time it took to get British ships—passenger liners and freighters, as well as Royal Navy warships—from Britain to India, the Raj. Once British ships no longer had to go all the way around Africa to make this vital journey, the Suez Canal became the most vital of all imperial arteries.

As Rudyard Kipling fans (especially of *Kim*) will know, Britain's biggest rival in Central Asia in the nineteenth century was Russia. This was the period of the "Great Game," with British spies trying to outwit their Russian equivalents in obscure parts of the Hindu Kush. (The strange shape of Afghanistan—the neutral zone between the two empires—demonstrates this.) Russia was a threat to the British not only in the Himalayas but in the Balkans as well. The Russians regarded themselves, not without cause, as the guardian power of the predominantly Orthodox Christian Ottoman subjects in the Balkans. Much of the nineteenth century, therefore, was taken up with the so-called "Eastern Question," the desire of Russia to expand and create client states in the Balkans and the struggle of other European powers, including Britain, to stop Russia from doing just that.

The main bulwark against Russian expansion in the Balkans was the Ottoman Empire. It was to stop Russia that Britain and other European nations spent decades shoring up the Sick Man of Europe, not so much because they wanted to help a repressive Muslim empire but because they feared the consequences of Russian imperial expansion. In retrospect, this was a mistake; as the late-nineteenth-century Prime Minister Lord Salisbury once lamented, Britain in effect backed the wrong horse.

All this is tied in closely with Iraq, as the matrix of the Ottoman Empire remained firmly under Ottoman rule right up until 1918. That included the Arab core territories of the Hijaz (the western section of the Arabian Peninsula, bordering on the Red Sea), where the holiest Islamic sites of Mecca and Medina are situated, Palestine, Syria, and the region then called Mesopotamia (which we now call Iraq). When the war to defend the Ottoman Empire came, in 1914, most Arabs stayed loyal to their fellow Muslim overlords, the Ottomans; the Kurds actually sided with them and, with the Ottomans' encouragement, massacred hundreds of thousands of innocent Armenians. This is why I am instinctively wary of what one might call the inevitability school of historic thought that considers the end of Turkish power a given— even to the extent of disagreeing with the great and deservedly fêted author Bernard Lewis and his many pre- and post-9/11 works on Islam.

It is a fact of history that the Ottoman Empire *in Europe* began to decline from 1689 onward and, but for British (and some French and Austro-Hungarian) assistance, would have fallen altogether to Russian-supported insurrections from the 1820s onwards. Nevertheless, it took until 1913 and the First Balkan War for the Ottomans to be driven conclusively out of most of the Balkans, though in the Second Balkan War, also in 1913, they were actually able to regain a small portion of their lost territory. The same pattern of Ottoman decline can be seen in Africa, beginning in the 1830s with the loss of Algeria and ending with the loss of Libya just before the First World War.

Nevertheless, right up until 1918, the heartland territories of the Near

East (to use an appellation popular at the time) remained firmly under Ottoman rule. Not only that; even though the empire had lost some territory in the Caucasus to Russia early on in the nineteenth century, its border with Iran remained undisturbed after that.

Yet because of the Ottomans' increasing weakness, the British and French were forever urging internal reforms on the empire's creaking administration. This proved to be a good thing—Ottoman rule became more efficient—and a bad thing—economically, the empire was nearly bankrupt, defaulting in 1875 on gigantic debts. A major rebellion in the Balkans saw a Russian invasion not long after. It was only the intervention of the other European powers at the Congress of Berlin in 1878, designed as much to prevent Russian expansion as to shore up the tottering Ottoman Empire, that enabled the empire to survive at all. Notice, however, that this decline was in the *European* part of the empire, the majority of whose inhabitants were Orthodox Christian. No such large-scale rebellion took place in the predominantly Islamic Near Eastern core of the Ottoman domain.

Up until the late nineteenth century, much of the Ottoman Empire, like the British Raj in India, was controlled through *indirect* rule. The British used local maharajas and other native rulers in the Raj, and the Ottomans similarly devolved a great deal of power to local magnates. However, indirect rule often brought with it serious inefficiency and corruption—and potential unreliability, since even the most ostensibly loyal local magnates were not always and entirely above rebellion. As a consequence, much more direct rule had to be introduced, and this upset many of the local notables who had hitherto been able to do more or less what they wanted without interference from Constantinople. Efficiency thus brought with it increasing discontent.

Worse still, centralization also brought increased "Turkification," or whatever word one wishes to use. Up until the late nineteenth century, the Ottoman Empire, while ethnically diverse, was above all a *Muslim* empire. The Ottomans, whatever their numerous faults, including their occasional tendency to massacre their subjects, were basically without prejudice toward non-Turkic peoples. Many of the grand viziers and other senior Ottoman officials were taken from the different racial, ethnic, and religious groups comprising the empire. But whatever the backgrounds of the high officials may have been, they were, as time progressed, mainly good Muslims. Not only that, but the fact that the Ottoman sultan, despite being non-Arab, was also Caliph of the Faithful meant that many Muslim subjects of the Ottoman Empire, of whatever origins, felt a strong sense of allegiance to their ruler on spiritual grounds. It is significant that, apart from the Bosnian Muslims and the majority of Albanians, this was not the case in the European reaches of the empire. That it was true of the Arab territories is an important distinction.

After 1908, however, when the Committee for Union and Progress (C.U.P.) became a force that began to bring about reforms, increasing numbers of good Muslim officials tended to be Turkish as well. While many of the early Arab nationalists were from Christian minorities that did not take kindly to *Muslim*—let alone Turkish—rule, Muslim Arabs, who had had no problems with Ottoman overlordship, also began to see it as oppressive.

As the power of the C.U.P., also known as the Young Turk movement, increased, along with Turkish chauvinism, the fortunes of the Ottoman Empire continued to decline. The instability of the Ottoman government prompted Austria-Hungary to annex Bosnia and Herzegovina; revolts took place in the Balkans; and the Great Powers were continually eyeing the remaining Ottoman territories.

Throughout most of the nineteenth century, the Ottoman Empire had been kept afloat by the support of Britain and France. Remember the Crimean War? The British and French fought on the Ottoman side against that empire's longtime enemy, Russia. In the early twentieth century, however, there was a major diplomatic revolution. Britain had traditionally regarded Russia as her enemy, especially in India, where the two empires collided. But in 1907, the United Kingdom and the Russian Empire patched up all their quarrels and came to a reconciliation. War on the remote passes and mountains of the Hindu Kush would no longer be a possibility.

Similarly, Britain and France, who nearly went to war over some obscure desert oases in Fashoda (now Kodok, in the Sudan) in 1896, in 1904 signed the Entente Cordiale, and never since has a Franco-British war been a possibility.

These ententes had what one could call an unintentional added consequence. Both Russia and France had for a long time been more than suspicious—justifiably, one could say—of the aggressive and expansionist German Empire, ruled over by the unbalanced and glory-seeking Kaiser

(Emperor) Wilhelm II. He had actively courted the Ottoman Empire, from which, over the previous decades, Britain and France had seized what the Ottomans had regarded as the jewels in their crown: Algeria, Egypt, Cyprus, and later, Morocco.

By 1911, the Ottoman Empire was shuddering from the attrition of its lands, internal political intrigues, and the threat of an increasingly militant Germany. France, Britain, and Russia were now aligned. The C.U.P. desperately needed an ally and made overtures to Britain, France, and Germany, none of which were interested in an Ottoman alliance, though Winston Churchill supported the Ottoman bid in Parliament.

Churchill had, in 1911, just become First Lord of the Admiralty, the political master of the mighty Royal Navy. He had entered politics in 1900 as a Conservative—the same party of which his father, Lord Randolph Churchill, had been a leading member in the 1880s. But Winston then switched sides, over the issue of free trade, to the Liberals, a move which, while consistent with his own beliefs, gave him a reputation for political inconsistency. He became a junior minister in the Liberal government that took power in 1905, and was soon in the Cabinet as Home Secretary, in charge of law and order. Here his swashbuckling methods—using overwhelming military force to besiege a few anarchists, for example—gave him a further reputation as a bit of an adventurer. His own politics became increasingly radical, and his closest ally in government was David Lloyd George, the fiery Welsh radical leader who, as Chancellor of the Exchequer, was responsible for the early beginnings of the welfare state in 1908 to 1909 and onward.

One of the problems of looking at a figure as outstanding as Winston Churchill is that we see everything through the prism of his heroic years as Prime Minister from 1940 to 1945; we too easily forget that for much of his life he was seen as a wayward genius, undoubtedly brilliant but utterly lacking in any kind of judgment. To begin with, although Churchill was one of the most distinguished Liberal members of Parliament during the period covered by this book, he had begun life, as his father had and as mentioned above, as a Conservative. People do not like turncoats, and most conservatives who were in a wartime coalition with the Liberals who followed David Lloyd George tended to perceive Churchill as a man who had betrayed his earlier allegiance. In fact, after our story finishes, in 1922, Churchill was to change party yet again and rejoin the Conservatives. This shows that he had an essentially pragmatic view of party allegiance, one not appreciated by the ideologues who usually make up a party's inner core.

Similarly, while we greatly admire Churchill's tales of daring in South Africa, the fascinating books he wrote about his many exploits as a soldier made him look like an egotistical self-publicist. Many people prefer the solid, reliable, and stable man who, while never as exciting, is dependable and down-to-earth. It was Churchill's burden that until 1930 he was deemed a buccaneer and a man whose judgment could not be trusted. This might not have mattered so much if things had gone well for him; but in the First World War they went spectacularly wrong, with near-fatal consequences for his political career.

In 1914, Russia went to war with Germany; Britain and France went to war on Russia's side; and the Ottoman Empire found itself with a problem. In the past, Britain and France had protected the Ottomans—against Russia. Now the Russians, British, and French were all on the same side, and the Ottomans were deeply divided about whether to remain neutral or enter the war on the side of Germany. Then an ambitious young Winston Churchill, the First Lord of the Admiralty, mobilized the British fleet without the Cabinet's authority and afterward seized two important Dreadnought battleships being built in British shipyards for the Ottoman fleet, and gave them instead to the Royal Navy. The intrigues that abounded in every quarter at that time obscure the impact Churchill's move may have had on the decision the Ottomans made shortly thereafter to join Germany in its war against Britain, France, and Russia.

Up until 1914, the Ottoman Empire had been a friend, or at least no foe; and so the Eastern Mediterranean, with its Suez Canal, so vital to Britain as a sea route to India, had not been in hostile hands. Now that the Ottomans were at war with the British, the whole perspective changed: British imperial interests were at stake.

While we now think of the Middle East primarily in terms of oil, it was not then as critical a factor as it is now. India was far more important to Britain, and so, too, was Persia, the country we now call Iran. There Britain did have oil interests, and few people were more aware of that fact than

Churchill. As First Lord of the Admiralty, he was always on the lookout for new sources of oil for the Royal Navy, preferably from places under British control. Up until then, most British oil for the Navy had come from the United States; but when substantial oil fields were found in Persia, Churchill was quick to exploit them to British advantage.

A new company, the Anglo-Persian Oil Company, was established, one in which the British government had a major controlling share. (It is now known as BP [British Petroleum], and following its recent takeovers of Amoco and Arco of the United States, it remains one of the biggest oil companies in the world.) When British Indian Army troops were sent in 1915 to the neighboring Ottoman-ruled province (*vilayet*) of Basra, on the borders of Persia, it was as much to protect British oil interests in Persia as it was to conquer Arab territory from the Turks.

It is easy to follow the thinking of the European powers at this juncture: Bringing down the Ottoman Empire would have had gigantic advantages for Britain in particular and the Allies in general. It would have made the route to India safe and it would have protected Persia. In addition, it would have helped the war in Europe enormously by opening up another front in the war against the Central Powers: Germany, Austria-Hungary, and their Bulgarian ally. We forget that until the dawn of the twentieth century, the Ottomans had ruled large swaths of Europe, including what is now Kosovo, Albania, Bosnia (nominally until 1908), and parts of Thrace.

If the Ottomans fell, then a new front could be opened up from the southeast, thereby forcing the Central Powers to divert troops from the carnage of the Western Front to protect their now-vulnerable Balkan rear. People like Churchill who supported this policy were known as the Easterners, and the key to such a plan's success was a knockout blow against the very capital of the Ottoman Empire, Constantinople. The key to that city was the narrow isthmuses of land on either side of the Dardanelles strait, the European side being Gallipoli.

In April 1915, British and Australian troops landed on the Gallipoli side of the Dardanelles. As the British had not first achieved naval supremacy, the Turks were able to bring in reinforcements and, worse still, dig in defensively in a way that made the expected swift Allied victory impossible. Consequently, the fighting was not unlike that on the Western

Front in Europe, with two highly entrenched sides trying vainly to gain
military superiority. This meant in turn that the knockout blow, designed
to decapitate the Ottomans by capturing their capital, Constantinople,
proved unachievable. As many Australians know, the Allied casualties
mounted rapidly in the face of growing and successful Turkish resistance.
In the end, the Allies were unable to break out of their bridgehead at Gallipoli, and the remaining troops had to be ignominiously withdrawn. The
whole brave attempt ended in humiliating failure, with great numbers of
casualties and with commensurate damage to Churchill's hitherto mete-
oric political rise.

It is well worth saying that the Gallipoli plan, if it had been successful,
could truly have ended the war earlier. If it had, hundreds of thousands, perhaps millions, of lives would have been spared on the Western Front. But as
it was, upward of two hundred thousand British, Australian, and New
Zealand troops were lost in the Dardanelles.

Very ominously for the future, the leader of the Turkish forces, Kemal
Pasha, proved to be a general of rare vision, talent, and competence. Kemal
Pasha, later to be known by the more modern name of Kemal Ataturk, or
"father of the Turks," is the great ghostly presence who is permanently in the
background for the rest of this book. Born in Salonika, now Thessaloniki in
Greece, the son of a poor Turkish man and an even poorer peasant woman,
he took what was to be the way out of poverty for many people of his background: the army. Fortunately for him, the Ottoman Army was a genuine
meritocracy, all the more so after the military coup of 1908, when some of
his fellow officers seized power—the Young Turks of the Committee for
Union and Progress (C.U.P.).

The key thing here is that he beat the Allies in Gallipoli, which meant
that, instead of a quick, fatal thrust that would capture the Ottoman capital
and knock the entire empire out of the war, the Allies would have to go the
long, hard slog of beating them slowly, using the only two routes left open
to them: Palestine and Basra.

The Gallipoli disaster also had a major effect on Churchill's career. This
is relevant because of the relationship he was to have with David Lloyd
George. After the debacle, Churchill lost office. To get it back, Churchill
depended entirely on the goodwill of Lloyd George, who by this time was

Minister of Munitions; he certainly could not expect any help from the Conservatives, who hated him for his defection to the Liberal side.

Lloyd George is another of the larger-than-life politicians of the twentieth century, perhaps matched only by Churchill himself, as both these men were to lead their country to victory in world wars. A fiery orator from North Wales, he was the first British prime minister from an unprivileged background, having begun life as a small-town lawyer and risen in the Liberal Party through sheer zeal and oratorical power. Not for nothing, therefore, was he nicknamed "the Welsh Wizard."

The year 1916 brought another disaster to a British expeditionary force, this time one en route to protect the oil fields of Basra from the Turks, as described more fully in the next chapter. Marooned for five months in the town of Kut on the outskirts of Baghdad, the troops suffered unimaginable hardships; by the time this debacle was over, more than twenty thousand British troops had lost their lives. Things were not going well elsewhere in the Middle East, either; but in June, an Arab revolt against the Ottoman Empire—long anticipated and much-hoped-for by the British—finally got underway.

At the end of the year, with all Britain's defeats in the Middle East and the continuing lack of success against Germany on the Western Front, there was a peaceful political regime change in London; the hapless and, sadly, increasingly inebriated Prime Minister, Herbert Asquith, was deposed. In his place, another Liberal, Lloyd George, who had been promoted on Kitchener's death to Secretary of State for War, became Prime Minister. He was the one senior Liberal politician whose unrivaled record for dynamism and competence since he had first gained office in 1905 had only improved with the war.

He had become famous in 1909 for a budget that attacked the power and wealth of the aristocracy and at the same time introduced the first measures of what would become the welfare state—of inestimable benefit to ordinary working men and women.

He was also, more privately, nicknamed "The Goat."

Lloyd George was to remain Prime Minister until 1922, so he is the leading politician in power for the rest of our main narrative. Ironically, despite his wild private morals, in public Lloyd George was the very model of Free

Church, or "Nonconformist," virtue, Nonconformist being the term given in Britain to churches that did not conform to the 39 Articles of the Church of England. If the Church of England was the Conservative Party at prayer, the Liberals represented the Nonconformist conscience in politics, and no one was more assiduous in cultivating this constituency than Lloyd George.

Both my family and Lloyd George himself knew their Old Testament inside and out, as did many Welsh Nonconformists of the time. This had more than spiritual relevance; it was to make a huge difference in the landscape of the Middle East, with repercussions right down to the present day.

Look at the Book of Acts and see where the Apostle Paul spent much of his time on his missionary journeys. Look at the Seven Churches in the Book of Revelation. Many of them are cities in what was then Asia Minor (in Roman times) and by the twentieth century, part of Anatolia. Many of the cities, notably Smyrna (now Izmir), were still predominantly Greek, and it was the dream of many a Greek nationalist to see them under Greek rule again. Lloyd George regarded the Greek politician Eleftherios Venizelos as the "greatest Greek since Pericles," and thought the aims of Greek nationalists and keen British Nonconformist readers of the New Testament went hand in hand.

Churchill strongly opposed Lloyd George on the Greek issue, and at times it was to make his political position relative to his political boss highly precarious, being entirely dependent as he was on Lloyd George's political patronage, because the Conservatives hated Churchill and because his wonderful idea of capturing Constantinople had failed so badly. That is a background factor we should always bear in mind: Churchill, until, I would argue, his hour of triumph in 1940 and 1941 in saving Britain, was always a politician whose political career was in severe danger of imploding, and of doing so permanently.

Churchill and Lloyd George did agree, nevertheless, on the other big issue that emerged from Lloyd George's reading of the Bible, though in Churchill's case one more than suspects that his reasoning was not of the biblical type. This was the major decision taken at the time, the one that has caused the most controversy since. The downfall and capture of Saddam Hussein in 2003 has not altered it—it is the Palestinian question.

This book is about Iraq. But as with the war between Turkey and Greece, the Palestinian issue was always in the background of people's minds, Churchill's very much included. At the Cairo Conference in 1921, he would spend as much time on the increasingly vexing issue of Palestine as he would on the problem of what to do with Iraq. So, while I am not concentrating on the Jewish dilemma, we should always also bear it in mind as part of the context in which Churchill and the other British decision-makers were operating.

If you read the Old Testament, you see countless references to a restoration of Israel from exile under the Assyrian Empire in what is now part of Iraq: Babylon. The issue of a *literal* return of all the Jews is one over which Christians of all stripes remain as divided today as ever. Do the biblical references mean a *physical* restoration of the Jewish people to their ancestral land, part of which did occur in biblical times, as recorded in the books of Ezra and of Nehemiah? Or was it a *spiritual* restoration, in which case it does not matter where Jewish people happen to live?

To non-Christian readers, all this might seem a bit arcane! But to many Christians—notably many devout Protestant Christians in both 1920s Britain and in the twenty-first-century United States, it is profoundly relevant. Consider, for example, the circles in which President George W. Bush moves (and his own personal Methodist beliefs). It was, I think one can argue, the same for Lloyd George and the equally devout Nonconformist religious circles that had as powerful an influence on the Liberal Party of his day as many neoconservative Christian groups have through the Republican Party in our own time. In fact, Lloyd George was to admit that he knew the geography of the Holy Land a lot better than he did that of many parts of Europe, something of very considerable significance when, after victory in 1918, he and the other statesmen got together to reconstruct the world.

When the war ended, a minority of Liberals, including Churchill, kept with Lloyd George and in office, with the now-majority Conservative group within the continuing coalition. A tiny Liberal Party—those who had been loyal to Asquith—remained and were now a spent force. (Asquith himself lost his seat and did not regain one for some time.)

One very unfortunate legacy of the now-defunct Asquith coalition government of 1915 to 1916 was the notorious deal made between the British

Middle East expert, Sir Mark Sykes, and his French counterpart, François Georges-Picot (usually simply known as Picot), to carve up the Ottoman Empire.

In March 1917, Britain got its first piece of it—Baghdad.

June 1917 saw a general who knew what he was doing, Field Marshal Sir Edmund Allenby, take charge of the British forces in Egypt. Now, with competent soldiers in command, the war to beat the Turks could begin in earnest.

CHAPTER TWO

THE ARAB REVOLT
AND THE GREAT BETRAYAL

Most French troops in the First World War were fighting a battle for the very survival of their own country—a struggle they very nearly lost as early as 1914. France had been resoundingly defeated by a new and renascent Germany as recently as 1870, losing the border provinces of Alsace and Lorraine to the new German Empire in the process. But while millions of British troops did fight on the Western Front, many others were engaged in the protection of the British Empire's wider dominions—in particular, of India.

The fact that Britain, France, and the Russian Empire were all on the same side, almost certainly more than Churchill's seizure of two Ottoman-bound battleships in 1914, tipped the scales of the Ottomans in favor of abandoning their old allies and siding with Germany and Austria-Hungary.

Russian ambitions did not go away, though, and now that Russia's old enemies were its allies against Germany, the Russians did not hesitate to advance their old nineteenth-century ambitions all over again, this time as Allied war aims. These were, first, to take sizable portions of eastern Anatolia, inhabited in large part by Armenians, most of whom had been under Russian rule since the late eighteenth century; and second, to gain free access from the Black Sea to the Mediterranean for their navy, possible only by going through the Dardanelles. (Russia had wanted this access for a long time, and it was to *prevent* it that the Crimean War had been fought, with Britain and France on the Ottoman side; and the Russians had been suffering from restrictions on their fleet movements ever since.)

Although the net result of the discussions between Sir Mark Sykes and M. Picot was to carve up the Middle East into British, Russian, and French zones, this was not their original primary purpose. What had prompted their deliberations was the need to respond to Russian claims that had existed for decades. Russian demands therefore required a Franco-British response, and here I agree with the very controversial book about the more recent Middle East, *Empires of the Sand,* written by a husband-and-wife team, Efraim and Inari Karsh. They argue that while there is no question that the British and French wanted to expand their empires, the dissolution of the Ottoman Empire—on top of its simple military defeat—was not originally one of their war aims (that was to come later, with Britain's support of the Arab Revolt). However, the Russians unquestionably *did* want their fair slice of Ottoman territory, so Britain and France had to formulate a policy. It was, in effect, that to balance Russia's ambitions, if Russia gained territory A, then Britain and France would need territories B and C for themselves.

The Sykes-Picot Agreement of 1916 now became notorious, entering Arab folklore as the savage and wicked Western desire to impose the evils of colonialism on the free peoples of the Arab world. When one looks at the redrawn map of the Middle East made by these two gentlemen, it is initially hard to think otherwise. The agreement certainly had enormous influence on T. E. Lawrence; he was to feel that its very existence was treacherous, so that in telling the Arabs he supported them, he was being duplicitous in all his dealings with them.

There is no question that the carve-up of the Middle East proposed by Sykes-Picot did indeed put large swaths of the Arab world under Western rule. It did, however, allow for an Arab state, under suitable Western guidance, in the middle, so that British protestations of support for an Arab country were not totally dissembling. But it is also true to say that, as the agreement stood, it was entirely inconsistent with the correspondence between British negotiator Sir Henry McMahon and Sharif Hussein, which made no mention of a colonial role by Britain but spoke only of supporting Arab freedom from Turkish oppression. To that extent, Lawrence was right to accuse his British colleagues of hypocrisy. Also valid is the Arab claim that the British were not being entirely honest with their Arab allies.

Facts are often disputable, their interpretation open to the influence of passionately held views that are wildly divergent. Beyond that, interpreting the past can be all too dependent on the effect of current events and issues. Never has this been more the case than in the history of the Middle East, and of the heavily disputed 1914 to 1921 period in particular. This book covers precisely that period; therefore, everything I write and you read is open to disputation and interpretation by zealous protagonists who have different ideas of what *really* happened, and why, during those seven years of war and upheaval.

This book is mainly a narrative about Churchill's creation of Iraq, but we do need to see, briefly, why it led to such dissension. In addition, while our discussion is mainly about Iraq (originally Mesopotamia), we cannot completely forget the other major area of British responsibility in the Middle East, the creation of a Jewish homeland in Palestine with the announcement of the Balfour Declaration in 1917 (so named after a letter from Lord Arthur James Balfour, the British Foreign Secretary, to Lord James de Rothschild).

Many of the facts of the post-Ottoman period are beyond dispute, such as the British capture of both Baghdad and Jerusalem in 1917; others are open to all kinds of interpretation, both at the time and now. The Arab Revolt against the Ottomans is just such a case. Exactly what happened in those Arabian deserts—and in the corridors of power—nearly a hundred years ago was and remains the subject of debate, with resonance in contemporary Middle Eastern politics.

The splendid Oscar-winning film *Lawrence of Arabia,* with Peter O'Toole as T. E. Lawrence and Sir Alec Guinness as a rather too old Prince Feisal, brought the story to a wide audience. But unfortunately, the film is based closely on Lawrence's own postwar memoir, *The Seven Pillars of Wisdom,* which is exactly where all the trouble begins. Most of Lawrence's biographers, particularly those writing after the British government decided to release all the documents relating to the First World War in the 1960s, discovered that large segments of the book are entirely imaginary. And since

Lawrence purported to be relating what really happened, chunks of his narrative go far beyond poetic license; they are blatantly untrue. That *Lawrence of Arabia* is full of inaccuracies is not the result of Hollywood's tendency to change the facts to make a "better" film, as so often happens; in this case, the filmmakers tried to tell something approximating the truth—it was Lawrence himself who fictionalized his past.

Many people fell under Lawrence's spell—even Churchill, who included a chapter on him in his famous book of biographical sketches, *Great Contemporaries*. And it was Lawrence's friend and cohort Feisal, who was installed as King of Iraq in 1921, who is pivotal to this whole story.

Certainly Lawrence did play *a* role in the Arab Revolt, but the actual scenario was a great deal less complex, if no less heroic, than Lawrence portrayed it. As one of his contemporaries ruefully put it, he was a man who was always "backing into the limelight," who pretended to be modest while always making sure that he was at the very center of everybody's attention.

Lawrence's whole life was a fantasy from its very beginning. Although his parents lived as husband and wife, they were never married—something Lawrence professed not to know until much later in his life. His father, while outwardly a pillar of society, had fled the life of respectability under a cloud. He took up with Lawrence's mother without marrying her and, in doing so, established a lifestyle his family strongly disapproved of. Lawrence's mother was a paradox, a devoutly religious woman whose adult life was based on an express contradiction of all the Church taught about the sanctity of marriage and family life.

Along with his rather unorthodox background, Lawrence himself was what can only be called a psychological mess.

Since the people who knew for certain have not told us, we cannot be sure whether Lawrence was a practicing homosexual or merely someone from a more repressed age than ours who had strong homoerotic feelings that he never actually acted on. Either way, in an age in which homosexuality was illegal, anyone with the inclination would have had a more difficult time than they would today. Repression can be said to have unfortunate psychological effects, and Lawrence certainly manifested many of them. He was always punishing himself for his achievements, psychologically and possibly physically as well: When he joined the Royal Air Force under a false name after retiring from public life, he was examined, and the doctors found many wounds that did not appear to be scars of battle but in all likelihood had been self-inflicted.

Lawrence studied both at Oxford and at Cambridge, where he became an outstanding young archaeologist. He made his first trip to the Middle East under the great Sir Leonard Woolley as part of the team that made some major discoveries at the biblical site of Carcemish, an especially rich source of knowledge about the great Hittite Empire that ruled a large part of the region in ancient times. While there, he formed a kind of attachment to the Arab peoples that was to change his own life and, through the profound influence he had on others, the Arab world as well.

While in Carcemish, Lawrence formed a close attachment to an Arab youth, a fondness that, even if not actually physical, was certainly homoerotic in some way. It seemed to have led him to an idealization of a certain kind of Arab lifestyle—that of the romantic nomad, or Bedouin—that has always afflicted dewy-eyed Westerners. This is a sentiment that can be entirely heterosexual or asexually imperialist, as was the case with many Britons and other visitors to the region for whom the nomadic Arab was an early twentieth-century colonialist version of Rousseau's eighteenth-century noble savage.

This perspective attaches much credence to those living, for example, nearer to nature—a traditionalist Bedouin living in his tent, riding on a camel across the desert—in preference to an educated town-dweller with progressive ideas and an anticolonialist frame of mind. It translated into a preference for more old-fashioned-looking, traditionally dressed, seminomadic Arab chieftains over Western-clothed, urban intellectuals who had ideas of their own—and the kind of nationalist sentiment that wanted a republic over a monarchy, preferably without any kind of strongly paternalistic Western interference, however well-meaning it might be.

It was precisely this advantage that a group of the Prophet Muhammad's twentieth-century descendants had over the educated urban elites of Cairo and Damascus. This applied in particular to the Hashemites, a branch of Muhammad's own Arabian clan, the Quraishi. Known also as Sharifs (our word sheriff comes from a similar root), an honorific given to proven descendants of the Prophet (hence the alternative adjective for them,

Sharifian), they were, because of their ancestry, much honored throughout the Arab world.

Heading the family was the ambitious Sharif of Mecca, Hussein, and some equally power-hungry sons, in particular Feisal and Abdullah. Ironically, the impression we get of them from *Lawrence of Arabia* and *The Seven Pillars of Wisdom*—as noble, primitive sons of the desert—is misleading, as much a projection of Lawrence's fantasies as anything else. Thirteen hundred years after the death of Muhammad, there were numerous descendants of the Prophet living in his homeland, and the post of Sharif was an appointed one, held by whichever descendant was deemed worthy by the Ottoman Sultan far away in Constantinople. Hussein was simply fortunate enough to be holding the position of Sharif at the right time in history. Possibly, when the war came, his fear of being deprived of so significant a post—Sharif of the very holiest city in Islam—may have steered him toward his momentous decision to rebel against his Turkish overlords.

As for Feisal, he had represented the part of Arabia from which their family came, the Hijaz, in the Ottoman Parliament. So, however traditional his outward appearance, he was in fact every bit as educated and sophisticated as the urban intellectuals romantic Englishmen so disdained. If Feisal spent much of the First World War in a tent or cave, it was due to the exigencies of war, not a statement of manly preference for a more rugged, in-tune-with-nature lifestyle. When we consider the heroic events of 1914 to 1918, we need to bear all this very much in mind. Much of what occurred in Lawrence's *Seven Pillars of Wisdom,* and thus also in the film, either did not happen as he said it did, or never happened at all. We all like a hero, and Lawrence's feats of heroism in the desert are very appealing, but we need to remember that what he relates does not have the veracity of prosaic logbooks and military telegrams that tell us what really happened; some of it has the same degree of relationship to reality as Tolkien's Middle Earth.

The fantasy element does not stop there; some of it had very serious political implications, many of which we have to live with today. One of the abiding senses one comes away with from both the book and the film is that of betrayal—Lawrence betrayed, Feisal betrayed, and as a result, the whole noble Arab race betrayed with them; all that desert-revolt heroism turned into dust and ashes at the hands of unscrupulous Western men plotting behind the backs of brave warriors who wanted no more than their freedom.

Most historians, whether Arab or Western, have tended to share this sense of bitterness and betrayal. It is hard not to, because the facts, outwardly at least, seem to point so overwhelmingly in that direction.

However, there are now two schools of thought being brought to bear on these events from very different perspectives, both of which would say that all the talk of betrayal is pure nonsense. There is the aforementioned *Empires of the Sand* by Karsh and Karsh, and a prize-winning account of the postwar Paris Peace Conference, called *Peacemakers* (*Paris 1919* in the United States), written by Margaret MacMillan, a Canadian descendant of Lloyd George. Those wanting a more academic look at these thorny issues will find them profitable reading.

These two books are very controversial, because history is not always as objective as we think. We all come to the past with our present-day prejudices fully intact, however much we try to get rid of them. Not only that, but the more recent the history we are dealing with, the more it is in and of itself an aspect of the prejudice of our interpretation.

I mention all this *before* we look at the exciting story of the Arab Revolt and its sad aftermath because until recently what has gone wrong with the Middle East has been deemed to be the fault of wicked, interfering Westerners; it had nothing to do with the unfortunate, betrayed Arabs, who won victory only to have it cruelly snatched away by the evil machinations of politicians in faraway Europe. This is why these new approaches to looking at the past are so controversial.

What Karsh and Karsh are saying is that the Arab Revolt was not just Western imperialism at work, but also the imperial ambitions of the Hashemite family. To summarize a very complex historical argument, the case they make is in effect that the mess of today's Middle East is the fault as much of local rulers—in particular the Hashemite clan, supported by people like Lawrence—as of outside European interference. This theory has been attacked because of the Israeli links of the authors, and it is fair to say such loyalties are bound to make some kind of difference, whether great or small. However, it is surely also the case that if you are an Arab, particularly a Palestinian, you are equally likely to be prone to sympathize with scholars who blame the West. (This is why, I feel, the late Palestinian intellectual Edward Said was so zealously opposed to the British Jewish expert on the Middle East, Bernard Lewis, a former Princeton professor whose writings since September 2001 have been especially influential, particularly on the Bush administration.)

Margaret MacMillan's book is interesting because she very bravely defends the record of many of the peacemakers who met in Paris in 1919 and their attempts to put together new countries from the wreckage of the old empires that had been defeated and destroyed the year before. I say "brave" because up until now most people have not hesitated to condemn men like Lloyd George of Britain, Clemenceau of France, and Wilson of the United States for Germany's unhappiness with the Versailles Treaty in 1919, which in large part was instrumental in the rise of Hitler and, ultimately far worse, the outbreak of World War Two.

My own prejudice—or at least the one of which I am aware—is that, in the end, we all have prejudices of some kind or another. I never see issues in black and white, I see them in shades of many different kinds of gray, like a mosaic. This does mean I regularly get shot at from both sides; it also means that I end up in partial agreement and partial disagreement with radical ideas, such as those of Karsh and Karsh, at the same time. (With Margaret MacMillan, I tend to agree in full.)

What we see in Lawrence's book, in the film, and in present-day Arab mythology is in reality an illusion. *Some* Arabs did indeed revolt against their Ottoman overlords and fight bravely on the side of the British. Others, however, did not and were quite content to remain Ottoman subjects under Turkish rule. The idea that the decision by the Ottomans to side with Germany against Britain, France, and Russia led to a massive, overwhelming, Arab-nationalistic, patriotic revolt is quite wrong. The importance of this cannot be overemphasized.

Here is a controversial new idea: that the only reason there was an Arab revolt against Ottoman Turkish rule in the first place was because the Ottoman Sultan took the fatal step of going to war on the German side.

The famous Arab Revolt is an event that so many, especially in the Middle East, regard as the origin of all their woes. In addition, its outcome directly affected the decisions with which Churchill was faced when he and all the experts, Lawrence among them, gathered in Cairo in March 1921. How, then, did the Arab Revolt actually begin?

In mid-1914, before World War One had even begun, a young, rather portly Arab Prince went to see the eminent British colonial official, Sir Ronald Storrs, the Oriental Secretary of the British administration in Cairo. The supplicant was Prince Abdullah, the brother of the soon-to-be-more-famous Feisal and a younger son of the Sharif of Mecca. This was a fishing expedition to see if the British would be prepared to provide weapons for a potential Arab revolt against the Ottoman rulers of the Hijaz.

Abdullah's was an explosive request in more ways than one. The British Empire was one of the world's greatest Muslim powers, not because of its loose, unofficial rule over Egypt, but because of the gigantic Muslim population of its empire in India. India then contained, before its independence in 1947, what is now Pakistan and Bangladesh as well as India proper, and we forget that even in the twenty-first century, India alone still has over 130 million Muslim citizens.

In 1914, the majority of India's Muslims, in the globally predominant Sunni branch, owed indirect spiritual allegiance to Islam's Caliph of the Faithful. The holder of this post (which was more akin to the pre-Reformation idea of the European Holy Roman Emperor than that of the present-day Pope, who has no Islamic equivalent) was also the Ottoman Sultan. What Abdullah was proposing—rebellion against the lawful Sultan—was also rebellion against the Caliph venerated by all of India's many Muslims. It was therefore a very high-risk strategy.

When World War One began, the British High Commissioner in Egypt, Lord Kitchener of Khartoum, was recalled to London as the Secretary of State for War. (It is his face on Britain's famous recruiting poster YOUR COUNTRY NEEDS YOU.) Kitchener realized that if the Ottomans were to side with Germany rather than stay neutral, Abdullah's offer could be the very thing the British needed. He knew that if the Turks did declare war on Britain and France, the Sultan, in his position as Caliph of the Faithful, would also declare a holy war, or *jihad,* on his Western enemies. There would be a major panic in Britain and France, since both countries had many Muslim subjects in their respective empires, the French mainly in Africa, the British in Egypt and other parts of the world, but mainly in India. If all their

Muslim subjects were to rise up against them, there would be a major military and political catastrophe, making their extensive imperial possessions virtually untenable, since millions of troops would also be urgently needed to fight the Germans on the Western Front in Europe.

If, however (Kitchener speculated), there was another major Islamic leader who was on the side of the Allies and against the Turks, it just might avoid a colonial meltdown in India. Sharif Hussein, Abdullah's father, was a *bona fide* senior descendant of the Prophet, and Sharif of Mecca in the bargain. British support for Hussein and his revolt would not only be militarily helpful in the Middle East; it could be a lifesaver in India as well.

Although the Indian colony of the British Empire is now long departed, in this period—1914 to 1921—it was still very much the jewel in the crown of Britain, the gigantic colony that accounted for so much of Britain's prestige in the world and which, better still, actually paid for itself, unlike most of the rest of the British imperial possessions. India had to be held onto at all costs. This meant, in geostrategic terms, hanging onto Egypt and the Suez Canal. It also meant keeping Muslim Indians happy and willing to fight in the armies of the Raj.

So now that Kitchener was back in London, he instructed his successor as High Commissioner, Sir Henry McMahon, to engage in correspondence with Sharif Hussein in Mecca with a view to helping the Arab cause against their Ottoman overlords.

Hussein wanted to be Caliph and to be rid of Ottoman rule. His son Abdullah sympathized with these aims, whereas Feisal, initially at least, was not so sure. He had discovered from some of the Arab secret societies in Damascus that the local Arab-nationalist groups had realized that getting rid of someone—the Sultan—who was not just a powerful political ruler but also Islam's religious leader would be no easy task.

In calling the groups in Damascus "Arab nationalists," I am walking straight into the minefield of the history of the Middle East. Nationalism was in many ways *the* great explosive force of the twentieth century, causing world wars, colonial rebellions, and much else besides. Its sheer power—seen as late as the 1990s' nationalist wars in Bosnia and Kosovo, in which hundreds of thousands died or were forced into exile—is surely obvious. Yet amazingly, there are those, including famous and revered authors such as Elie

Kedourie and his followers (such as the Karshes), who actually deny that such a phenomenon as *Arab* nationalism even existed. Yes, they argue, people supported their tribe, or their clan, or perhaps a charismatic sheikh; but nationalism, in the sense of a powerful feeling of national identity uniting all or most of the Arabs, simply was not there.

This notion completely alters the picture when we look at the Arab Revolt. It is why we need to work out which prism we are looking through when we consider the rebellion that was about to unfold.

If, as many other writers have argued—most recently the well-known popular historian John Keay in *Sowing the Wind*—Arab nationalism genuinely did exist from the mid-nineteenth century onward, then we can really see Hussein's correspondence with Sir Henry McMahon and Abdullah's earlier request for military support as the origins of a genuinely Arab revolt against alien Turkish rule. Yes, it is true that in asking to lead this revolt himself, Hussein wanted to aggrandize his own clan—on that, surely, everyone can agree. But there is a major difference between saying that Hussein was doing so sincerely on behalf of Arab nationalists everywhere, albeit with plenty of side benefits for himself, and saying that there was no such thing as Arab nationalism—saying, in effect, that Hussein was one imperialist out entirely for himself, asking for help from another bunch of imperialists, the British.

I tend to think that while Hussein was out for himself, there was also a genuine—even if still small—sense of Arab nationalism he was able to tap into. This is important, since our main focus is Iraq, and one of the key factors in Iraqi history from this period up until the downfall of Saddam Hussein in 2003 is that Arab nationalism is usually innately secular. The fact that it was a descendant of Muhammad who was conspiring to revolt against the Ottoman Empire makes Hussein's action rather ironic, but it was, I think, the case. One could be a faithful Arab nationalist and a Christian, just like the Syrian founder of a small group that was to go on to become notorious—the Renaissance or, in Arabic, Ba'ath Party.

Equally controversial was the correspondence between the increasingly beleaguered Hussein in Mecca—his phone number was Mecca 1—and the ever-cautious Sir Henry McMahon. As many historians have told us, it is probably the most minutely picked-over correspondence in history, possibly, one writer has suggested, even more scrutinized than the New Testament Epistles! The reason is that in the year or so during which their letters went to and from Mecca and Cairo, Hussein and McMahon, unbeknownst to them at the time, were carving up what was slowly becoming the Middle East we know today.

In 1916 the British were getting desperate. There was a stalemate on the Western Front, and tales of horror were coming from Flanders, where millions of young men from all sides died needlessly in endless rounds of carnage between the trenches without any real major victories being won. Thankfully, in terms of casualties, things were not quite so bad on the Eastern Front; but if the Western forces, mainly British, Australian, and New Zealander, with strong support from Indian troops dispatched from the subcontinent, had thought that "Johnny Turk" would be a pushover, they were very sadly mistaken.

In Sinai the British were getting nowhere at all, and it was just as well that there was stalemate, since the alternative would have been a successful Ottoman seizure of Egypt (something that Rommel himself only just missed achieving in 1941 and again in 1942). British attempts to capture Mesopotamia—then thought of only as the Ottoman *vilayets* (provinces) of Basra and Baghdad—were proving equally fruitless and soon resulted in one of the biggest British disasters in either world war—at Kut.

The British commander, General Charles Townshend, like many of the leading officers in Mesopotamia, had been relocated from India, where conditions were very different. As nearly happened to the Americans in 2003, he managed to get to Baghdad quite quickly, and then discovered that he was hopelessly overextended. So he retreated to the nearby town of Kut to settle in for what he thought would be a brief wait until reinforcements came. He was also hoping that Russian troops, fighting the Ottomans in the Caucasus, would be able to sweep in from the north, thereby forcing the Turks to withdraw forces from the Arab part of the empire to defend the Turkish heartlands in Anatolia.

Townshend was, however, to be gravely disappointed on all counts. The Russians became more interested in getting rid of their own despotic ruler, the Tsar, than in fighting Turks. The reinforcements from Basra in the south never got through; and the Turks, contrary to all expectations, were turning out to be first-class soldiers. When a rather effete young Arabic-speaking British officer named T. E. Lawrence was sent to Kut in early 1916, it was not to announce that help was imminent but to help with negotiating as honorable and face-saving a British surrender as possible.

After months of increasingly dire siege conditions, the British troops were led off into captivity—luxurious in the case of the officers like Townshend; grim and brutal for the ordinary soldiers, thousands of whom died in a forced prisoner march out of the town. As for the unfortunate Arab inhabitants, who had had no say in hosting their foreign visitors, perhaps as many as thousands of them were put to death by the avenging Turkish victors.

Also preying very heavily on McMahon's mind would have been the debacle of Gallipoli. Without understanding the background to Britain's two disasters, Gallipoli and Kut, we cannot really see why the prospect of an Arab revolt against the Ottomans, a military operation that would not require many British troops, would be such a godsend to the increasingly frustrated and concerned British High Command in Cairo.

The Gallipoli campaign was another large-scale military catastrophe, again involving many Australian and New Zealand troops—the ANZAC Division—a blow to these two infant countries that rankles with many of their citizens to this very day. Whereas Kut could be put down to sheer military incompetence, the disaster of Gallipoli ranks as one of the great military tragedies of the twentieth century. This is, I would say, because it was so close to being one of the most brilliant masterstrokes of military genius ever, one which, had it been successful, would have ended the war months, if not years, earlier. It might also have rendered the Arab Revolt unnecessary, as the revolt of the Bedouin tribes did not really get going until the debacle in the Dardanelles was already over and lost—in which case too, of course, the whole history of the Middle East might have been very different.

In June 1916, Hussein raised the Hashemite standard, and the revolt began. A triple strike against the Ottomans could now get underway: the Arabs in revolt, a dynamic British-Australian army under Allenby attacking through Sinai and Palestine, and a renewed British invasion of what was then Mesopotamia, now Iraq (along very similar lines to those followed by British and American forces in 2003).

Initially, the revolt was highly successful—with large parts of the coastal areas of the Arabian peninsula falling to Hashemite forces (I describe them that way because, in contrast to the scenario of *Lawrence of Arabia* and the many myths that have grown from the story of the revolt, many Arabs stayed entirely loyal to their secular and spiritual overlord, the Ottoman Sultan.)

As David Fromkin, in his best-seller *A Peace to End All Peace,* put it rather starkly:

> In the event, the Arab revolt for which Hussein hoped never took place. No Arabic units of the Ottoman army came over to Hussein. No political or military figures of the Ottoman Empire defected to him and the Allies. The powerful secret military organization that al-Faruqi [the Syrian resistance group and its eponymous leader] had promised would rally to Hussein failed to make itself known. A few thousand tribesmen, subsidized by British money, constituted Hussein's troops. He had no regular army.

Fromkin is right. Most Arabs, including those in the Ottoman *vilayets* of Basra, Baghdad, and Mosul—the *vilayets* making up the present Iraq—stayed loyal to the Ottoman Empire.

Nor, historians now say, were the original Arab rebels, led by Feisal, very effective. What they were good at was guerrilla raids, something that under Lawrence's leadership, they handled quite well. When it came to pitched battles against well-trained Ottoman forces, they were sadly out of their league. What *did* help was the recruitment by the British of Ottoman Army prisoners of war, mainly Arabs from the future Iraq. They were trained soldiers and were thus far more effective than Lawrence's irregulars. Among the most prominent of them was Nuri al-Said, who was to spend twenty years, from 1938 to 1958, as the key strongman in the Hashemite Kingdom of Iraq. Finally, there was also a small French contingent under Colonel Edouard Brémond, whose considerable skills with artillery made up for an important lack in Feisal's forces.

Many of the feats of derring-do mentioned by Lawrence in the *Seven Pillars of Wisdom* did take place: the capture of the port of Aqaba, raids on trains carrying Ottoman supplies and forces, episodes of that kind. All of them were no doubt profoundly irritating to the Ottomans and their German allies. In addition, guerrilla raids often forced the occupying forces to keep troops stationed in areas where they would otherwise have been unnecessary. This, one could argue, was the case with the Arabs fighting under Feisal's command, and to that extent they were doubtless of enormous help to the British and Australian troops engaged in the main conflict with the Turks.

It is also the case that Djemal Pasha, the overall Ottoman commander, alienated many Arabs by committing punitive raids and atrocities against the Arab population.

Up until 1908, Ottoman policy had been that if you were a Muslim, you were a loyal subject of the empire and would be given considerable leeway locally in what you did—something the overwhelmingly Muslim Arabs subscribed to. However, in 1908, the Young Turk regime had started to introduce what one might call a Turkification process, slowly changing it from a Muslim empire whose ruler was a Turkish Muslim, the Sultan/Caliph, into much more of a Turkish empire, with Turks as a ruling class.

In addition, by 1913, the Turks had lost most of their remaining empire in Europe, retaining only a tiny European foothold around Adrianople, now known as Edirne, the remaining part of what had once been an enormous Ottoman domain over most of the Balkans and even much of present-day Hungary.

The state of the Ottoman Empire makes the failure of the Arab peoples to revolt *en masse* against such oppression all the more remarkable. A group of Arabs who did rebel were the Egyptians—against *British* rule after the end of the war in 1918; and another group, the Arabs in the British-liberated provinces of what is now Iraq, later did the same in 1920. But as for an Arab revolt against their fellow Muslim Turks, this did not happen on anything like the scale that Lawrence portrays and popular legend has had it since.

By the end of 1916, military and political conditions for the British had changed dramatically. Victories were urgently needed, and there was Lloyd George—and new dynamism—in No. 10 Downing Street to make sure that things started to happen.

While the Arab Revolt was floundering in March 1917, the United States entered the war. Plenty of historians in addition to Karsh and Karsh have argued that many Arabs thought the Ottomans *would* win. These included some of the leading Arab chieftains, who remained loyal to their

Ottoman masters throughout the war, as also did—with disastrous long-term effects—many of the leading Arab citizens of what was, in 1921, to become Iraq. As we know from the failure of Churchill's intended master-stroke at Gallipoli, the war certainly could have had a very different out-come. There are many who argue, with much good sense, that without the intervention of the United States, it might have ended in a draw or possibly even in a victory for the Central Powers. In that case, the Ottomans would have chosen the right side, and they, not their Arab subjects, would have been on the winning team.

Late in 1917, the imperial Russian government was overthrown. Since one of Lenin's main platforms was to take Russia out of the war, that hap-pened in 1918 with the Treaty of Brest-Litovsk. Karsh and Karsh and others of like mind are thus right to say that the Sykes-Picot agreement then became irrelevant to the later map of the Middle East, including the new Iraqi state created by Churchill in 1921. To the embarrassment of many, one of the other things the Bolsheviks did was to publish all secret treaties under-taken by their tsarist predecessors, including Sykes-Picot: so if the Arabs did not know about it earlier, they certainly learned of it then.

Field Marshal Allenby, the British commander on the Palestinian front, was very aware of the power of symbolism. When it came to the liberation of Jerusalem in 1917, he did it himself, but when it came to entering Damascus, he decided that it would be much better if it were to look as if it had been cap-tured by Arab forces under Feisal. The Australians and British, who would otherwise have seized the city, therefore held back and allowed Feisal's forces to enter first. So symbolically it was Arabs who captured the Arabic city of Damascus, with T. E. Lawrence among their number.

But the Turks had already left; some local Arabs not sympathetic to Feisal already ruled the city. One of the first tasks of the Arab forces, there-fore, was to get rid of the local Arabs in order to install Feisal as Syria's legit-imate ruler.

In Lawrence's written works, the film, and the legend in general, it looks as if the Arabs were betrayed by British and French perfidy, with the brave Arab liberators being ousted by the wicked and scheming Westerners. Recent work by Lloyd George's descendant, Margaret MacMillan, among others has shown that this was not the case at all.

To begin with, it was the Australian/British invasion under Allenby that truly liberated the whole area from the Turks, along with the parallel Indian Army–based invasion through Mesopotamia, led by British troops, that captured Baghdad in 1917. But for this, the Turkish forces would have been triumphant, and Hussein's revolt would have been swiftly crushed into oblivion, along with the dreams of Arab nationalists in Syria and throughout the Arab world.

This is not to say that there were not plenty of Arabs who disliked Turkish rule; Turkish atrocities, committed on a genocidal scale against the Armenians during the war, would sooner or later have alienated an increasingly large part of the Arab population. But the proportion of Arabs who *actually* revolted following Hussein's rebellion in 1916 was rather small. The Arab intellectuals in Damascus and elsewhere who feared that any revolt would be crushed were surely being realistic. What made all the difference was the twin-pronged British invasion through the Sinai on one front and Basra on the other. That was what dealt the deathblow to the Ottoman Empire and its five centuries and more of rule over the Middle East.

So was there a betrayal, as Lawrence felt at the time and many an Arab nationalist and Islamic zealot have argued since? I think the answer is both yes and no.

Historians now think that Hussein *did* know about Sykes-Picot-and he knew at the time it happened. So either Lawrence once again was lying, or he really did not know about it. Margaret MacMillan shows conclusively in her book that the British regretted Sykes-Picot from the outset, but in reality it was not the Arabs they were deceiving, it was the French. MacMillan, as well as other historians, points to the fact that the British, now that the war was won—and in the Middle East, overwhelmingly by troops from the British Empire—did not want to give major territory to the French. The French, with some justification, pointed out that it was mainly French dead in the war against Germany, and had the French not fought so hard on the Western Front, the victorious British troops in the Middle East would have been obliged to fight in Europe and not against the Turks.

It was British troops who controlled Damascus, even though it was in a part of the world—Syria—that France wanted for itself. Feisal was there as the *de facto* local ruler, but he was bolstered by the presence of a mainly British army alongside his own fighters, many of whom, like Nuri al-Said, were in fact from Mesopotamia, not Syria. It does now seem that as far as the British were concerned, it would not have mattered if Feisal had stayed. In that case, he would have been able to rule in Damascus as King of Syria after all, and his brother Abdullah, the first choice of the local leaders in Mesopotamia, would have become King there instead. The Middle East would thus have been a very different place from the one it became.

To me, at least, the reason for the Arab sense of betrayal was that once the idealistic Americans had entered the war and made self-determination the key, the British were hoist with their own petard in the Middle East. The French were at least consistent: They wanted direct colonial rule when they gained new territory from defeated enemies in Africa, the Middle East, and elsewhere. Britain had often ruled indirectly, such as through the maharajas in India, native rulers in Africa, and various local sultans in Malaysia. To the British, having an Arab King and also having some form of indirect British rule were not incompatible objectives.

In any case, those who argue that the British spent much of the rest of the war trying to get out of their commitments under Sykes-Picot are surely correct—to the benefit of the Arabs and in particular Hussein and his sons Abdullah and Feisal.

But in 1917 and 1918, President Woodrow Wilson's commitment to the principle of self-determination threatened to change the rules of the imperial game; at least, so he and many of the peoples of Europe and the Middle East devoutly hoped. To a very great extent, the Big Four did not fully finish the business of the Middle East during their time in Paris in 1918 and 1919, for while the peacemakers in Paris were able to solve many postwar problems, there was still the huge difficulty of determining what to do with the remains of the defeated Ottoman Empire. It was precisely those *unfinished* issues Churchill had to deal with, which is why, I would argue, *his* decisions made all the difference in what happened then and in what is *still* happening in the twenty-first century.

Sadly, we know from the causes of the Second World War that matters were really far more complicated than that, for all empires—almost by definition, one could say—are a self-determinist's nightmare.

Yugoslavia had only a brief period as a democracy before the different national component parts started to fall out with each other—Croats, Serbs, Slovenes, Macedonians, Albanians, and so on. The solution took three different forms—a royalist Serb-dominated autocracy before the Second World War; a violent and bloodthirsty civil war in addition to a fight against external enemies in the Second World War; and finally, the Communist dictatorship of Marshal Tito. It did not take long after Tito's death for the country to collapse, break into its component parts, and endure an even more bloodthirsty war in which well over 250,000 people perished, most of whom were innocent civilians. Now no such country as Yugoslavia even exists.

The Ottoman defeat ended the rule of the one major Islamic superpower, the Ottoman Empire. The empire was a Muslim power that at its peak had terrified the less powerful Europeans and, following the Ottoman defeat of the Hungarians at the Battle of Mohacs in 1526, had very nearly allowed the Islamic conquest of Western Europe as well. Had the siege of Vienna in 1529 gone the other way, that is indeed what might have happened. But now, in 1918, the empire was defeated, and Western armies stood guard over its very capital, Constantinople. The once mighty Ottoman Caliphs, the Commanders of the Faithful, stood impotent before the victorious West.

So if the Ottomans had not been so foolish and ungrateful as to go to war with their former friends Britain and France in 1914, particularly since they were allied with Russia, would the Ottoman Empire have vanished when it did?

On the one hand, the decision of the Ottomans to Turkify the empire made its *long-term* decline and eventual disappearance inevitable, since being Turkish became more important than being Muslim. On the other hand, the process of Ottoman decline could have been drawn out for far more than the ten years it lasted after the advent of the Young Turks; what made the empire's fall *in 1918* a certainty rather than just an ultimate inevitability was the decision of the Young Turk government to go to war with Britain and France in 1914.

The Ottoman Empire would surely have fallen apart anyway at some stage during the twentieth century. The Turkification policy of the Young Turks would have reminded the Arab regions of the empire that they were

Arabs as well as Muslims; therefore Arab rebellions certainly would have emerged. It would have been a very different Middle East from the one we see today.

In 2001, one of the things that puzzled many people, especially in the West, was Osama bin Laden's frequent reference to the suffering of the past *eighty* years. One can see why, say, *fifty* years might have made more sense—the Israeli state was established in 1948, and thousands of Palestinians were evicted from their ancestral homelands following the defeat of the Arab armies both that year and in 1967. But to bin Laden and his fellow followers of the more extreme *salafiyya* version of Islam—the kind that wants to re-create the pure Islamic and Arab-led Islam of the seventh century—the defeat and betrayal of 1918 was the real disaster.

In the Islamist view, *the map of the Middle East as we know it now is entirely the result of the invasion of that region by Britain and France, and their plans for it. It is not the map that would have been drawn if the Ottoman Empire had imploded from within.*

It was a nominal Muslim, however, a nationalist secularist, the Turkish leader Kemal Ataturk, who abolished the Ottoman Empire in 1922 and then, with the agreement of the Turkish Parliament, abolished the Caliphate in 1924—the office that had, with a few gaps, stretched back to Muhammad's first successor in 632. In other words, it was not the wicked West that abolished the ancient Caliphate and destroyed the Ottoman Empire—it was a Muslim-born Turk. His aim was to modernize Turkey, the country that emerged from the ashes of the old empire. He wanted to bring it up to par with the West so that never again would Turkey be defeated by Western powers or be helplessly dependent on them, as the Ottomans had been throughout the nineteenth century. Finally, Turkey, under his leadership in 1923, became the only defeated power of World War I to get a revised treaty in its favor.

As the continuing history of Egypt demonstrates, and as the story of Iraq under Ba'athist rule also showed, you did not *have* to be a Muslim to be an Arab. The founders of the Ba'ath Party that overthrew the monarchies of Syria and Iraq in 1958 were Christians. Many later Arab leaders, like Gamal Abdel Nasser, the Egyptian dictator, and later Saddam Hussein, while nominally Muslim, were essentially nationalist secularists rather than Islamists.

They regularly put Islamic leaders to death and employed Christians in key posts in their regimes.

So while Islamic extremists like bin Laden might lament 1918, why *they* do so is, I would say, very different from why so many Arabs feel betrayed by what happened that year.

The Arab Revolt did not do much to beat the Turks, but it did give the Arabs a powerful argument for legitimacy in the very changed circumstances of the end of the war; for, as many of them argued—notably in Egypt, which had become a British protectorate in 1914—the right to self-determination that Wilson was granting to the oppressed peoples of Europe—the Czechs, Poles and others—applied to Arabs as well. They, too, had the right to an independent sovereign nation of their own.

Now that British and Australian troops had conquered the old Ottoman Empire, local Arab populations were bound to see things differently. In Egypt, there were nationalist riots against both the British, who ruled indirectly, and the Egyptian Sultan, who was descended from the powerful Albanian-born Muslim ruler, Mehmet Ali, who had himself nearly destroyed the Ottoman Empire back in the 1820s and 1830s. These rebels were known by the Arabic word for "delegation"—they wanted to send delegations to the victorious Allies meeting in Paris—the *wafd*. Egyptians, being in a British-ruled state, had obviously taken no part in the Arab Revolt, but when it came to nationalist tumult, they led the way.

When the Ottoman Empire was defeated in 1918, Kemal Ataturk did not take the view of the corrupt and failing Ottoman government in Constantinople that all was over. He refused to accept the viciously harsh Treaty of Sèvres—which was never adopted—that not only gave all the Arab lands their independence, but gave Greece and other Allied countries large chunks of Turkish Anatolia as well, along with a large, independent Armenia. He was to launch a war of resistance, which he had won militarily by 1922, driving the Greeks out of Anatolia, reclaiming all the Turkish parts of the old empire (including much Kurd-inhabited territory), and getting a brand-new treaty to recognize it: the Treaty of Lausanne, signed in 1923.

The first difference one notices in looking at the map of the Middle East after 1918 is that the Russian zones are obviously gone; no one was going to allow the Bolsheviks any land. But look, too, at what is now Iraq.

Under Sykes-Picot, Mosul, with all its oil-bearing areas, is in the French zone. Not only that, but so is much of what is now Israel. Only an international zone around Jerusalem, and the port of Haifa, allocated to Britain, are not French. But in 1920, Britain got the mandate for all of Palestine—not the French—and Mosul was also under British rule and formally part of Iraq when that country gained full independence in 1932.

In other words, helping the Arabs rather than hindering them was a key part of British policy that, many writers argue, was to continue as Britain's main Middle Eastern goal until the Suez fiasco of 1956 and the violent and bloodthirsty overthrow of the Iraqi monarchy in 1958. The Arab Revolt began a long process of British sympathy for the Arab cause, albeit one made considerably more complicated by Britain's other wartime promise, the grant of a national Jewish homeland in Palestine.

The British had their obligation to the Zionists, and the French were determined to get Syria, including Damascus. France's often-brutal rule in Syria, its creation of a Christian-ruled state in Lebanon, and the very existence of a Jewish state are all now seen as savage betrayals of Arab-nationalist hopes. It was, however, not meant to turn out quite that way.

CHAPTER THREE

HOW TWO MEN IN LONDON CHANGED THE WORLD

O n 1 December 1918, two men met in London and accidentally changed the world. The conversation between them went roughly as follows:

"Well, what are we to discuss?" said the older man.

"Mesopotamia and Palestine," replied the younger one.

"Tell me what you want," replied the first one.

"I want Mosul," answered the second.

"You shall have it. Anything else?"

"Yes, I want Jerusalem too."

"You shall have it," the older man replied, "but Pinchon will make difficulties about Mosul."

The older man was Clemenceau, the walrus-mustached Prime Minister of France; the younger of the two, Britain's dynamic 55-year-old Prime Minister, David Lloyd George. The two men were meeting in order to try to square away as much as was possible in advance of the whirlwind—President Woodrow Wilson, with all his ideals and nonimperialist views—that was about to sweep into Europe and change everything. The United States was, after all, a country born as a result of a war of independence against the

British Empire. Wilson's passionate advocacy of self-determination—for the peoples of the Ottoman Empire included—would mean carving it—and all other empires—up, making things rather complicated for Britain and France, still imperial powers.

Mosul *vilayet* presented a problem: It was overwhelmingly Kurdish, not Arab. Its main city, Mosul, was home to many Arabs as well as Turcomans, an ethnic group very close to the former Turkish Ottoman rulers. But the Kurds, an Indo-European people closer to the Iranians than to any Arabs, did not want to be part of an Arab-ruled state; in fact, many of them would have even preferred continuing living as a minority people under Turkish rule to being part of a new and essentially Arab-nationalist kingdom. In an Arab-nationalist state they would be non-Arabs, but in a multinational Islamic Empire they would, as devout Muslims, be equal to the Islamic, even though non-Arab, Turks.

Under the infamous Sykes-Picot agreement that parceled out the Ottoman territory to Britain, France, and Russia, the Ottoman *vilayet* of Mosul, which bordered Russia, had been allocated to France. But after the Bolsheviks seized power from the Russian Tsar, I would argue, the entire Sykes-Picot agreement was rendered meaningless. This was greatly to Britain's advantage, in that the British Empire could now acquire possessions whose ownership had not previously been open for negotiation.

Lloyd George was dimly aware of Mosul's oil potential, as were some of the British officers in the field, such as Major Noel, who represented Britain's interests to the Kurdish tribal chieftains. But Lord Curzon, the British Foreign Secretary in whose political hands all this lay, was not. When he consulted with his colleagues on how to formulate policy for this area, oil was not mentioned as a factor—and in that the region's oil did not begin to gush until some years later, it may be that he was right. The *prospect* of finding oil, and actually *finding* any, as major exploration companies can attest, can often be two very different things. Leaders such as Churchill, who knew how important reliable sources of oil supply were for modern navies and armies, were still comparatively rare. We cannot read the twenty-first-century importance of Iraqi oil back into the discussions of the 1920s and presume that petroleum was as vital in their thinking as it is in ours today.

As a result of his conversation with Clemenceau, Lloyd George was able to feel confident that he could have his own way in the Middle East. For Clemenceau, revenge on Germany for seizing Alsace and Lorraine in 1871 was a far greater priority than a few acres of sand a long way from Europe. Unfortunately, as always, it was not that simple, as Clemenceau hinted to Lloyd George. There was a very strong colonial expansion lobby in France, one that did not greatly concern Clemenceau but that was nonetheless important in domestic politics. He knew he could not alienate them, even if he thought making France safer from German invasion was more important than who governed what part of the Middle East.

The result was that, although British and Australian troops had liberated Syria with the help of Arab troops, they were not able to keep the promises they had made in good faith to Feisal, who was now living in Damascus with many of his followers. However little Clemenceau cared personally for the Levant (the region including Syria, Lebanon, Israel, and Jordan), and however much leading British generals, politicians, and Arab sympathizers might also want to claim Syria, abandoning the region was too great a step for the French to take. Consequently, although the British would have liked Feisal to rule in Damascus, priorities back home ultimately dictated that they were not positioned to offer it to him, certainly not on a permanent basis.

So what Feisal was expecting—and Lawrence, too, on his behalf—the British were eventually unable to deliver. This was, though, no deliberate betrayal; the British had not offered Feisal a kingdom that they knew in advance they would not be able to give him. Rather, a series of mistakes and crossed wires ended up with Feisal getting a kingdom—but not the kingdom of Syria.

In 1918, the British did not have any real idea of what any of the boundaries would be of the area they had just conquered. Worse still, they did not agree among themselves on the status of the territories. Some officials, mainly those who had served in the British Raj in India, wanted full colonial rule. Others, in the new spirit of Wilsonian self-determination, were happy to offer the Arabs a country or countries of their own, so long as Britain was able to pull the strings behind the scenes. We can see this if we look at attempts that were made to draw maps of the newly British-occupied territories, split up along the lines agreed upon by Lloyd George and Clemenceau during their brief chat in London.

The real problem was how to square imperial designs with the professed public agreement of Britain and France *and* with Wilson's policy of self-determination.

To start, we can best describe British policy on "Kurdistan" (no such unitary and independent state has ever existed) as a mess. No one had any idea of how great an area a Kurdish state could cover and how any new country to be created would relate to the nascent Armenian and Arab states they also wished to see blossom. Nor was there any one Kurdish leader, as Feisal was for the Arab parts of Britain's new dominions, whom the British felt they could rely on as a useful and compliant native ruler.

The other problem the British had in Kurdistan was the potential existence of oil there. Here I agree with John Keay's excellent book *Sowing the Wind: The Seeds of Conflict in the Middle East.* He shows how, for politicians at the time, oil was simply not an issue, since the vast oil reserves we now know to be there were at that time unproven. Lloyd George was not unaware of the potential for oil from Mosul *vilayet,* but even he did not greatly press the issue.

Surprising, from our twenty-first-century perspective, oil was the missing factor in Britain's ill-fated decision to become involved with Iraq, at least during the period in which Churchill was involved. Most of the world's oil came from the United States or Mexico, and it was not until 1914 that the Anglo-Persian Oil Company's major refinery at Abadan, in Persia, came onstream. According to Peter Sluglett's *Britain in Iraq: 1914–1932,* Anglo-Persian was "the sole oil *producing* undertaking in the Middle East until 1927."

Eager prospectors were not deterred from trying to find oil elsewhere in the region, though, and the Ottoman *vilayets* that now make up Iraq were being explored even before the First World War. In 1912, a British, German, and Dutch consortium formed the Turkish Petroleum Company to see if there was oil in the Mosul and Baghdad *vilayets.* They were, it seems, as keen to stop the United States from finding oil there as anything else, until the outbreak of war in 1914 considerably altered the geopolitical landscape, placing Britain on the opposite side from the Turks and Germans.

Churchill's lack of interest in Iraqi oil is all the more ironic since he was the person who, as First Lord of the Admiralty, was responsible for the

British government's decision in 1914 to secure 51 percent of the shares in Anglo-Persian Oil. This was a holding that the government was to retain until Margaret Thatcher's privatization policy in the late 1980s (by which time the company had become the BP we know today).

After the war, Britain's policy seems to have been to deny others the chance to get the oil rather than actively to prospect for it herself; that is, that no country should have the ability to stop the United Kingdom from obtaining oil from the region.

As Colonel A. T. Wilson, Britain's acting ruler for the area, suggested in late 1918, "oil is the only immediately available asset of the Occupied Territories, the only real security. . . ." In his later memoirs, he wrote that:

> The daily press in Europe and the USA was during the latter part of 1919 and the whole of 1920 full of reference to the fancied connection between the reputed oil deposits of Mesopotamia and the acceptance by Great Britain of the Mandate, and nothing that British statesmen could do or say availed against the attacks and innuendoes appearing in the daily press of Europe and the USA.

This was, however, slightly disingenuous, since the British, while not having themselves dug wells in the area, knew that the Germans had begun active work there during the war. As one report put it:

> It is not possible to give any estimates of the potential production of Mesopotamia as this can only be determined when deep drilling has been carried out over a wide area. There is no doubt however, that this region can safely be regarded as extremely promising.

By 1919, though, all prospecting had been halted by the British occupying authorities. The Americans had become very interested in the region, and the British government had not yet decided on whether to let the United States in or not. The main issue was that the United Kingdom wanted to be in control of who exactly got what, where.

At the Conference of San Remo in 1920, the Allies decided to allocate the former German share in the Turkish Petroleum Company to the French, and put the company "under permanent British control." Needless to say, this was not at all acceptable to the United States, whose free-trade "open door" policy meant that all countries had an equal right to whatever could be discovered in the newly liberated areas. (There were also some legal niceties that the United States regarded as invalidating the original prewar Ottoman grant.)

All this contributed considerably to what by 1922 was to be serious British isolation on the issue. As Churchill noted:

> There is some reason to believe that neither the United States nor France would be sorry to see the Turks back in Mosul in a position to give their nationals the oil concessions which are at present claimed by H.M. Government for the Turkish National Petroleum Company.

Not, in fact, until 1923, when Churchill was out of office but Lord Curzon was still Foreign Secretary, was the issue finally resolved, by which time there was also a notional Iraqi government. And not until 1927 did any serious prospecting begin, and in 1929 the company's name become, more logically, the Iraq Petroleum Company. But it "was not until the early 1950s that oil receipts began to make a substantial contribution to the economy of Iraq."

May 1919 was to be a month with permanent repercussions for the world we live in today. Britain was severely overstretched militarily, with commitments greater than it had the capacity to absorb in peacetime, as Churchill, the Secretary of State for War and Air, well knew.

The Greeks, on 15 May, with full Allied authority, landed 20,000 troops on the Anatolian mainland and occupied the town of Smyrna, which had had a large number of Greek inhabitants since biblical times (it is one of the Seven Churches of Asia in the Book of Revelation). The very next day, Mustapha Kemal, the victor at Gallipoli, left the essentially defunct Ottoman capital of Constantinople and demanded the total evacuation by the allies of both Anatolia and Turkey-in-Europe. The Turkish counteroffensive had begun, an offensive that was to continue until, by 1922, the Turkish nationalists were militarily successful and, by 1923, were able to force the Allies to recognize their victory.

All this—British overreach and the war between Greece and Turkey—forms the essential background to what Churchill wished to do with the Middle East. His prime aim as the minister in charge of both the army and the infant Royal Air Force was to save money, and that meant drastic troop cuts and withdrawals. It was also an axiom of British military doctrine that the British Empire should have to face as few enemies as possible. This policy, which, in the light of Britain's very limited resources, made considerable sense both financially and militarily, has often been called "limited liability."

While no one could outdo Churchill in saving money, it is also fair to add that throughout the main period of this book (1918 to 1922), he was stymied by Lloyd George's decision to back the Greeks against the Turks. This and Britain's shaky postwar financial state were Churchill's two priorities; they outweighed everything else. And as he realized at the start of May 1919, if Britain had to maintain large forces in Constantinople and other parts of the Dardanelles, reductions would have to come from somewhere else.

In the short term, Churchill's policy made a lot of sense; but its long-term repercussions were to prove dire. Britain had troops not only in Turkey but also in Egypt, Mesopotamia, Palestine, Persia (defending the country against Bolshevik attack), Russia (trying in vain to get rid of Lenin and the Bolshevik regime), Ireland (protecting it against the increasingly successful Irish rebels), and India (where Mohandas Gandhi was beginning his career as the person to get the British out of the subcontinent). All this was far too much for a war-weary and very battered United Kingdom that was still reeling from the effects and horrors of four years of global war.

As Churchill wrote to Lloyd George on 1 May:

The responsibilities of the Army will have been increased by the war. . . . The whole East is unsettled by the disintegration of Turkey, and we shall have large additions of territory in Palestine and Mesopotamia to maintain.

The problem was, as Churchill well knew, that all this was far beyond the resources of the frail British Empire to sustain. Some months later, in August, he wrote to the former British Prime Minister and now Peace Conference delegate, Arthur Balfour:

We have maintained a force of some 40,000 men in Constantinople and on the Black Sea shores ever since the 11th November [1918]. The strain of this upon our melting military resources is becoming unsupportable.

Unfortunately, as Churchill knew, it was not for him to make the decision on peace with Turkey, a drawn-out process that took until 1920, longer than any of the other negotiations for peace treaties that followed World War One. Since cuts had to come from somewhere, given the gigantic and ongoing expense of British occupation in Turkey, Churchill chose what he thought would be an easy option: Mesopotamia.

On 30 August 1919, he wrote to the commander in the region, General Sir George MacMunn, that of the 25,000 British troops stationed there, at least 13,000 had to be sent home "within the next three months." Of the 80,000 native Indian Army forces, 45,000 were also to be sent home, along with 60,000 "Indian followers" (camp followers and civilian workers). It was, he told the general, "absolutely necessary to get down to it at once."

All this, though, was at a time when Churchill was also pestering his colleagues to send a considerable number of British troops to Murmansk, at the northwest tip of Russia, and to the Caucasus. They were to be part of the larger army designed to defeat the Bolsheviks and install a "White" (anticommunist) government in Russia. There was perhaps one thing that was more important to Churchill than saving money: getting rid of the Bolsheviks. (The fact that as Prime Minister Churchill fought alongside the U.S.S.R. against Nazi Germany is one of the many ironies of his long political life.) But for now, reducing unnecessary expenditure was what mattered. As he reminded Sir George:

There can be absolutely no question of holding the present enormous forces at your disposal, and you must make the best military plan you can in the circumstances. I would remind you that under the Turks Mesopotamia not only paid its way but supplied a revenue to the Central Government. The military establishment you are maintaining at the present time would simply crush the province and possibly prove fatal to its retention by Great Britain.

However, without a peace agreement with the crumbling Ottoman Empire anywhere in sight, Churchill was having to operate under a policy of demobilization without knowing the long-term need for British forces abroad.

Churchill also now had an unsympathetic prime minister. On 22 September, Lloyd George found Churchill:

> so obsessed by Russia that I felt I had good ground for the apprehension that your great abilities, energy and courage were not devoted to the reduction of expenditure.

Churchill replied the same day, protesting that his political master was being "unkind" and "unjust." Much of the letter is about Churchill's very real obsession with Russia, which Lloyd George was surely right to put in the realm of fantasy, since British troops alone could not possibly have had any realistic chance of overthrowing Lenin and the Bolsheviks. But on the Middle East, Churchill made a fair point:

> Even now what you are asking will butt up against the impossible at many points. You will not be able to reduce the garrison of Ireland to its prewar figure without an Irish policy. You will have to maintain exceptional forces in Palestine, Egypt & Mesopotamia till you have settled with Turkey & till the provocation of Turkey by the Greeks has come to an end. . . . Of course in a gigantic sphere like that of our dissolving armies with all their litter scattered about the globe, there are many things wh[ich] may serve the purposes of unfriendly or captious criticisms.

This meant a total reorganization of both the Army and the Royal Air Force, of which Churchill could fairly claim to be a parent, along with Lord Trenchard. Much of the debate on reorganizing defense is beyond the scope of this book, but Mesopotamia was one of the biggest headaches Churchill inherited and should be seen in the context of the reorganization debate.

Churchill was often in the habit of writing stern letters to people and then, tactfully, not actually sending them. One hopes that getting any anger out of his system made him feel better; it certainly gives us great insight into how affairs of state affected him emotionally. A missive to Lloyd George a few days later, on 24 September 1919, is a good example:

> It is clear to me from your letter that you have no idea of the work which has been done here, or of the very considerable difficulties which have been surmounted. Let me remind you that I took over a dissolving army, gigantic in size and to a very large extent permeated by mutiny and discontent. . . . Side by side with all this, I have to be ready to meet repeated emergencies in Egypt, in India, in Ireland, on the Rhine and in this country, and have been forced to continue in war occupation of Constantinople, Mesopotamia and Palestine under conditions of great unrest.

In Churchill's attempts to reduce military expenditure, he frequently found the generals more than obdurate. The British army of occupation in Mesopotamia, under General MacMunn, was one of the worst offenders. Take this letter, which actually was sent, on 25 September:

> I asked for a provisional and immediate reduction of 98,000 as specified. In reply you propose successive reductions amounting to 120,000 by the Spring of next year. I cannot accept this. . . . [When MacMunn's new reduction estimates had been] completed, the provisional post-war garrison will have been reached. But even this garrison, as reduced, will crush the province with military charges and ruin its future development. Even its retention by Great Britain would be questionable on these terms. You should therefore prepare without delay a scheme for creating a special police and military instrument for maintaining order in Mesopotamia.

Since Churchill was not the minister politically responsible for the province, it was brazen of him to ask for such a force. But he was never put off by the prospect of interfering in things that were not directly his business. This can be seen in a memorandum he wrote for his colleagues in the government on 25 October, in which he makes recommendations for the entire fate of the dying Ottoman Empire. He was, as things turned out, entirely right to be worried about the Greek army of occupation and also about the very high-handed attitude of the French, whose treatment of the inhabitants of Syria was far more draconian than anything the British had attempted in similar territories. He was especially concerned because, in addition to Britain's rule over millions of Muslims in the Raj, as a result of its new responsibilities in the Middle East, the British Empire had become unquestionably "the greatest Mahommedan [*sic*] power" in the world. Churchill worried that the Greeks and the French could upset it all:

> India, Egypt, Mesopotamia and Palestine are all affected prejudicially. In regard to Egypt, Mesopotamia and Palestine, we are forced to maintain military establishments the cost of which far exceeds the resulting revenue and throw [*sic*] a burden on Army Estimates of the gravest kind.

To him, the British policy of abetting the carve-up of the Ottoman Empire was thus a "mistake" that included deserting the Arabs who had fought on Britain's side during the war. He realized that the chances of the United States taking on any of the hoped-for mandates in the Middle East were now slim. His course of action was therefore drastic:

> whether the European Powers should not, jointly and simultaneously, renounce all separate interests in the Turkish Empire other than those which existed before the war. That is to say, the Greeks should quit Smyrna, the French should give up Syria, we should give up Palestine and Mesopotamia, and the Italians should give up their sphere.

He then propounded the very radical scheme of placing the League of Nations headquarters in Constantinople, not Geneva. The League would rule the Ottoman Empire itself, with a "secular Government" under an Inter-Allied Council of Control directly under the League. Constantinople would be a Turkish version of the District of Columbia, preferably under an American governor.

He realized, of course, that it would be:

> found very hard to relinquish the satisfaction of those dreams of conquest and aggrandisement which are gratified by the retention of Palestine and Mesopotamia. As a matter of fact we have far more territory in the British

Empire than we shall be able to develop for many generations. . . . The need of national economy is such that we ought to endeavour to concentrate our resources on developing our existing Empire instead of dissipating them in new enlargements. We can only compel the other Powers to give up their exploitation claims against Turkey by ourselves being willing to set an example.

Churchill was surely right to say that for Britain to extend its empire would be a grave mistake, and the major rebellions that were just about to erupt in Mesopotamia against the British and in Syria against the French bear him out. But would the Arabs have been any more quiescent toward a League-ruled empire? For them, one could well argue, *any* European presence, whether directly British and French, or an amalgam of all the white powers under a League banner, would have been equally unacceptable.

In any case, Churchill's bold initiative was ignored. He continued in his endless attempts to save money and, ironically, in so doing, reduced British troop levels so effectively in the newly conquered territories that he unwittingly helped precisely those nationalist rebels who wanted Britain to leave, for soon there would not be enough troops in the region to crush *any* nascent Arab revolt. To be fair, Churchill understood this. He also realized, as 1920 began, that the only way to keep order in the area would be to use Indian Army troops. But since many of these troops would be enraged by the overall British decision to block the growing nationalist movement under Mustapha Kemal, this would, Churchill saw, compromise the very Indian troops on which Britain relied.

On 7 February, Churchill submitted his Army Estimates for 1920 to 1921. The cost of maintaining British armies in the Middle East was, he explained to his colleagues, quite excessive. When it came to Mesopotamia, he told them that the cost would soon be as much as eighteen and a half million pounds sterling a year. As a result:

The cost of the military establishment in Mesopotamia appears to me to be out of all proportion to any advantage we can ever expect to reap from that country . . . it seems high time that our general policy in regard to Mesopotamia should be fundamentally reconsidered. Apart from its importance as a link in the aerial route to India and the air defence of the Middle East, and apart from the military significance of the oil deposits, the General Staff are not pressing for the retention of Mesopotamia, or any part of it, on strategic grounds of Imperial security.

Churchill's allusion to oil is interesting—it is the *military* significance of the potential oil discoveries, not the economic, which is important.

He continued:

Personally, I believe that the military forces in Mesopotamia are out of all proportion to what is justifiable or reasonable to employ in that part of the world.

What Churchill wanted was for Britain to occupy, if necessary, a much smaller and thus far cheaper area that would cost only five and a half million pounds a year. He would have withdrawn from Mosul altogether, the area in which the Kurds predominated and where most of the oil would eventually be found—a policy the leading generals both supported and opposed. Economies were fine with some of them, but they saw—accurately, as it soon turned out—the dangers inherent in withdrawing too many troops from Mosul too soon. As General Radcliffe put it to the acerbic Chief of the Imperial General Staff, Sir Henry Wilson, a scuttle (withdrawal) would harm the British Empire's prestige. Furthermore:

In Mesopotamia, or especially in the Mosul Villayet [*sic*], is the one potential asset which has come to us from the war. It is surely worth some sacrifice in the present to reap its unbounded possibilities in the future.

Even if Churchill and Curzon were oblivious to the future potential of Middle Eastern oil, the generals were not. Churchill's concerns continued to be to save money and to spare the world from Bolshevism.

Unfortunately for Churchill, his rosy plans for withdrawal all depended on general peace in the Middle East; on 7 March 1920, the Allied governments made the fateful decision to declare Allied occupation of Constantinople and the Straits. Then, on 10 March, Feisal, who had been aspiring to a throne for a long time, declared himself King of Syria, despite the fact that the French were now in military occupation of much of his supposed kingdom.

On 1 April 1920, Churchill was on vacation in one of his favorite holiday spots in southern France, in this case near Bordeaux rather than at one of his more usual Côte d'Azur resorts, when he decided to write to the new commander in chief of British forces in Mesopotamia, General Sir Aylmer Haldane, whose appointment, from many points of view, was unfortunate for Churchill.

In 1900 Churchill had been captured while a young officer in South Africa during the Boer War. His brave escape and his considerable ability to write about it and publicize it to his own advantage were among the exploits of his youth that had made him famous.

Haldane had also been one of those captured, and he greatly resented all the fame and fortune that their mutual capture—and Churchill's escape—had brought his erstwhile fellow officer. Haldane was to spend the next two years intriguing against Churchill, something that was not to advance the chances of the many things that Churchill wanted to do. In the end Churchill proved forgiving, but theirs was not to be an easy relationship.

Churchill's first telegram to Haldane, who was now in Baghdad, set out what he thought was British policy. Since he was Secretary of State for Air as well as for War, Churchill's enthusiasm for a role for the RAF in the region probably did not help. He told Haldane:

> The fate of the province depends . . . entirely upon whether a reasonable scheme for maintaining order can be devised at a cost which is not ruinous.

Since rebellion was brewing, this was not to be the case; but Churchill's mind, for the time being, remained on cutting costs. He wrote a memorandum a month later on the whole Mesopotamian situation. He wanted, he told his colleagues, to draw their:

> attention . . . to the waste of money entailed by our present military and

administrative policy in Mesopotamia, and to invite them to take certain general decisions of principle which will enable a prompt and drastic curtailment of expenditure to be effected.

Being a strong proponent of airpower, Churchill understood that the RAF could do far more than ground troops to keep order in a place as widely flung and comparatively uninhabited as Mesopotamia.

In his dispatches, Churchill's depth of feeling on the issue is apparent. The prevailing system of placing garrisons all over the country made no sense to him, and he saw it as completely wasteful. He was also not without many of the white colonialist prejudices of his time:

> The result of this vicious system is that a score of mud villages, sandwiched in between a swampy river and a blistering desert, inhabited by a few hundred half naked native families, usually starving, are now occupied, have been occupied for many months, and are likely to remain occupied in the future. . . .

All this was to him "ruinous expense."

He now came up with an idea that was to haunt him—the creation of a special "Department of State" for the Middle East. He had a good case for it, though whether he realized that he would himself soon be burdened with running it is open to debate.

The region was the overlapping zone between several different, often feuding, major government departments. For historic reasons, much of the Middle East, including the *political* control of Mesopotamia, was under the India Office. The Foreign Office dealt with states which were already independent and also Egypt, whose exact status was under discussion at the time. Troops in the region were under both the War Office (if British) or the India Office (if Indian Army). Nearby British colonies were under the Colonial Office. All this led to endless bureaucratic infighting which, as Churchill fully realized and did not hesitate to point out, was all very unhelpful to coordinated British policy in the region. He therefore requested that "Mesopotamia be handed over immediately to the Colonial Office," which was then being presided over by the former British ruler of South

Africa, Lord Alfred Milner. Military control would be under the RAF, which would need far fewer bases than a fully equipped army. These two decisions would, he explained, save Mesopotamia and the British taxpayer from the current "profuse and futile expenditure of the taxpayers' money."

In one of his rare mentions of the local oil reserves, Churchill concluded his memorandum on Mesopotamian expenditure by adding:

> In considering the future profit which may be drawn from the Mesopotamian oil fields, it is necessary always to bear in mind the capital charges which are accruing. Every year we go on at the present rate of expenditure adds £1,000,000 a year at 5 per cent to what Mesopotamia will ultimately have to produce in order to yield a profit. Even if the oil-fields bear out our most sanguine hopes, we are burdening them to an intolerable extent with capital charges, and what would be a thoroughly good business for the British Empire, if developed gradually and thriftily is being daily deteriorated by the sterile charges which are mounting up.

One wonders how many similar discussions, balancing Iraqi oil revenues against the cost of occupation, have vexed British and American minds ever since.

In April 1920, the Allies made the fatal decision to dismantle the old Ottoman Empire; Churchill's notion of keeping it together proved unable to stand up to Britain's desire to acquire as much territory as possible. Sad, too, was the fact that the United States was no longer in the equation. Wilsonian idealism had given way to conservative isolationism in the United States, with all the dire consequences for Europe that were to follow over the next nineteen years, from the San Remo Conference in 1920 to the outbreak of World War Two in 1939.

One could say, with justice, that we still live with the consequences of the decision of a few Allied leaders at San Remo, in April 1920, to give France mandates for Syria and Lebanon. Here lie the origins of the Lebanese civil war of the 1970s and 1980s, since, in order to give the purely Christian parts of Lebanon effective economic support, the French artificially added large swaths of Muslim and Druze territory to the area inhabited solely by Maronite Christian Arabs. Arab-nationalists in Syria were deeply unhappy with this decision, and it is no coincidence that today, following the years of destruction of the Lebanese civil war, the notionally still-independent Lebanon is entirely occupied by Syrian troops, who control the country behind the scenes.

But the most lasting and controversial decision at San Remo was to award the mandate for Palestine to Britain, whose commitment to the Jewish people to set up a permanent homeland there clashed with its postwar promises to give the Arabs some measure of independence. One could say that this is a dilemma that remains unsolved and is causing deaths and conflict right up to our own day, with no end in sight.

As this book is on Mesopotamia/Iraq, I will not enter the Palestine/Israel minefield. Suffice it to say that it was to be a matter of immediate concern to Churchill, both as Secretary of State for War in charge of security policy and then as Colonial Secretary with direct political responsibility. At that time, though, the costs of the Palestinian garrisons were nowhere near as high as they were in Mesopotamia, so from that point of view, the expenditure vexed Churchill less. He was to find, though, that his instinctive Zionism and the contrary wishes of the local Arab peoples, who wanted to keep out the growing tide of Jewish settlers, were to be in permanent conflict.

The other decisions that affected him were the grant of the mandate for Mesopotamia to Britain, our main theme, and the dismemberment of mainland Anatolian Turkey. This last decision, soon to be forced on the Turks in August 1920 by the signing of the Treaty of Sèvres, would, understandably, inflame Turkish opinion. While the crumbling Ottoman government in Constantinople agreed to sign the treaty, the nationalist alternative government in Angora, under Mustapha Kemal, refused to do anything of the kind. The humiliation of the treaty—which went far beyond anything imposed on Germany by Versailles—now encouraged them to launch a war that would within just a few years bring Turkish victory and destroy the British government of which Churchill was so eminent a member. As soon as the treaty had been signed by Constantinople and the Allies, Mustapha Kemal, in Angora, summoned a Grand National Assembly and declared that Turkey was at war with the Allies who had imposed it.

The fact that Churchill fully realized how foolish the treaty was did not help; he was to spend much of the next two and a half years as a lone voice crying in the wilderness. When justification came in October 1922 with the defeat of Greek forces in Anatolia, it was too late for him; his political career was to go down along with that of the increasingly rabidly anti-Turk, pro-Greek British Prime Minister, David Lloyd George.

Churchill's acute dilemma for the next two years (1920 to 1922) has been neatly summarized by his official biographer, Sir Martin Gilbert:

> This hostility threatened to bring war to Britain's new Arab territory, Mesopotamia, and to antagonise Muslim feeling both in Mesopotamia and in Palestine. Concerned above all with economy, Churchill feared Muslim antagonism, and warned that the policing of these two territories could become extremely expensive unless Turkey were appeased. Unwilling to see his War Office budget drained in Middle Eastern conflicts, he had taken a lead in urging a policy of withdrawal and disengagement. But just as Lloyd George supported the Greeks against the Turks, he was also eager to see British power retained in Palestine and Mesopotamia. Churchill therefore persevered in a joint policy of control and economy, but remained sceptical that either could really succeed if they were forced to run together.

As someone who passionately believes in what Churchill stood for in opposing Hitler, I would never want to defend Neville Chamberlain's appeasement of the Nazis and the catastrophic policies he pursued—ultimately unsuccessfully—as prime minister. But there is a good case for saying that what was morally so wrong in relation to Nazi Germany *did* make a lot of sense when applied a decade earlier to Turkish nationalism. Mustapha Kemal was no saint—he had committed many major atrocities. But rather like the Spanish dictator, Franco, who came to power in the following decade, he was a dictator who at least did not fight wars of aggression outside his own main territory. This does not excuse him at all, as Armenians remind us to this day. But he did end decades of religious repression and obscurantism, and he began a rapid process of modernization that resulted in what Turkey is today, the one fully democratic, religiously Muslim state in the Middle East. Whatever the faults of Kemal Ataturk's modern Turkey, it did not join the Axis in World War Two (Churchill's attempts to persuade the Turks to join the Allies were unfruitful until 1945, Turkey remaining neutral until then) and launched no wars of invasion on neighboring countries, not even to reclaim Mosul, despite Churchill's deepest fears in 1920 to 1922. All in all, Britain could have done a lot better listening to Churchill during this period than to the philhellene Prime Minister, David Lloyd George.

In the summer of 1920, the lack of foresight of Churchill's many cuts in Mesopotamia became all too apparent. In May, a rebellion broke out in Tel Afar, in Mosul *vilayet,* over the arrest for debt of a local sheikh. Four British soldiers were killed by local Arab insurgents. The British thereupon sent two armored cars, but they were ambushed, with the loss of two officers and fourteen men.

Regrettably, the British response was extreme: The entire population of Tel Afar was driven out into the desert; this resulted in the whole of British-ruled Mesopotamia being in revolt by July.

Churchill, though, was still worrying about the expense! He wrote to Lloyd George on 13 June about the "weakness of the Army in relation to its commitments." In relation to Mesopotamia and Mosul province, he asked:

> Next are we to clear out of Mosul or not? There is going to be fighting in this district in the near future, & no possibility of reducing the Mesopotamian garrison exists unless a definite contraction of responsibilities is accepted. . . . We cannot go on sprawled out over these vast regions at ruinous expense & ever increasing military risk. If it is decided to hold Mosul, the garrison of Mesopot[amia] must be fully maintained, the railway must be prolonged into Mosul, & Parliament must be told that the expectation, of reduction in expense cannot be made good.

If a major war were to break out, he told Lloyd George, there were *"no reserves anywhere."*

As he said to his Cabinet colleagues two days later, he was all in favor of a decision to abandon Mosul and to "withdraw everywhere to our railheads."

> This means leaving our many half-fulfilled responsibilities in the extended

regions which have been occupied to the mercy of the Arabs and Kurds. On the other hand, a decision to make our will effective by vigorous action in the Mosul area must delay indefinitely that process of military reduction which I have been enforcing severely upon the Commander-in-Chief in Mesopotamia.

By mid-June both Churchill and his acerbic Chief of the Imperial General Staff (CIGS), Sir Henry Wilson, were in favor of pulling out of Mosul. When Wilson met "Lawrence of Arabian fame" on 17 June, Lawrence told him "baldly that we should be kicked out of Turkey, Mesopot[amia] and Persia."

But while Wilson was pro-Turkish, and Churchill was in favor of appeasement, Lloyd George himself remained as anti-Turkish as ever, and thus strongly in favor of staying put in Mosul and the rest of Mesopotamia.

While all this was going on, a rogue British general, General Reginald Dyer, massacred scores, probably hundreds, of innocent protesters in Amritsar, India, in the notorious Amritsar Massacre. British forces were now in India, Ireland, Persia, Turkey—and Mesopotamia—with action in each place that was seriously overstretching Britain's slender postwar resources.

On 15 July, Wilson was with the Prime Minister on the Continent at an Allied conference when he heard the news from Mesopotamia—the rebellion was spreading like wildfire. Highly perturbed, he sent a telegram to Churchill urging:

> the despatch of the whole Div[ision]: from India & not only a Brigade for
> it was essential to give those Arabs on the Lower Euphrates a good lesson.

What precisely "a good lesson" meant is still a highly controversial subject. Rebel tribesmen with comparatively primitive weapons were attacked from the air by the Royal Air Force using the latest ordnance against them.

Churchill, to Wilson's despair, continued to worry primarily about cost. As Sir Henry noted in his diary the next day, "A wild wire from Winston about Mesopotamia & expense!"

In Mesopotamia, the rebels were soon making major progress. When General F. E. Coningham's forces reached the town of Rumaitha, they succeeded in halting the rebel siege but lost five British officers and thirty Indian soldiers. On 24 July, yet worse news came; General George Leslie of the Manchester Regiment was in retreat from the town of Kifl. No fewer than 180 of his men had been killed and 160 captured. However much Churchill was worried over the expense, a British scuttle was clearly no longer an option.

Part of the predicament was that Britain was also facing major problems elsewhere, Ireland included. Not until 30 July was Churchill prepared to order the dispatch of a whole military division from India to Mesopotamia; yet by the beginning of August, General Haldane was telling his War Office colleagues that not even Baghdad could definitely be held against the rebels.

Then the former Acting Commissioner, A. T. Wilson, had an idea that would eventually come to Churchill's rescue. Up to this point, Wilson, like many other India Office officials, had been against the notion of an Arab regime. Yet he now proposed that an Arab government be set up in the region, headed by Feisal, who had only just been brutally expelled from Syria by French troops.

Churchill knew that cutting expenses and crushing a rebellion in which British troops were being slaughtered was an impossible combination. He had wanted to reduce British troop levels, but Lord Curzon, the Foreign Secretary, and Lord Milner, the Colonial Secretary, had opposed him. Now the issue had to be discussed. On 5 August he wrote to Lloyd George:

> I have not hitherto thought it right to do more than place on record my protest . . . [and the CIGS] . . . against the position of increasing danger to which our troops are exposed. I feel, however, that matters have now reached a point where my responsibility to prevent a great disaster has become a very real one.

But the only decision taken by the Cabinet the next day was to send the veteran diplomat Sir Percy Cox to Baghdad. Sir Percy had been the Chief Political Adviser to the ill-fated Indian Expeditionary Force to Mesopotamia from 1914 to 1917 and more recently the Acting Minister to Persia, where he was in charge of the diplomatic side of the British effort to prevent that country from being taken over by the Bolsheviks.

That same day, a Cabinet Finance Committee met in Lloyd George's room in the House of Commons, and both Churchill and Sir Henry Wilson "impressed upon the Committee with the utmost earnestness the risks that were being run by the dispersion of our forces in different theatres."

> The military authorities were unanimous in thinking that it was out of the question for them to assent to the suggestion . . . that the Lower Euphrates position should be temporarily abandoned.

But Britain was also fighting in Persia, and that could not be abandoned, even if doing so would free up troops to help the increasingly hard-pressed British forces in Mesopotamia. So the dilemma continued.

Sir Percy Cox, in London temporarily, but now en route to Baghdad, suggested to the Cabinet that they create a special Department of State exclusively for the Middle East. This made enormous sense, as it would prevent the endless bickering between the many government departments dealing with the region and the endless turf wars that were preventing what a later British government would call "joined-up government."

Churchill was still principally obsessed—Lloyd George had been right to describe him as such—with the Bolshevik issue. He was also most concerned with the likely decision of his colleagues to recognize independence for Egypt. Still, he did not altogether forget the fact that British troops were having a very hard time in the Mesopotamian desert; on 13 August, six British officials were killed by Arab rebels in the town of Shahraban. So when he wrote a letter to the Prime Minister on 26 August, mainly about Russian issues, at the end of it he did remember to mention the issue of Mesopotamia:

> With regard to Mesopotamia, I have told Sir Henry Wilson that the Cabinet have definitely decided that we are to plough through in that dismal country [and that] every effort must be made to procure vigorous action and decisive results. You will see that Haldane thinks that with the reinforcements we are sending he should be able to quell the revolt by the end of November.

Twenty new battalions were on the way, sixteen Indian and four British. Churchill wrote to Haldane the same day:

> The Cabinet have decided that the rebels must be quelled effectively, and I will endeavour to meet all your requirements. . . . Thus by the middle or end of October you should be possessed of effective striking forces, and a vigorous use of these to put down and punish disaffection combined with the policy of setting up an Arab state should bring about a better situation.

One of the main features of British forces in the area would be increased use of the Royal Air Force. In a letter to Sir Hugh Trenchard of 29 August, Churchill made a decision which has now become notorious, mentioned in virtually every television documentary in recent years, but never published in full. This is the complete letter:

> I think you should certainly proceed with the experimental work on gas bombs, especially mustard gas, which would inflict punishment on recalcitrant natives without inflicting grave injury upon them.

One can look at this infamous request in two ways. Yes, Churchill wanted to gas the rebels. No, Churchill did not want them killed, just put out of action. In fact, it would have been hard to drop mustard gas on Arab rebels without "inflicting grave injury upon them," and this proved to be the case, since many hundreds of Iraqi rebels died in the attacks. But on the other hand, his correspondence shows it was not true that Churchill wanted the rebels gassed *to death,* though that is the inevitable conclusion of more recent commentators, television broadcasters, and journalists. We cannot excuse Churchill from what actually happened as a result of the use of poison gas. But, while he did not intend the final results, we can therefore conclude that his suggestion to Trenchard was, however phrased, a highly unfortunate one. There is also the fact that it was made in the context of the ever-mounting British losses and defeats; more British officials had been murdered only a few days before.

Not surprisingly, General Haldane was getting desperate, and asked for even more troops—more than the twenty battalions already on the way.

Churchill had to write back on 30 August with the bad news that it was "very difficult to see how or to what extent this demand can be met." After asking Haldane many very specific questions on how, exactly, the fighting was going, he then asked him to speculate:

> In a recent telegram you explain that you had been anxious to withdraw from Mosul but did not feel yourself strong enough to do so. Let me know exactly what you mean by this. Suppose, for instance, you gave the troops in Mosul orders to concentrate on Mosul or Shergat or some other suitable point and come back into closer proximity to Baghdad, sacrificing of course the entire Mosul province? What would happen?

If British troops quit Mosul *vilayet,* would the Arab forces then attack Baghdad, Churchill wondered. He was also worried about the many vulnerable women and children and about the "Assyrian and Chaldean refugees," who were ethnically Arab but Christian in religion. Finally, he asked Haldane:

> Do you consider it impossible, with the reinforcements now on the way, to draw your troops into Baghdad and retire to Basra? How would you do it if you had to? Naturally everything in human power must be done to avert such a withdrawal, but for the information of the Cabinet I wish to know whether it is physically impossible in a military sense. What would you do if there were no reinforcements available. Would you be able to collect your Army and make your way to the coast or would you be destroyed en route.

This was indeed very serious, and as Churchill wrote the next day to Lord Curzon, "we are at our wits' end to find a single soldier."

Churchill then drafted a letter to the Prime Minister, which in the end he did not send. He realized that Haldane's pleas for more soldiers could not actually be met, since it would involve, for instance, having far fewer troops in Constantinople. Not only that; there was the continuing chaos in Ireland to consider. And troops could not reasonably be withdrawn from India.

Churchill now recognized that:

Evidently we are in for a long, costly campaign in Mesopotamia which will strain to the uttermost our military resources. I hope that may be the worst.

What worried Churchill considerably was that if Haldane tried to evacuate his troops before reinforcements arrived, it "might produce a disaster on a scale much greater than Kut." He no doubt would have recalled that not only had Britain's ignominious defeat there been a military and psychological disaster, it had also led to the resignation, albeit temporary, of Austen Chamberlain, the minister responsible for it. Churchill's political self-preservation was now surely playing a major part in his decisions.

As he put it to Lloyd George:

There is something very sinister to my mind in this Mesopotamian entanglement, coming as it does when Ireland is so great a menace. It seems to me so gratuitous that after all the struggles of war, just when we want to get together our slender military resources and re-establish our finances and have a little in hand in case of danger here or there, we should be compelled to go on pouring armies and treasure into these thankless deserts.

A better case against the perils of empire and of imperial overreach could not possibly be made! And in a way that many a politician of today could identify with, Churchill continued:

We have not got a single friend in the press on the subject, and there is no point of which they make more effective use to injure the Government. Week after week and month after month for a long time we shall have a continuance of this miserable, wasteful, sporadic, warfare marked from time to time certainly by minor disasters and cuttings off of troops and agents, and very possibly attended by some very grave occurrence.

Here, too, in 2003 and 2004, many a British or American administration figure must have echoed Churchill's inner and heartfelt sentiments on the nature of guerrilla war in the deserts of Iraq.

Despite all the disasters, Churchill had not forgotten his original over-riding aim—trying to save money:

> Meanwhile the military expense of this year alone will probably amount
> to something like fifty millions, thus by this capital expenditure knocking
> all the bloom off any commercial possibilities which may have existed.

Churchill now understandably vented his frustration with the British administration and their clear lack of competence, again expressing a view many a twenty-first-century politician or soldier could relate to:

> It is an extraordinary thing that the British civil administration should
> have succeeded in such a short time in alienating the whole country to
> such an extent that the Arabs have laid aside the blood feuds that they
> have nursed for centuries and that the Suni [sic] and Shiah [sic] tribes are
> working together. We have even been advised locally that the best way to
> get our supplies up the river would be to fly the Turkish flag, which would
> be respected by the tribesmen.

As for the new High Commissioner, Sir Percy Cox, in whose skill so much was being invested, Churchill had to confess:

> I do not feel any complete sense of confidence in him. His personality does
> not impress me, and all his recent prognostications have been falsified.

Churchill was doing his best:

> Every possible soldier that we can find is being set in motion for rein-
> forcement to the utmost limits of our available transport. This is equally
> necessary whether we decide to stay or quit. There is nothing else to do
> but this and it will take some time.

Churchill then made the extraordinary decision—unthinkable in today's manic age—to take two weeks' vacation in his beloved South of France! After returning briefly to London, he was off for France again on 25

September. By this time, the Mesopotamian revolt had effectively been suppressed. The rest of 1920 saw the British forces undertake all kinds of vicious reprisals—not just confiscating all the weapons the rebels had used, but also burning down villages and engaging in other actions that today we would regard as overly punitive if not downright barbaric. (The infamous "Black and Tans" activities of British troops in Ireland that were taking place at the same time created equal controversy.)

By the time Churchill had finally finished his vacation, returning to London on 12 October, the rebellion in Mesopotamia and in Mosul province had finally been totally crushed. Sir Percy Cox had taken charge in Baghdad the previous day, and the area was now under civilian control and nominally, at least, under the India Office in Whitehall.

The same period saw great tragedy; in November 1920 the Turkish nationalist forces under Mustapha Kemal finally ended the vain attempt of the Armenian people to have a genuine homeland of their own, the Republic of Armenia, established in May 1918. As one historian has commented, by the time the Armenian state was snuffed out, over one million Armenians had been slaughtered in one way or another by Turkish soldiers since the first large-scale massacres had taken place in 1915. Proportionately, this was a much higher percentage of the overall population than perished in the later and much more widely-known mass murder of the Jews by Hitler. (In fact, Hitler was to justify his genocidal policies later, in the 1940s, by saying "Today, after all, who speaks of the annihilation of the Armenians?") This was the template, the first genocide of the twentieth century, one made worse by the fact that it is so little remembered today. The Armenians can justly say that they are the primary victims of the failure of the peacemakers in Paris to keep all the promises they had made and of Wilson's failure to persuade his own people to allow the United States to take up mandates, since Armenia was designed to be under American protection.

The only good piece of news was the fall of the Greek government's warlike Eleutherios Venizelos. Churchill hoped this would lead to a major change in Lloyd George's policy; sadly, in the long term, this did not turn out to be the case, but not for want of trying on Churchill's part. He understood that British policy in Turkey had major repercussions in the new Middle Eastern possessions.

In early November, Churchill had told Lloyd George that all the financial cuts he had hoped for had become unfeasible as a result of the "very unpleasant" business in Mesopotamia; the savings he had hoped for would now be "an excess." But there were wider strategic issues as well.

As he informed his colleagues on 23 November:

> An opportunity now presents itself of securing an effective abatement of the strain and pressure put upon our troops and interests in the East and Middle East. We ought to come to terms with Mustapha Kemal and arrive at a good peace with Turkey which will secure our position and interests at Constantinople and ease the position in Egypt, Mesopotamia, Persia and India.

Churchill still hoped that the Armenians and other peoples of the Caucasus could be rescued from the Bolsheviks as well as the Turks; but in this his hope was futile. On the wider issue, however, he had a significant point to make:

> In our present state of military weakness and financial stringency we cannot afford to go on estranging the Mohammedan [sic] world in order to hand over a greater Greece to King Constantine. . . . Finally I must point out that the burden of carrying out the present policy at Constantinople, in Palestine, Egypt, Mesopotamia and Persia is beyond the strength of the British Army, and is producing [the] most formidable reaction upon the Indian Army, upon which we are compelled to rely. I see the very greatest difficulty in maintaining that situation through the new financial year unless our military measures are aided by a policy of reconciliation and co-operation with the Turks and with the Moslem world. It is far better to do this than to give up a province like Egypt, where we have been . . . established for so many years.

Churchill's main concerns continued to be the collapse of the anti-Bolshevik forces in Russia and the ongoing turmoil in Ireland. But on 4 December he decided to send an appeal to Lloyd George to reconsider his Middle East policy, about which he was now gravely worried. He was very "sorry how far we are drifting apart on foreign policy," but equally concerned at how harmful the Prime Minister's actions were:

> Moreover it seems to me a most injurious thing that we, the greatest Mohammedan power in the world, [should] be the leading Anti-Turk [*sic*] power. The desire you have to retain Mosul—& indeed Mesopotamia— is directly frustrated by this vendetta against the Turks. The terrible waste & expense [that] the Middle East is involving us in brings the subject forward in a practical & urgent form. I deeply regret and *resent* being forced to ask Parl[iamen]t for these appalling sums of money for new Provinces—all the more when the pursuance of the anti-Turk policy complicates & aggravates the situation in every one of them, & renders cheaper solutions impossible.

Churchill's determination to save money was to continue to dominate his thinking in the weeks and months ahead. Not only that, but as he asked the Prime Minister:

> But is y[ou]r policy going to be successful? I fear it is going wrong. First you are up against a shocking bill for Mesopotamia, Palestine and Persia. More will have to be spent in these countries next year than the Navy is demanding to save our sea supremacy.

Lloyd George's very personal policy, as Churchill pointed out to him, was doing him no good politically, either, and had alienated him from his old friends on the radical left, whose hero he had been before the war.

Churchill was in a vulnerable political position, though, to be pointing out these many home truths to the Prime Minister, since he owed everything to Lloyd George for bringing his political career back from ruin after the Gallipoli disaster: "I can never forget the service you did me in bringing me a fresh horse when I was dismounted in the war." Churchill's powers of persuasion over his rescuer were, perforce, to be sadly limited.

When Churchill met with his Cabinet colleagues on 13 December, he argued strongly for Britain to withdraw to Basra province, which would have left the *vilayets* of Mosul and Baghdad effectively outside British control. This would, he assured them, save at least fifty million pounds a year. For the long-term future of Iraq, this could have been a much better solution. The Kurds would then have formed a mini-state of their own, of that part of Kurdistan under neither Iranian nor Turkish rule. Most of the inhabitants of the Baghdad province would have been Sunni—albeit with significant Jewish and Shia Arab minorities—and Britain would have ruled over just the Shiite south.

Unfortunately for both Churchill and the hapless inhabitants of the area, he was overruled by his colleagues. As one of them pointed out, possibly with justice, "the Turks, possibly in collusion with the Bolsheviks, would enter into the vacuum thus created." This argument proved decisive, and a further step was taken to create the Iraq we know today.

As Churchill had been compelled to give in, he felt obliged to defend the government in public; he did so two days later, on the 15th, when he presented the financial estimates to the House of Commons. Talking of the rebellion and the extra expenses thereby involved, he informed the Members of Parliament (MPs) that: "We have had to face real responsibility and real difficulties, and we have to face them not with hysteria or irritation, but with firmness and courage."

If his colleagues were to deny further money for Mesopotamia, they could dismiss the British government as well. But all this, he warned the MPs:

> would not alter the difficulty which exists in that country, nor would they diminish the expenditure which we shall have to incur on account of it. If at this moment we were to order the troops in Mesopotamia to begin evacuation it seems very probable that we should be involved in very heavy fighting in many parts of that region which would last well into the next financial year.

He then attacked the press for giving indirect aid to the rebels, which, since most Arab tribesmen were unlikely to be reading British newspapers, seems rather strange:

> I am quite certain that the loose talk indulged in the newspapers about the speedy evacuation of Mesopotamia earlier in the year was a factor which provoked and promoted the rebellion.

Surely Arab (and also Kurdish) nationalism was far more potent a force; maybe Churchill, being a colonialist of his time, simply did not see it.

Finally, he reminded his colleagues of the moral case for Britain being in the region, and here he struck what, to twenty-first-century readers, is a more understandable note:

> Whatever your policy may be, it would certainly be in the highest degree imprudent to let it be thought that this country, having accepted the mandate, having entered into territory of that kind, having incurred, accepted, and shouldered responsibilities towards every class inhabiting it, was in a moment of irritation or weakness going to cast down those responsibilities, to leave its obligations wholly uncharged, and to scuttle from the country regardless of what might occur. Such a course would bring ruin on the province of Mesopotamia, and it would also impose a heavier expense on the British taxpayer than I believe would be incurred if we actually and firmly resumed the policy of reducing our garrisons, of contracting our commitments, and of setting up a local government congenial to the wishes of the masses of the people.

Since Churchill disagreed with much of the policy he was having to defend in the House of Commons, this is a remarkable example of the British doctrine of Cabinet responsibility at work—that of defending collective government decisions even if you as an individual minister do not agree with them.

In private, however, Churchill continued to press his case, writing to his Cabinet colleagues a day later, on the 16th:

> Our own military forces are extremely weak and maintained with great difficulty and expense, and we have not secured a single friend among the local powers.

For France and Italy were already proving treacherous to Britain and were subtly beginning to befriend the nationalist Turks.

As Churchill again stressed:

We are the greatest Mohammedan power in the world. It is our duty, more than any other Government, to study policies which are in harmony with Mohammedan feeling.

This was all in tune, too, with the thinking of the CIGS, Sir Henry Wilson, who wanted to withdraw altogether from most of Palestine, Mesopotamia, and Persia.

On 31 December, though, there was good news for Churchill. He was able to tell the Cabinet that the revolt in Mesopotamia had been conclusively crushed. Not only that but, against stiff opposition from those losing out, the Cabinet agreed that he would be in charge of a new department based in the Colonial Office that would oversee all the affairs of the Middle East. At last Churchill would have the power to deal with problems in the way he thought best.

Chapter Four

Churchill and His Forty Thieves

Churchill now knew that he had a serious task ahead of him. As he bemoaned to Lord Curzon, the Foreign Secretary, his was a "difficult & embarrassing task," in which he could "look forward only to toil & abuse." But he was determined to get on top of things as soon as possible, and he therefore immediately dispatched his views to Sir Percy Cox in Baghdad.

His main priority was money, and he was blunt with the British proconsul from the outset. "It is impossible," he told him on 8 January 1921, "for us to throw upon the British taxpayer the burdens for military expenditure in Mesopotamia which are entailed for your present schemes for holding the country." Fighting over the border in Persia was continuing, and Britain had to hold Mosul and the oil fields against enemy invasion. Some kind of army would therefore remain necessary through 1921 into 1922. But, Churchill's dispatch to Sir Percy Cox continued:

> The presence of these forces for many months to come and the effects produced upon the Arabs by the suppression of the rebellion and the surrender of [their] rifles, give me the hope that by the effective use of the resources at our disposal we may be able to set up an Arab Government,

through whose agency the peaceful development of the country may be assured without undue demands upon Great Britain. It is to this policy that we must devote our efforts.

This was therefore to be Churchill's main goal: an Arab regime that would preserve British imperial interests but would also cost as little as possible.

Meanwhile, Feisal's intrigues in London were bearing fruit. He met with his old Arab Revolt friend, Kinahan Cornwallis, director of the Arab Bureau from 1916 to 1920 and now a Foreign Office adviser on behalf of Lord Curzon, and the next day the Cabinet asked Curzon what he thought of the now-footloose and kingdomless prince. He was asked to let Sir Percy Cox "know the position in reply to his own not altogether judicious or feasible proposals."

Feisal had made just the impression he had hoped to make on Cornwallis. "Feisal," Lord Curzon glowed to Churchill, "behaved like a real gentleman & with a fine sense of honour & loyalty. Furthermore, his attitude is in my view the best possible one for us in the present [circumstances], for it postpones a decision regarding himself, the very point for which you pressed in the Cabinet."

Churchill had pressed for a delay because he needed full convincing of the Hashemite case himself. He had also been persuaded by Lawrence that an immediate decision was not necessary. As Churchill revealingly wrote to Sir Percy shortly afterwards:

Do you think Feisal is the right man and the best man? Failing him do you prefer Abdullah? Have you put Feisal forward because you consider taking a long view [that] he is the best man or as a desperate expedient in the hopes of reducing the garrisons quickly?

This shows us two things: that Churchill himself had not reached any final decision, and that he wondered if others, such as Cox, shared his priority of getting out as fast as possible. While some historians are right to say that Hashemite ambitions knew no bounds, it can also be argued that Churchill was no pushover either.

Churchill also wanted any decision on a ruler to look good and to be handled in a way that did not alienate the French in Syria. As he reminded Cox, if the High Commissioner was "really convinced that Feisal is necessary," Cox could "make sure he is chosen locally . . . do not let us slip into taking the wrong man against our better judgement."

A modern-style referendum was not needed, though. In order to select a ruler and for a National Assembly to make an invitation, Churchill presumed that:

> These conditions will be prescribed in relation to the end we have in view, namely the good government of the country and the honourable discharge of our mandate without undue expense. Western political methods are not necessarily applicable to the East and [the] basis of election should be framed.

Churchill was, though, coming around to Feisal. As he told Curzon, he now had "a strong feeling" that:

> Feisal is the best man, and I do not think that there is much to be gained by putting forward an inferior man in the hopes that he will be rejected and smooth away certain difficulties in the selection of the best candidate. . . . We must certainly see that we get the "turtle" and not "mock turtle."

Churchill now decided on some sunshine and once more departed for what would remain one of his favorite haunts for the rest of his life, the South of France. On his way to Nice, he decided to drop into Paris and see some leading French officials. Much of the conversation was on wider issues relating to Churchill's fear of Soviet expansion and the problems of the newly vanquished Germany. But conversation inevitably came around to the Middle East, and Churchill was far more optimistic about the situation there than were his colleagues back in London.

The French, he observed, were getting fed up in Syria and were therefore "pretty much in the same position there as we are in Mesopotamia, namely utterly sick of pouring out money and men on these newly acquired territories."

Churchill was a consistent opponent of the pro-Greek stand of his boss, Lloyd George, against the rise of Turkish nationalist power under Kemal Ataturk (the issue that was to overthrow both Lloyd George and Churchill in 1922 and end the tenure of Britain's last Liberal Prime Minister). This meant that he was particularly sensitive to how the Muslim world was feeling. Now Greece was at war with Turkey—with Britain effectively supporting the Greeks—and the threat of Soviet invasion in the region was looming ever greater on the horizon.

Britain, however, was stuck, and not just because of its isolation over Turkey, a renascent power with whom the French were becoming especially friendly (as always; Franco-British rivalry is nothing new). But there was also a large British army in the Middle East—not to mention one in Ireland, where the civil war was continuing to rage. As Churchill wrote to the Archbishop of Tuam, a leading Irish cleric, "I need scarcely tell you how intensely I feel the desire and need for a truce and appeasement in Ireland."

Appeasement is not a word we normally associate with Churchill, yet here he was advocating it in the Irish struggle. He was at the same time suggesting exactly the same appeasement policy in the Middle East. He realized that a war-weary Britain could not possibly fight wars in several countries at once—the Soviets in the Middle East, the Turks possibly in both Mesopotamia (for the oil of Mosul) and to help the Greeks, and in Ireland to protect the rights of the pro-British minority. So appeasement was the only feasible option, something gloriously ironic in light of Churchill's later patriotic and resolute opposition to Britain's appeasement of Nazi Germany.

He also knew that because of the presence of Britain not just in the Middle East but also in India, the British Empire was now "the greatest Mohammedan power in the world." As a result, he reminded his colleagues, it was:

> our duty, more than any other Government, to study policies which are in harmony with Mohammedan feeling. It would appear therefore that we should initiate and steadily and consistently pursue a policy of friendship with Turkey and with the Arabs, and that we should not hope for any effective assistance either from the Bolshevik Russians or the pro-German Greeks.

As he wrote to his friend, the Tory grandee and landowner Lord Edward Derby, he wanted to use Kemal Ataturk "and a reconciled Turkey as a barrier against the Bolsheviks and to smooth down all our affairs in the Middle East."

Now, in Paris, he pursued his own foreign policy, even though it was entirely different from that of his own Prime Minister and their colleague, Foreign Secretary Lord Curzon.

As he told the French officials, Britain and France were now in "the same boat" over the Arab issue, "that we had a common interest in the appeasement of the Middle East." After he and the French discussed their respective woes with the Turks, Syrians, and Mesopotamians, Churchill continued:

> I pointed out the absolute need from both [the] British and French point of view of appeasing Arab sentiment and arriving at good arrangements with them. Otherwise we should certainly be forced by the expense of the garrisons to evacuate the territories which each country had gained in the war.

Churchill now realized that if his colleague Lord Curzon retained responsibility for relations with much of the Arab world, then Churchill's own overall schemes for the area were sure to be thwarted. So from Nice he wrote to Lloyd George, asking that his new Middle Eastern Department be given responsibility for the whole Arab world, not just the mandated territories of Mesopotamia and Palestine. As he rightly perceived, the Arab issues were "all one" issue, and:

> any attempt to divide it will only reintroduce the same paralysis and confusion of action which has done so much harm during the last two years. It will be fatal to all prospects of success to introduce conflicting or divergent policies—Feisal or Abdullah, whether in Mesopotamia or Mecca; King Hussein when at Mecca; Bin Saud at Nejd . . . and King [in reality the High Commissioner Sir Herbert] Samuel at Jerusalem are all inextricably interwoven, and no conceivable policy can have any chance which does not pull all the strings affecting them. To exclude Arab relations [as Foreign Secretary Lord Curzon wanted to do] would be to disembowel the Middle East

Department. . . . All affairs in the triangle Jerusalem–Aden–Basra must be dealt with in their integrity by one single Minister and from one single point of view. Otherwise muddle, failure and discredit are certain.

All this shows us is that the turf wars which bedevil politicians in our own age are not new: Churchill was fighting for total control over his own bailiwick every bit as much as the Colin Powells and Donald Rumsfelds or Tony Blairs and Gordon Browns of our own day.

As he put it, "I must have control of everything in the ringed fence. . . . What is vital is the internal control of the Arabian triangle" of the key city of Jerusalem; of Basra, the port entry into Mesopotamia; and of Aden, the British-ruled entry into the Red Sea.

It was not all work for Churchill, though. He went to an art gallery to admire the paintings of a little-known artist named Charles Morin. This was, in fact, Churchill himself! The pictures were being exhibited for the first time, and though Churchill had originally wanted to call himself Mr. Spencer, he had opted for this more discreet pseudonym instead.

Not surprisingly, those government departments on whose turf Churchill was so cheerfully trespassing reacted vigorously to his attempts to seize their territory. Churchill, still enjoying the winter sun in Nice, wrote to Lloyd George again. He reminded him of the "utter impossibility of conducting the affairs of the Middle East while the management of the Arabian problem is split up between the Foreign Office, the India Office and the Middle Eastern Department," only the last of which was under Churchill's control.

He also realized, after reading the extensive briefing papers he had been given by his officials on:

Mesopotamia, that the impression forced upon me is that the mandates are so drawn as to make it very difficult for Britain to gain any real permanent advantage out of the country. We seem to have tied ourselves up in every detail to give it all back to the Arabs without compensation for our expenses as soon as they are able to stand alone. I know of course that you think a different interpretation will be put upon these mandates in practice. But as they stand they certainly constitute a very firm starting point for an attack on Mesopotamian expenditure.

Needless to say, Churchill's overarching desire to save as much money as possible did not go down too well with Sir Percy Cox, especially since Cox had told everyone in Baghdad that British troop levels would remain high, and Churchill's policy in effect completely overruled what had been decided. He was equally incensed about the fact that it looked as if his scheme for Feisal to rule the new Iraq was being put on ice. On receiving Churchill's telegram asking him to introduce major cuts, Sir Percy immediately offered his resignation. This was indeed a problem, since, as Churchill's officials did not hesitate to remind their vacationing "secretary of state," no one else held the same degree of prestige in the Middle East that was enjoyed by Sir Percy. If he resigned, they would "want more troops & not less!"

More bad news then reached Churchill in Nice. The French Government he had gotten along with so well—and so recently—had lost office. And now the India Office, under its prickly Secretary of State, Edwin Montagu, was insisting that it, too, should have a vital stake in the Middle East process, and at Churchill's expense.

Churchill therefore had to write begging letters to Lloyd George to fend off the India Office and to Cox to stop him resigning. With Cox though, he was firmer, reminding him of the facts of financial life and telling him that in trying to sort out the Mesopotamian mess, he had the "right to loyal aid and support from the men on the spot."

Churchill then heard from Curzon that Lloyd George was proposing to send him, Churchill, "out to Mesopotamia." As Curzon joked:

In the atmosphere that produced Nebuchadnezzar, Darius, Xerxes & other military heroes of the past I am hopeful that you will institute sound ideas about the importance of the Middle East. Whatever you do, do not follow the example of Alexander, who found Babylon too much for him.

Meanwhile, Lawrence got in touch with Churchill's long-term personal assistant, Edward Marsh, with the latest on Feisal's thinking. After his expulsion from Damascus by French colonial troops, Feisal had clearly learned his lesson with the French. He promised never to mention it again to the British government and also to abandon his father King Hussein's rather awkward claim to Palestine.

But Feisal was still interested in Mesopotamia, on which he wished to have a "watching brief," and on Transjordan—the part of Palestine being excluded from Jewish settlement—which he wanted to be an independent Arab state "with British advice." He was also concerned with Ibn Saud's predatory designs on his father's kingdom in the Hijaz and with the region we now call Yemen, some of which was annexed by the Saudis, including the area from which many of the later 9/11 terrorists were to come.

As Lawrence pointed out, Feisal's new attitude in effect cleaned the slate of exactly what had been promised to whom in the past. There were no more broken promises, and this was "so much more useful than splitting hairs." If Feisal was on board, then he could accomplish great things.

Lawrence ended by saying the one thing that would be music to Churchill's ears: All Feisal's cooperation on the key areas would "tend towards cheapness & speed of settlement." This played, I believe, the key role in Churchill's agreeing to install a Hashemite regime not just in Baghdad but, as it turned out, in Amman as well, where a Hashemite king, Abdullah II, sits on the throne to this very day.

Churchill now discovered that Lloyd George was going to Paris, so he arranged to go and see the British Prime Minister at the Ritz. Churchill was still hesitant about going to Mesopotamia, which not only Lloyd George but also the nervous officials in London wanted, now having realized that the exponential growth of British expenditure in the area was becoming "a bottomless pit to pour money into." The British in Iraq, grumbled Sir Arthur Hirtzel, head of the India Office Political Department, to Churchill, were being "recklessly extravagant" and there was "inadequate control" of where all the money was going.

Churchill was also worried about the continuing prospect of a Turkish invasion of the Mosul *vilayet,* something made all the more ominous by Britain's ongoing failure to decide what its actual policy was in that troubled area.

As it was for the appeasers of the 1930s, Churchill's aim was to try to reduce the number of Britain's enemies by as many as possible. The situation was not helped by the fact that the Turks, under the leadership of Mustapha Kemal, who were now being invaded by the Greeks, were proving as impossible to beat as they had been under Kemal's decisive leadership back at Gallipoli.

To Churchill—as to the French, who had made a separate peace deal with the Turks that left Britain highly exposed and isolated—the simple thing for the British to do was to agree to Turkish terms. After all, one of the main reasons so many British troops were needed in the region was to protect Mosul against a possible Turkish invasion. As Churchill wrote to General Haldane:

> Please telegraph fully what evidence you have pointing to a Turkish invasion during the present year. I am naturally doing my utmost to procure a settlement with the Turks which will ease our position throughout the Middle East. Evidence tending to show the dangers to our Mesopotamian position by Turkish hostility will be useful.

Here again, since Lloyd George was as persistently pro-Greek as ever, Churchill was flagrantly pursuing his own foreign policy. From one point of view, things had improved, as the new French government now rendered impossible Britain's position with Turkey. But while this helped Churchill's cause, the official British position remained unaltered, since Lloyd George, according to the increasingly hysterical Secretary of State for India, Edwin Montagu, was "violently anti-Turk," so much so, Montagu wrote to Churchill, that the Prime Minister was even "dreaming in *Greek*."

At this time, Britain's situation was arguably worse than it would be a decade later against Hitler, because the French and Italian deal with the nationalist forces in Turkey under Kemal meant that the British were completely isolated. The days of hopes of an American mandate over some of the region, such as Armenia, were now truly gone, and, as Montagu was aware, a "new Greek stunt" could lead to a war in which Britain would find itself on the losing side.

Meanwhile, the military men were pondering the situation. The Chief of the Imperial General Staff, the irascible and violently anti–Lloyd George Sir Henry Wilson, was desperate to pull out of the area altogether. As he confided to the General Officer of the troops in Egypt, General Sir Walter Congreve:

> I will never stop trying to pull out of Constantinople [where there had been a British army since 1918], Palestine and Persia, and pull back in

Mesopotamia to the railheads. In fact, if it was not for the oil at Ahwaz, I would like to pull out of Mesopotamia also, but the oil problem is a real difficulty, since the Admiralty insist on the vital necessity of covering those fields. . . . This rather inclines one to pull up and occupy Baghdad as well as Basra, but the difficulty of that again, is that it makes an increase of some 8 millions to the total cost of occupation.

Wilson then damned Churchill with faint praise, in a way that many a leading general, admiral, and air marshal to do throughout Churchill's great leadership of Britain during the Second World War, and which has become familiar to us from the Alanbrooke *Diaries*:

However, Winston, who proposes starting for Mesopotamia on the 7th February, can be guaranteed to box up the whole situation quicker than almost any other Frock [the military term of insult for civilians in World War One] I ever met. Give him my love as he passes through, for on the whole he and I have got on famously together. He has many good qualities, some of which lie hidden, and he has many bad ones, all of which are in the shop window.

Churchill, meanwhile, oblivious to all this, was dining with Sir Henry, Lloyd George, and other leading British officials at the luxurious Hotel Crillon in Paris on 23 January 1921. Churchill and Lloyd George disagreed vehemently on Turkey and Greece. When the Prime Minister had gone to bed, Churchill told Wilson that he would now not be going to Mesopotamia in February after all. So worried was Churchill about the level of military expenditure and over-reach that he wondered, when speaking secretly with Wilson in his room, whether the British would have to withdraw all their forces back to Basra.

Soon Churchill was back in London, and his first move was to ask his new officials for the one-page summaries of essential facts for which he was to become so famous as Prime Minister. He wanted maps, to see who ruled which bit of desert in the many different regions of Arabia. He insisted, too, that all Arabic names had to be spelled consistently, as he had gotten fed up with everyone following "his own caprice." (How one wishes that the press had taken his advice, or would take it even now.)

More worrying for the Hashemites was that Churchill was beginning to grumble about the many weaknesses of their claims to rule an Arab empire in the Middle East. Writing to his chief adviser in London, Sir Arthur Hirtzel, about Feisal's father, King Hussein of the Hijaz, he asked:

> I had not appreciated the weakness inherent in King Hussein's position. He is only a member of the Sherifian family selected by the Turks on political grounds. What other candidates were there in the Sherifian family at the time when the Turks made this decision? When did they make it? What other important chiefs of the Sherifian family are there still alive? It seems to me that all this has bearing upon our committing ourselves irrevocably to one of King Hussein's sons as ruler of Mesopotamia. If the father's title is defective, the son's influence may fall within it. Probably you will be able to re-assure me. Write a brief opinion on this.

Churchill also realized that by far the strongest Arab ruler was Ibn Saud—and that he would be capable of far more "mischief and blackmail" than any other Arab ruler, especially if the son of his Meccan rival, Hussein, were to be given the Mesopotamian throne.

Churchill, like many of us since, was also confused by the numerous similar-sounding Arabic names: "I have succeeded in disentangling Saud bin Rashid [another rival clan leader] from Ibn Saud. It will simplify matters once and for all whether you will call them 'Bin' or 'Ibn.' "

He then asked another important question, one that has very considerable relevance for us in the twenty-first century. He asked Sir Arthur:

> The Wahabi sect is at feud with the Sunni. Is it also at feud with the Shia? What are the principal doctrinal and ritualistic differences involved between the Shia, the Sunni and the Shabi Mohammedans? A very brief answer will suffice.

Here Churchill had unwittingly hit upon one of the most dangerous points in relation to the decision to make Feisal the king of a new Iraq. For it was certainly true, as the complex family tree Sir Arthur provided showed

Churchill, that there were several branches of the Hashemite/Sharifian clan, all with cast-iron proof of descent from the Prophet Muhammad.

But even more important were the religious problems Churchill raised, problems that still haunt the Arab world today—not just in how to maintain a unitary state but also in the version of Islam that arguably led directly to the horrors of 11 September 2001 and all that has flowed from that day.

First of all, the majority of people living in what was about to become Iraq were—as Churchill was aware—Shia, not Sunni, Muslim. In fact, the *theological* differences between these two ancient branches of Islam are not very great. Rather, the differences are in many ways political and cultural, all stemming from a seventh-century debate on who was the legitimate successor of the Prophet Muhammad following his death in 632. Shiite Muslims followed Muhammad's cousin and son-in-law Ali, whereas the majority of Muslims, the Sunni, supported those elected to the post and later the dynastic ambitions of the Umayyad and Abbassid caliphs. While the Hashemites were unquestionably descended from the Prophet, it was not through the line recognized by the Shia.

The Hashemites are Sunni Muslims, and in 1921, while the overwhelming majority of the world's Muslims were Sunni (85 percent or more today), the majority in both Iran and the new Iraq were (and are) Shia. So even if Feisal (and his branch of the Sharifian clan) could be said to be the right ruler for Iraq, as his supporters argued, that would still not have given him any degree of legitimacy among the vast majority of his new—and loyally Shia—subjects. It would also mean minority Sunni rule over a predominantly Shia population.

Minority rule has been the fate of Iraq's majority Shiites ever since and is thus a massive problem for any genuinely democratic Iraqi state that may try to emerge in the twenty-first century. All the Hashemite kings, the various generals and others who ruled after the 1958 coup, and the Ba'athist leaders such as Saddam Hussein were Sunni Muslims *and* Arabs—even the Hashemites local to Iraq. Since Iraq's independence, given that its large population of Kurds is Sunni—but not Arab—the rulers of Iraq have been drawn from a small minority of Sunni Arabs. Democracy would bring Shia majority rule and the possibility of endless Sunni intransigence after having lost control of a state they had dominated for over eighty years.

All this stems from the question that Churchill raised but that was not effectively answered then and has not been since. The path to Saddam Hussein and the domination of an entire country by a small clan of Sunni Arabs from Tikrit had, unwittingly, begun.

Unfortunately, Hirtzel felt that whatever the father's position, the credentials of the son, Feisal, were impeccable; he could be ruler of Mesopotamia even if his father were to lose the Hijaz throne (which he did in 1924).

Churchill, meanwhile, had other battles to be getting on with, notably the serious reluctance of the War Office to downsize the British armed forces in the region, to be replaced by the new and upstart branch of the military, the Royal Air Force. Sir Henry Wilson exploded with wrath at what he felt was Churchill's interference: "the man is a fool," he exclaimed. Churchill was equally angry with Wilson, complaining that the War Office's "attitude" was one of "inveterate hostility and obstruction . . . a form of warfare [which] I have never seen the like in all my (now long) experience."

Britain, Churchill found out, was now financially responsible for not only nearly 20,000 British personnel but almost 90,000 "natives" and just over 46,000 "native followers" or ancillary civilians and families as well— along with the maintenance of 53,198 donkeys! All told, Britain was responsible for 225,785 people, far more than was affordable. This was, to Churchill, "no doubt one of the reasons why we are being driven out of the province by expense."

Back in London, Churchill found himself in a verbal war with the Prime Minister over Churchill's account of how Turkey got into the war in 1914. Putting aside that issue, Turkey in 1921 was at the heart of the problem facing the British government—this time with Churchill in favor of doing a deal with the Turks, not attacking them.

As Roy Jenkins has shown us in his award-winning biography of Churchill, his relationship with Lloyd George was mercurial. They had now been in government together for fifteen years, excepting Churchill's post-Gallipoli spell in the wilderness, from which Lloyd George had rescued him by bringing him back in as Minister of Munitions in 1917. During his two-year tenure of this post, Churchill had regularly threatened to resign if he could not get his way, and what is perhaps amazing is that Lloyd George never accepted his resignation, sorely tempted though he must surely have been at times to do so.

The history of such correspondence now caused Churchill to write a letter to Lloyd George offering his resignation—again—but this time, wisely, he did not send it. Fortunately for us, though, he did keep it, so we can read it in his archives.

While we can feel of two minds about defending Churchill the appeaser in light of his later resolve against appeasement in the 1930s, his rationale for wanting to emulate the French and make a deal with the Turks in 1921 does at least make sense. For it was to be Lloyd George's equally stubborn refusal to do so that was to overthrow both him and Churchill in October 1922, destroying Britain's last Liberal Prime Minister.

Churchill's unsent letter is also important in that it places his Iraq policy firmly in context: what on earth to do about the huge financial and military responsibilities in that part of the world. As he had put it to one of his officials the day before he wrote the unsent letter, he was most concerned about "allowing twenty or thirty millions to flow away in Mesopotamia."

To Churchill, all went back to the disastrous decision to back the Greeks in their invasion of Turkey in May 1919, with the resultant "deplorable massacres and destruction of property." This had naturally inflamed Turkish opinion and caused the rise of Mustapha Kemal, the man whose successful generalship in 1916 was surely singed into Churchill's consciousness.

As Churchill wrote in the letter he never sent to Lloyd George :

The present misfortunes from which we are suffering throughout the Middle East are in my opinion the direct outcome of the invasion of Smyrna by the Greeks. The fact that we are the greatest Mohammedan power in the world makes us the chief sufferer in all our vital interests in the East from a policy which makes England the bitterest enemy of the Turks and which exalts the Greeks over them.

Not merely did the Treaty of Sèvres have clauses in it that were now unenforceable, but the French and Italians had pulled out and were refusing to ratify it. Britain was thus on her own.

Churchill went on:

If now Britain is to proceed alone to ratify this Treaty we shall draw upon ourselves the whole hostility of the Mohammedan world and our position in the Middle East will only be maintained by the expenditure of enormous sums of money such as have been poured out during the present year.

While the letter was not sent and Churchill did not resign, he nevertheless began to make inquiries of the key people in the field about the possibility of Britain withdrawing altogether from Mesopotamia. He then went on to the newly donated Chequers, now the country house of the Prime Minister but then only just converted from being a private home. Despite their very recent acrimonious correspondence, he found Lloyd George "agreeable, evasive, elusive & indefinite as usual." At least Churchill had some good news, though; a leading magazine, the *Strand,* had agreed to pay him a thousand pounds tax-free for articles by him on his painting.

Back in London, and now formally sworn in as Secretary of State for the Colonies, Churchill decided that he could not after all go to Mesopotamia itself. Rather, he would go to Cairo and summon all the chief people involved in Middle East decisions to meet him there. These people he nicknamed his "forty thieves." Thus the Cairo Conference was born, to take place on 12 March 1921.

The gathering was to make some key decisions:

First, the new ruler. Second, future size, character and organisation of the future garrison. Third, the time-table of reduction from present strength to that garrison. Fourth, arising out of the above the extent of the territory to be held and administered.

While Churchill decided not to include Baghdad in his itinerary, he did feel he ought to visit Jerusalem. Though this is not a book about the Palestinian problems—of which there are many—the decisions Churchill was to make there have proved as momentous and long-lasting as those made in Cairo. The map of today's Middle East and the problems that have beset the region for the past eighty years owe their nature to a small group of British experts meeting in the area over the course of just a few days.

Meanwhile, Churchill continued to battle with the British Army, especially when he discovered that the military were being used not just for defense but also for tax collection, thereby causing a "great deal of the waste of force and money." As he grumbled to Sir Arthur Hirtzel, why had Britain "got to pay £300,000 a year for wretched shanties in Baghdad?" particularly since the number of British troops would, all being agreed, soon be drastically reduced.

One piece of expenditure Churchill did agree to, however, with dire consequences: King Hussein of the Hijaz was being paid royally, and now Churchill agreed with Sir Percy Cox that Ibn Saud's subsidy should also be £100,000 a year, renewable on an annual basis. As for long-term value for money, this was a sad waste. Three years later, in 1924, Ibn Saud conquered the Kingdom of the Hijaz, thereby giving himself the prestige, held by his descendants ever since, of being the Guardian of the Two Holy Places, Mecca and Medina. Spiritually, this was to give much greater importance to the austere Wahhabi form of Islam, since they now imposed their eighteenth-century interpretation of the Koran on all the lands under Saudi rule. This remains true today, with the result that contemporary pilgrims on the annual *Haj* to Mecca learn a far more severe and innately anti-Western form of their faith.

It was also unfortunate financially: When Ibn Saud named his new kingdom after himself—Saudi Arabia—in 1932, he was to give all the main oil concessions to the United States and to the new company it would create—Aramco. The close relationship between the Saudis and the United States was based on their mutual interest in oil, an idea so offensive to Al Qaeda that its consequences were seen by everyone on 11 September 2001.

In retrospect, it might have been better if the British had not subsidized Ibn Saud, or at least had defended the Hashemites against his predatory instincts. Whatever the faults of the Jordanian Hashemites, state-sponsored religious extremism has not been among them since they came to power in 1921.

Churchill was seen as friendlier to Muslims than the British Foreign Secretary, Curzon, had been, so his new post as Colonial Secretary was welcomed by those who realized that his support for Turkey against Greece was a good sign. As Lord Henry Rawlinson, the Commander in Chief of the British Army in India, wrote to Churchill on 10 February, "I know full well, from conversations that we have already had together, that the cause of Islam will receive more sympathetic treatment at your hands than could ever have been the case with Curzon."

Churchill was now able to make some key staff appointments, and one of the first was of T. E. Lawrence, whose fame as "Lawrence of Arabia" was now widespread. He also engaged an old colleague of Lawrence's, Major Hubert Young, who had served both in Damascus and in Mesopotamia and more recently in the Foreign Office. Lawrence's post, that of Adviser on Arabian Affairs, was temporary for one year; Young's, the Assistant Secretary to the Middle East Department, was to be the first of many jobs he held in the Colonial Service until his retirement in 1942.

Needless to say, the appointment of the unorthodox Lawrence immediately aroused suspicions among more sober-minded officials. Sir James Masterton Smith, the Under-Secretary of State for the Colonies, rather alarmed, wrote to Churchill:

> Are you sure that Col Lawrence should come? I had gathered the impression (but perhaps wrongly) that he did not wish to hold a Government appointment in connection with the Arab problem. He is not the kind of man to fit easily into any official machine, and I consider it important that Mr Shuckburgh [a seconded India Office official] and Major Young should have their position as your responsible departmental advisers made clear beyond challenge. I gather that Col Lawrence has got used to dealing with Ministers—and Ministers only—and I see trouble ahead if he is allowed too free a hand. But no doubt you have already weighed this.

Fortunately, Churchill, a somewhat unorthodox character himself, had no problem with people who thought "outside the box," and Lawrence was duly appointed his Adviser on Arabian Affairs, his possible irresponsibility notwithstanding.

Meanwhile, Churchill's turf wars continued, this time with the Foreign Office. In the Cabinet there was a "long wrangle between Winston and Curzon as to spheres of interest." As Curzon grumbled to his new American wife, Grace, Churchill wanted to "grab everything into his new Dep[artmen]t & to be a sort of Asiatic Foreign Secretary." Fortunately for

Curzon, Lloyd George took his side, and Churchill had to continue his struggle to get everything coordinated by himself. He had won this turf war.

To Churchill, everything in Mesopotamia ultimately boiled down to money. He sent a note to his Cabinet colleagues on 10 February, asking them:

> what they would consider would be a suitable grant-in-aid for Mesopotamia after the present evacuation of the main body of troops has been effected and the reduced force is holding the country. . . . Unless I know the length my colleagues are prepared to go, it is impossible for me to ascertain whether a suitable force can be formed to hold the country and how much of the country can be held. Unless the Cabinet can see their way to authorise plans to be made on the basis of about seven million pounds a year [i.e., about one third of what was being spent annually to date], I doubt very much whether it will be possible to discharge the conditions of the mandate [over Mesopotamia].

It is interesting that such a cost-free kind of empire was in his mind *before* he set out for Cairo. To use a twenty-first-century expression, one could say that this was *empire lite*. The problem about this is that it can easily end in the worst of both worlds, and it was precisely such a policy that Churchill was about to embark on.

Some of the officials in Mesopotamia had wanted to rule the three provinces directly, as a colony of the British Empire. Their reasons were that then the British would be directly responsible for everything that happened and, more important, they could run everything themselves. Mesopotamia— or Iraq, as people were now beginning to call it—would be a British colony no different from, say, Uganda in Africa or Malaya in the Far East.

In the new post-Wilsonian world, such an option was no longer realistic. Arabs could and did point out that they were as entitled to freedom as the Czechs and Poles had been following the downfall of the Austro-Hungarian and Russian Empires in 1918. Indeed, the British had themselves exploited exactly such nationalist sentiment in backing the Arab Revolt against the Ottoman Empire, however limited that rebellion had in fact been in practice. So Britain could hardly now renege on her promises, particularly after the debacle of the rebellion in Mesopotamia in 1920.

On the other hand, vital British interests were at stake: While Lord Curzon may not have been aware of the region's potential oil riches, others were. And, at that time, more important still was the route to India, and that could not possibly be left in potentially hostile hands.

So Britain had to have a half-way house, a country it controlled but did not actually rule—at least not overtly. This was what was now being proposed for Iraq.

It goes without saying that if you want to run an empire on the cheap (the British dilemma of 1921 and the American one of 2004), then there are massive risks involved, particularly if the imperial government is risk- and cost-averse. This was unquestionably behind the case Churchill made in February 1921 and presented to his Cabinet colleagues on 14 February. Significantly, he included his right to determine Kurdish policy himself. Kurdistan, he proposed, should be organized as a "friendly State providing a barrier against Turks and Russians." That he was soon to be persuaded out of a separate Kurdish state was to be a tragedy with present-day consequences.

As usual, though, Churchill's main concern was money and the need to save it. But getting costs down would need an Arab government. It would, he argued to his colleagues, be "shameful if Great Britain threw the Mandate aside without making an effort to set up an Arab Administration in the place of the Turkish Government which she had destroyed." Churchill had now decided that all would be resolved in Cairo. Though he had managed to get Lawrence made into an Assistant Secretary of the Colonial Office, Lawrence was having to "put on a bridle & collar" because of the hostility of others. He was now to see Feisal, and Churchill covered his bases by clearing what Lawrence was to say by copying his instructions to the jealous Curzon, who felt that "Lawrence will be very useful if he will cease to intrigue."

Lawrence was therefore asked by Churchill (and Curzon) to tell Feisal that he was now working for Churchill. There would be a Cairo conference at which a Hashemite candidate for Mesopotamia would be discussed, as well as the subsidies to King Hussein—and those to Ibn Saud, who was busily harassing the Hijaz kingdom.

Meanwhile, Churchill told Lawrence to pass on to Feisal that there was much concern about the armed force under Abdullah's leadership making its way to fight the French in Syria. Abdullah was currently in Transjordan; were

Feisal's brother to mess things up and attack the French-ruled territory from which Feisal had been expelled, "all chance of a decision favorable to your house [would be] destroyed." This was all the more the case since the French were highly suspicious of Lawrence, let alone the Hashemites.

Churchill now began preparation in earnest for his great Middle Eastern excursion. His concerns were still primarily financial, meaning how to reduce military expenditure by as much as possible. But the question of who the new ruler should be also weighed heavily on him; he even considered the possibility of offering the throne to Ibn Saud. And there was the ongoing problem of what exactly to do with the Kurds. He was also perturbed by another crisis beyond the scope of this book but which influenced his thinking: It was the ever-present Soviet threat to Iran (or Persia, as it was still called) and the need to maintain a large British force there in order to prevent Persian oil from falling into Soviet hands. This made him all the more anxious to cut costs in Mesopotamia, since maintaining British troops there at the levels needed to fight a war against a European power was, to him, "terribly wasteful."

Churchill was a man of precise habits. All his office papers had to be kept in special dockets, just as they had been when he first became a Cabinet minister. Even the exact details on how the dockets should be fastened and presented was of enormous importance to the new Secretary of State for the Colonies. Likewise, the color coding had to be the same as when he was the wartime Minister of Munitions. Churchill was not the easiest of men to work for, and the towering genius that made it just about bearable for his officials during the Second World War was not, at this stage in his political life, so apparent or agreed-upon by all.

In choosing Cairo for the conference, Churchill was also walking into a political minefield, since there was considerable difference of opinion between the Foreign Office and British officials in Egypt, led by the former victorious Field Marshal Lord Edmund Allenby, on how Egyptian nationalist unrest should be handled. (Allenby was now the High Commissioner and not unsympathetic to some of Egypt's more moderate nationalist sentiments.) One can add here that Egypt's stance was unique in emphasizing national bonds due to its rather large Christian population and the continuity of its ancient past. None of this fell within Churchill's purview, yet his very presence would provoke nationalist opinion and possibly, through any well-meaning interference by him, upset the feelings of the local British officials as well.

Not surprisingly, therefore, even though Churchill was not supposed to be discussing any Egyptian business during his stay, the British authorities in Cairo were, as Churchill confessed, "getting rather excited about my coming, as they seem to think that it has something to do with them."

Despite his resolve not to get involved, his propensity for speech- and policy-making well beyond his domain did not desert him. Just before his departure, he made a speech in which he likened Egyptian-British problems there to those the United Kingdom was having in Ireland. While Churchill was cheerfully telling his wife Clementine how much Lord Allenby was looking forward to having them as his guests, the High Commissioner was writing a scorching telegram to Curzon, saying that Churchill's speech had "given great offence, naturally."

Now came the issue of the agenda, and Churchill laid out his ideas for his officials to implement. He requested that there be "six days of discussion":

We shall begin with Mesopotamia—

(1) The new ruler. Methods of Election. The Mandate generally. Kurdestan [sic], Bin Saud, etc.

(2) The permanent garrison for the three years 1922–1923, 1923–1924 and 1924–1925: size, location, permanent barracks; co-operation with or control by the Air Force.

(3) Critical examination of present military charges, station by station, unit by unit, category by category. After a general discussion on this, a sub-committee will sit separately to formulate proposals for immediate economy and report before the Conference separates.

(4) The rate of reduction from the present force to the permanent garrisons. My hope is that one third of the present troops can leave the country before the hot weather and another third immediately after it is over. [They should work out means of] accelerations of evacuation. The shipping question must also be studied.

(5) The system of taxation and the scale of the civil Government to be maintained must also be reviewed in the direction of having lighter taxation and a less ambitious Government.

(6) [About working out the grant in aid for 1922–1925 inclusive.]

(7) Final review of the political situation in the light of the above and decisions as to the actual territory and positions to be held.

The rest of the memorandum dealt briefly with other issues, such as Transjordan, Somaliland, and Aden, all territory within Churchill's triangle.

All these items show how much was still up for grabs at the Cairo Conference. Churchill was still leaning strongly toward a Hashemite solution, though he realized that intense ill-will between Feisal's and Abdullah's father, King Hussein of the Hijaz, and the predatory Ibn Saud of the Nejd, could complicate things greatly. Nor were the borders finally settled. The San Remo Conference and the Treaty of Sèvres had been unhelpfully ambivalent about Kurdistan, not least because the northern part of it was in territory the Turks regarded as an integral part of their own country, and the southern part was a region that should have been under their rule rather than that of any newly created Arab state.

But predominant in Churchill's thinking was finance. Compounding his worries about the escalating costs of the army in Mesopotamia was the issue of Persia, right next door. A considerable British army was there, too, fighting to protect the Persians against Soviet invasion. Churchill was prepared to lose northern Persia if necessary, "but South Persia," with its "great Anglo-Persian oilfield," ought, he thought, "certainly not to be thrown away without an effort." The problem was that all this cost a lot of money too, even though some of this expense was borne by the British Raj.

As a result, the high-spending British forces in Mesopotamia had no chance. Why, Churchill continued to ask the military men, was it so necessary to maintain full European cavalry regiments in the region, with all their additional expense? He noted exasperatedly:

> Divisions are tactical formations for fighting European armies. One could quite understand half a dozen mobile columns being organised and other troops being put into small garrisons; but all this idea of reorganising the troops keeping order in Mesopotamia as if they were part of one of the armies which fought on the Western front must be terribly wasteful.

Churchill was now writing therapeutic letters to Lloyd George again, venting his feelings against what he felt was the increasingly foolish pro-Greek policy of the Prime Minister, a policy that was having so deleterious an impact on Britain's standing in the Middle East. (What similar papers will be read by historians in 2033 to 2034, one wonders, when the British Cabinet papers for 2002 to 2003 are released?) To Churchill, it was just so obvious "that our Eastern & Middle Eastern affairs would be enormously eased & helped by arriving at a peace with Turkey." Not only that, but such a peace would directly affected what he was about to try to do in Cairo:

> The reactions from this state of affairs fall mainly upon us [and partly on France]. They are all unfavorable. The Turks will be thrown into the arms of the Bolsheviks; Mesopotamia will be disturbed at the critical period of the reduction of the army there; it will probably be quite impossible to hold Mosul & Baghdad without a powerful and expensive army; the general alienation of Mohammedan sentiment from Great Britain will continue to work evil consequences in every direction; the French & Italians will make their own explanations; and we shall everywhere be represented as the chief enemy of Islam.

Apart from the fact that Italy sided with the United States in 2003 and the fact of the fate of the unfortunate Armenians—about to be crushed between Turkish nationalists and Soviet forces—Churchill's unsent but heartfelt memorandum could easily have been written in 2002 or 2003.

Back in the 1910 to 1914 period, Churchill and Lloyd George had been the great dynamic radical duo, the forward-thinking, progressive pair leading the forces of change in the prewar Liberal government. Now they were sorely and deeply at loggerheads over Turkey. This was painful for Churchill, especially since he was so dependent on the Prime Minister for retaining his seat in an overwhelmingly Conservative and thus unsympathetic Cabinet. When Churchill wrote the next paragraph, he was not being flattering but, sadly, sincere:

> In these circumstances it seems to me a fearful responsibility to let loose the Greeks & to reopen the war. I am deeply grieved at the prospect and

at finding myself so utterly without power to influence your mind even in respect to matters with which my duties are specially concerned.

(Churchill, remember, had been interfering massively in the affairs of Egypt, which Lord Curzon zealously regarded as his own area, and Lloyd George was, at the very least, failing fully to take Churchill's side.)

"All the more I am distressed," Churchill concluded:

because of my desire to aid you in any way open to me in the many matters in which we are agreed, & because of our long friendship & my admiration for y[ou]r genius & work.

These, then, were two major constraints on Churchill as he planned for Cairo: money, and the impending debacle in Turkey, the two issues being inexorably intertwined. Britain had isolated herself over the Greco-Turkish War and been left in the lurch by France and Italy. The British government also simply did not have the money to conduct major military operations abroad, especially so soon after the carnage of the Western Front. Churchill was in charge of Iraq policy, but he was now increasingly aware that he had been handed a very unsatisfactory deck of cards.

Fortunately for historians, Churchill decided to explain exactly what he was being asked to do in a letter he wrote to Sir George Ritchie, a wealthy businessman in Churchill's Parliamentary constituency of Dundee, the major jute-manufacturing town in Scotland.

Taxpayers, Churchill wrote, had misunderstood the reason why the new Middle Eastern Department had been established, and the popular press had not helped either. They clearly thought that his aim:

in undertaking the charge of this department will be to build up a costly and vainglorious Middle Eastern Empire at the expense of the British taxpayer. My object is exactly the opposite. The present position is as follows:—We have accepted, by the Treaty of Versailles {Churchill is technically wrong here—it was the Treaty of Sèvres} mandates for Palestine and Mesopotamia and we have also incurred certain responsibilities in regard to Arabia which are of profound significance to the Mohammedan subjects of the Crown. The discharge of our task both in Palestine and in Mesopotamia is now threatened by the enormous military expenditures required for the garrisons of these two countries. During the present financial year 1920–1921 the cost of the garrison in Palestine has been about eight million pounds, and the cost of the garrison in Mesopotamia, including the fighting to suppress the revolt, over thirty-three million.

Churchill had hoped that he could reduce these costs for Parliament:

Unhappily, the reductions so far effected in Mesopotamia are wholly inadequate. It is estimated that [to hold the country safely] over twenty-five million pounds will be required in the present year. It is also estimated that, even if complete evacuation were to be decided upon, the rate at which the troops could leave the country is so slow, owing to the bad communications and the need of collecting the outlying detachments, that very little of this sum could be saved. I am not convinced by either of these propositions. I have found it impossible to deal with these by telegraph. It is therefore indispensable that I should be able to confer with the officials who are responsible.

Since both he and these officials had vital tasks, he could not go to Mesopotamia. So they had chosen a half-way house (which Churchill did not mention in the letter was Cairo). He continued, cogently outlining his and the British government's dilemma:

On the one hand it is perfectly clear that we cannot go on spending these enormous sums on Mesopotamia and that the forces that we maintain there must be promptly and drastically reduced. Even the reduced forces which it is hoped will be sufficient after this year are estimated to cost ten or eleven millions. This is far more than we should have any right to spend in such a quarter, more especially when we remember the immense fertility and values of our West African and East African territories and the far better opportunities that they offer for Imperial development than the Middle East.

This is interesting: We would not think today that Ghana or Kenya offered better opportunities than the oil-rich Gulf. Even though Churchill, as a former First Lord of the Admiralty, had helped to create the Anglo-Persian Oil Company, he, in this letter to an eminent businessman, did not mention the abundant oil reserves of Iraq.

Churchill continued, expounding on the difficult decisions in further detail:

> Therefore, unless some better and much cheaper scheme than those with which we are at present confronted can be devised and carried through, we shall have to withdraw altogether from Mesopotamia. This would at any rate terminate our expense after the present year.

This would, Churchill clearly realized, be a scuttle, a rapid departure in ignominious circumstances, something that would be politically impossible:

> On the other hand, the disadvantages and even disgrace of such a procedure should not be under-rated. We marched into Mesopotamia during the war and uprooted the Turkish Government which was the only stable form of government in that country at that time. We accepted before all the world a mandate for the country and undertook to introduce much better methods of government in the place of those we had overthrown. If, following upon this, we now ignominiously scuttle for the coast, leaving sheer anarchy behind us and historic cities to be plundered by the wild Bedouin of the desert, an event will have occurred not at all in accordance with what has usually been the reputation of Great Britain.

Churchill went on to outline some of his hopes:

> It is my hope, therefore, that by means of an Arab Government supported by a moderate military force we may be able to discharge our duties without imposing unjustifiable expense on the British Exchequer. The fact that we shall be calling into being an Arab administration [under an Arab ruler] in Bagdad [sic] makes it indispensable that we should treat the Arab

question as a whole so far as it concerns British interests. Unless Arabian affairs can be handled as to secure tranquillity among the tribes at this critical time, the early withdrawal of large numbers of troops from Mesopotamia, and consequently of the reduction of the expense, may be very greatly hampered.

Churchill concluded his epistle to Sir George by re-emphasizing the reluctance with which he had picked up the task of dealing with the whole area. How genuine this was is hard to tell. He had been very keen at the beginning to undertake a major political project to improve his political reputation. Even though he had been a great success as Munitions Minister in 1917 and 1918, the whiff of failure and of the Gallipoli fiasco still hung heavily on him. But by now, as he had come to realize the enormity of the task at hand and the possibility of further failure, his reluctance may have become very real.

When we look at the conspiratorial chat between Sir Henry Wilson, still Chief of the Imperial General Staff, and his former boss at the War Office, Lord Derby, as they strolled along the beach at Biarritz, we can see what Churchill's reputation was with the Army. When Lord Derby asked Wilson whether Churchill could ever run a government—Churchill's desire one day to be Prime Minister was hardly a secret—Wilson replied that, in his judgment:

> Winston is quite incapable of laying out a policy & then sticking to it; & that although he has lucid & bright intervals these never continue for any length of time, & at other times he is frankly stupid in the mad things he does.

None of this augured well for Churchill, whose main concern now was to get a policy that he could convince the government and then the House of Commons to adopt. Even now, it seemed, a complete scuttle—or ignominious withdrawal of the humiliating kind he wanted to avoid—was still in the cards.

As always, the French still had to be dealt with. Churchill, feeling terrible from the side effects of some antityphoid medicine he was having to take, had a meeting with them in London on 24 February 1921.

The French were holding on to Syria, now legitimately theirs following League of Nations approval of the San Remo allocation of the mandates. As Churchill and his officials learned, the French had already successfully negotiated their own ignominious withdrawal from Turkish Cilicia, which would enable them to move their forces to Syria, the better to rule it. On their new mandate, they announced that France was "not thinking of wholesale cessions of territory and that their interest in Syria was undiminished."

France had recently expelled Feisal from Syria, destroying his chances of ruling that territory, so their bolstered military presence there was bad news for him. But from Feisal's point of view, worse was to come: M. Berthelot, the Secretary General of the French Foreign Ministry (who was not long after sacked for nepotism and corruption that was clearly too much even for France), went on to tell his British hosts:

> for the French to be in a position to carry out their programme it was essential that the British should not instal the Emir Feisul [sic] in Mesopotamia.

Worse still, M. Berthelot insisted, he had evidence from General Henri Gouraud, who was at the meeting. Gouraud was French High Commissioner for the no-longer-French Cilicia; Commander in Chief of French Forces in the Levant; and still High Commissioner for Syria. Berthelot told Churchill that Gouraud; Lord Londonderry, Churchill's Parliamentary Under-Secretary; and their aide, General Spears, could show them "offers made by Feisul to the French suggesting his turning against the British." Gouraud immediately confirmed that this was true. In an attempt to kill Feisal's chances, the General added that the Emir:

> was in reality a stranger whose only influence rested on his xenophobia; that he was responsible for the deaths of some 20 to 25 French officers and 500 to 600 French soldiers, and that it was impossible to accept him.

M. Berthelot then added that for Britain to put Feisal on the Mesopotamian throne "would be entirely misunderstood in France."

Gouraud emphasized Feisal's powerlessness, and Berthelot confessed that he had once been in Feisal's favor (presumably, though, when the French thought that they could make him their tame puppet in Syria). But now, the French diplomat expostulated:

> It was evident that Feisal was most treacherous, principally out of weakness of character. The only support he could claim was on the basis of hatred of both French and English. He returned from France having taken all sorts of engagements to the French who on their side made it clear that their continued support depended solely on his loyalty. Hardly had he arrived when he completely changed, simply because he was not a strong man, and it was evident that he would have no following if he held to his engagements . . . the Sheriffiate [sic—the Hashemite ruling family] had no popularity, but it appeared that the French [noted General Spears] had not the same objections to other members of the Sheriffian family, although they emphasised that Hussein and his sons had no real standing. It was made abundantly clear that the whole of the French programme in Syria would be upset, and public opinion in France much roused should the British instal the Emire Feisul in Mesopotamia.

The French position, then, could not have been any clearer. Churchill was certainly not going to be told what to do by the French, even though his friend in the delegation, M. Loucheur, added his own harangue about the damage Feisal's enthronement would do in the Near East.

However, I do think it is fair to say that at this point Churchill genuinely had not fully made up his own mind, even though he was now strongly inclining toward a Hashemite solution. I do not think, in other words, he was the pawn of the pro-Hashemite faction—including Lawrence of Arabia, Sir Percy Cox, and the redoubtable Gertrude Bell—that some historians have made him out to be. He was going to Cairo in order to decide what to do, and to be open to all arguments. He therefore played for time and informed the French of his own "open mind." He did, though, remind them that Cox and others were all in favor of Feisal, and, perhaps we can deduce, most important in his own thinking was the advice that to install "a Sheriffian [sic] government . . . would enable a British Protectorate to be run cheaply."

What Churchill says here is doubly significant. It reemphasizes the key centrality of money as the overarching factor in his policy; he was going to choose whatever was cheapest. But second, he saw Mesopotamia— Iraq—as a *protectorate,* not as a proper state in its own right at all. This was, of course, implied in the nature of any League of Nations mandate—benign Western supervision of a country that was not yet, for whatever reason, fully capable of ruling itself alone. But Britain was, as Churchill spoke, experiencing riots in its protectorate in Egypt, so rashly proclaimed in 1914. Britain was to exercise many other similar colonial protectorates—in Africa, such as in present-day Botswana, so beloved of Alexander McCall Smith fans; and in Aden, in the Arabian peninsula—right up until the late 1960s. Whatever idealism there may originally have been in the concept of protectorates, the British and French saw things very differently.

Churchill's colonial mentality was as strong as anyone's. Indeed, the main reason for his being out of office in the 1930s was not, as many suppose, his antagonism to Hitler as early as 1933, though that did not help him, but his resolute opposition to any form, however mild, of independence for India.

It is also possible that the very passionate objections of France to Feisal actually helped Feisal's cause rather than hindered it, however accurate the French may have been in laying out his double-dealing in an attempt to secure a throne.

Churchill made his position clear to the French as the meeting ended:

> He mentioned how difficult it would be for him—he up to date of course keeping a perfectly open mind on the subject—to return to the House of Commons and state that all British local advisers were in favor of the instalment of the Emir Feisul and that nevertheless he had to recommend the evacuation of all save a bridgehead because of the French point of view.

As General Spears laconically noted: "This the French quite saw." Whatever Churchill was going to decide in Cairo, it would be for British reasons, and for those reasons alone.

The Mesopotamian problem, and the Turkish crisis that was worsening it, never left Churchill's thoughts. He wrote to the Prime Minister again, this time on 28 February. Various commissions were attempting to find a solution to the Greco-Turkish War and were investigating the ethnic makeup of Thrace in Europe and Smyrna in Anatolia. Churchill was hopeful that this would help him in dealing with Mosul; it was, he wrote, "of great importance to my affairs."

For it was, as he well knew by now, the threat of Turkey to the Mosul *vilayet,* with its small but nonetheless vocal Turcoman population, that was one of the reasons Britain was having to keep such a large army in the region. As he reminded Lloyd George:

> It is . . . all important to us that the Mosul district be included [in the remit of the Commissions], and that the Turks should be made to undertake not to disturb this region in any way. [Lloyd George would know] that they have been busily making preparations to put pressure on us here; and that any such pressure will fatally hamper my schemes for a more rapid with-drawal of our large army. Perhaps tens of millions of money depend upon tranquillity in Mosul and the absence of external pressure. If therefore there is going to be an armistice [between the Turks and their opponents], which I devoutly hope will be the case, it is of the highest importance that the tranquillity of this region should be a definite part of it.

Once more, this was to impose a solution for the region based on British interests, not on those of its inhabitants. While some local British officials were all in favor of a genuinely free Kurdish state, for others it was British imperial considerations that came first and last. The situation was not helped by the way they had gone about trying to gauge local opinion, prin-cipally by asking the views not of ordinary people but of their tribal chiefs. Needless to say, local Kurdish leaders did not reply in the interests of the Kurdish people as a whole but in those of their particular tribe or local area. Kurdish nationalists, such as existed, tended to be middle-class and urban— as in Syria during the Arab Revolt—and were thus often ignored by the more traditionalist and hierarchically biased British local officials. As some histo-rians have pointed out, many leaders also gave the answer they thought the British wanted to hear, with the result that an accurate gauge of Kurdish opinion in the region was even more difficult to obtain.

Churchill's final missive was to Lord Allenby, the British High Commissioner in Cairo, with details of his forthcoming arrival. No conference secretary had been arranged, so Churchill asked Allenby to provide one—somebody with "knowledge and experience of Eastern affairs but without strong personal views on the Arab question." Churchill's own select invitees—his "forty thieves"—had plenty of strong views on all matters Arab, so presumably yet another opinion on the issues would make a cacophony.

Churchill then set off, ready to travel luxuriously to Egypt for the conference that would permanently change the borders of the Middle East, creating the turbulent region we know today.

Visiting the Pyramids March 20, 1921. Left to right beginning with figure in white robe and hood: Clementine Churchill, Gertrude Bell, Winston Churchill, T. E. Lawrence, and W. H. Thompson (Churchill's detective). (Courtesy of the Broadwater Collection at the Churchill Archives of Churchill College Cambridge)

Churchill on his polo pony, May 11, 1921. (Courtesy of the Broadwater Collection of the Churchill Archives of Churchill College Cambridge)

Prince Abdullah (Feisal's brother), Sir Herbert Samuel, and Winston Churchill, in Jerusalem, March 1921. (Courtesy of the Broadwater Collection at the Churchill Archives of Churchill College Cambridge)

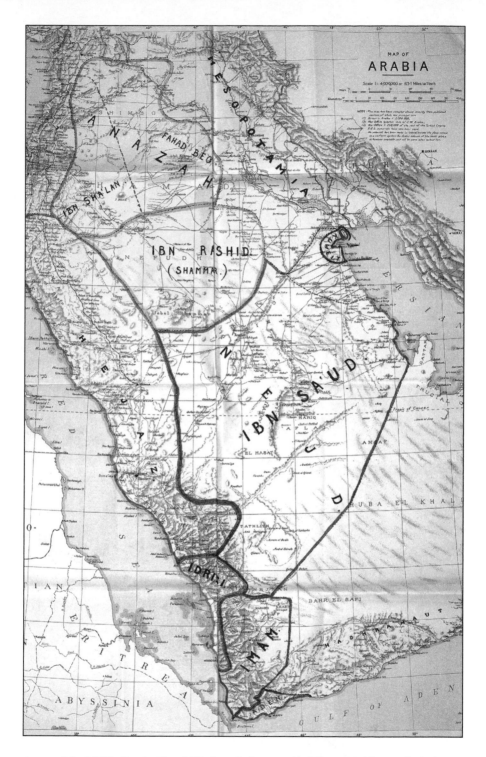

A map of the Middle East in Churchill's time. It shows a very different Middle East from the one we know today. (Courtesy of the Broadwater Collection at the Churchill Archives of Churchill College Cambridge)

The Cairo Conference, Official Photo, March 1921. The Churchill Archive does not identify most people in this photograph. Those who are identified are as follows. Front row, from left to right, beginning with man in military uniform and cap, holding cane: General Congreve, Sir Herbert Samuel, Winston Churchill, Sir Percy Cox, General Haldane, General Ironside, Radcliffe. Second row: (second from left, in flowered hat) Gertrude Bell; (center, standing behind Sir Percy Cox, in civilian clothes) T. E. Lawrence; (to the right of Lawrence) General Salmond; (to the right of Salmond) Hubert Young. Extreme top row, center, wearing bow tie: Sir Archibald Sinclair. Below Sinclair and slightly to the right, also in bow tie: Joseph Crosland. (Getty Images Collection

CHAPTER FIVE

CHANGING THE MAP: THE CAIRO CONFERENCE OF 1921

I t is no exaggeration to say that the experts who gathered together in the elegant Semiramis Hotel in Cairo in March 1921 created the map of the Middle East that we know today. Here we are concentrating on one part of their deliberations—the creation of the artificial state we now call Iraq. But present-day Jordan also owes its existence to the men and women who assembled in the Semiramis. So too does the fact that we still have a major problem between Israelis and Palestinians, in particular, whether or not that territory constitutes one single state—Palestine—or an Israeli state for Jews and a land with areas in which Palestinian Arabs are permitted to live.

The Semiramis was evidently *the* place to stay. T. E. Lawrence wrote to his more respectable brother Bob—soon to be a missionary in China—that it was "a marble and bronze hotel, very expensive and luxurious: horrible place: makes me a Bolshevik. Everybody Middle East is here."

From the beginning, Churchill was the life and soul of the gathering. Jessie Raven, a university lecturer married to Joseph Crosland, the Director of Finance at the War Office, related her memories to Churchill's official biographer, Sir Martin Gilbert. The Croslands were from a staunchly Plymouth Brethren background, a behaviorally very strict

Protestant denomination, but they attended the Cairo Conference. Their son was Tony Crosland, the *bon viveur* Labour Foreign Secretary and ideologue. Their grandson, the eminent cell biologist Denis Alexander, years later himself lived for many years in the Middle East, the world his grandfather and Churchill were busily creating in Cairo in 1921. As Jessie Raven recalls:

> When things were boring in the Hotel everyone would cheer up when Winston came in, followed by an Arab carrying a pail and a bottle of wine . . . [Churchill] was unpopular with the Egyptians—many carriages had notices *"à bas Churchill"*—but he didn't care. He took his easel and sat in the road painting—he also talked so loudly in the street that the generals got quite nervous. He was always telling people not to give up their painting. He didn't like Arabs coming into the Hotel, not even into the garden.

Since he was about to determine the fate of millions of Arabs, this was, perhaps, rather unfortunate.

What we now call the Cairo Conference opened on 12 March 1921, presided over by Churchill himself. He had arrived in Egypt two days earlier and had already had talks with both T. E. Lawrence and two leading members of the Royal Air Force: Lord Trenchard and Sir John Salmond, the Air Officer Commanding in the Middle East; for without the assurance of airpower that could transform the military situation in Mesopotamia, Churchill's desire to save Lloyd George serious millions would not be possible.

Fortunately, the airmen had good news. Trenchard was able to tell Churchill that "all the machinery" was available, and Sir John assured him that all the money needed to begin the Cairo-to-Baghdad air route was on hand.

The assembly was divided into two committees—one to discuss the political issues, the other the military. Churchill chaired the political committee and General Congreve the military. The main aim of both committees was to figure out how to save as much money as possible.

In their book *Empires of the Sand,* Efraim and Inari Karsh point out that most of the experts at the conference were protagonists of the "Hashemite solution," the placing of the Hashemite princes Feisal and Abdullah on the respective thrones of what would become Iraq and Transjordan. Churchill's main goal in Cairo, however, was financial, not the advancement of one rival dynastic claim against another. If the "Sharifian solution" (to give the Hashemite claim its alternative name) was the one best suited to saving money, then that would be the best way forward.

We see this in what Churchill announced to the political committee on its very first day. He told them that the British High Commissioner, Sir Percy Cox, and the General Officer Commanding, General Haldane, had "already arrived" at a military conclusion. This was the preliminary withdrawal of troops from Mesopotamia, something that had become possible because of what airpower could now do to maintain law and order. Consequently, Churchill informed them, preliminary withdrawal could now be taken off the agenda.

The question of whether military withdrawal was a good or bad thing was not even open for discussion; the decision had been made. In this context, surely one can guess at the next item on the agenda—the identity and suitability of the various candidates for the soon-to-be-created Iraqi throne. While Karsh and Karsh are quite possibly right to say that the Hashemites were powerfully ambitious, they are not right in saying that putting the Hashemites on the throne was the primary purpose of the Cairo Conference. Looking at it from Churchill's point of view, the Hashemites were simply the best means to an end—getting British troops out of Mesopotamia and saving millions for the Treasury in the process.

So Churchill, having dealt with what to him was the main issue—troop reductions—went on to the other key decision: the new ruler. He asked Sir Percy Cox first for his view, and Cox replied that Feisal was by far the best candidate. The reason Sir Percy gave is significant, in that it spoke to Churchill's primary aim—the creation of a native Iraqi army that could work alongside the Royal Air Force, Britain's new means of maintaining order as cheaply as possible in the newly independent mandate state. Sir Percy said he "considered Feisal's previous experience during the war placed him in the best position for raising an army quickly."

In other words, the "Sharifian policy" was the one that would enable the British army to withdraw and save millions without leaving chaos behind.

Lawrence's views were more complex and tinged with the kind of benign, paternalistic, but nonetheless still imperialist racism he had exhibited during the Arab Revolt. As the Cairo Conference minutes record:

> *Colonel Lawrence* supported the candidature of Amir Faisal not only from his personal knowledge of and friendship for the individual, but also on the ground that in order to counteract the claims of rival candidates and to pull together the scattered elements of a backward and half civilised country, it was essential that the first ruler should be an active and inspiring personality. Amir Abdullah was lazy, and by no means dominating.

This is something of a caricature of both brothers, Feisal and Abdullah, and in fact Abdullah was the easier of the two to manipulate. But whether or not Lawrence's preference for Feisal over Abdullah was fair, such Orientalist notions of rescuing a backward race were not much on Churchill's mind: His thinking was altogether more pragmatically based:

> *The Chairman* [Churchill] pointed out that a strong argument in favor of Sherifian policy was that it enabled His Majesty's Government to bring pressure to bear on one Arab sphere in order to attain their own ends in another. If Faisal knew that not only his father's subsidy and the protection of the Holy Places [Mecca and Medina] from Wahabi attack, but also the position of his brother in Transjordan was dependent on his own good behaviour, he would be much easier to deal with. The same argument applied *mutatis mutandis* [necessary changes having been made] to King Hussein and Amir Abdullah.

Churchill then reminded the political committee of Feisal's failed attempt to seize a kingdom in Syria. The "French Government had tried to convince him [Churchill] that by adopting a Sherifian policy he risked being destroyed, like Frankenstein, by a monster of his own creation."

Was Churchill doing what the French had warned him against? The revolt the previous year had cost enormous amounts, and with fiscal retrenchment urgently necessary, any policy that saved expenditure was worthwhile. But to remove the British troops too soon could result in the return of chaos, and that was equally undesirable. Just as complex was the issue of working with the locals, something that British commentators in 2003 referred to as the "British policy," or the British way of doing things. We can see this—and the twenty-first-century parallels—in the meeting that took place at the Semiramis Hotel on 13 March.

Churchill opened the political committee with a very significant telegram that he proposed to send to Lloyd George, the Prime Minister, who was anxiously awaiting the outcome back in London. "I think we shall reach a unanimous conclusion among all the authorities," Churchill read, "that Feisal offers hope of best and cheapest solution." He told the committee that he had every confidence that Lawrence would be able to persuade Feisal to take the throne of what would become Iraq, and that Feisal would be able to reach Mesopotamia either the very next month, or at least by May.

Not only that, but the committee members all agreed that Feisal's presence in the new Iraqi kingdom being established "would have such an inspiring effect on the majority of the population that there was little fear of any opposition to his candidature."

This was, in fact, untrue, since both the Naqib of Baghdad and Sayyid Talib were themselves actively hoping to become the ruler of Iraq. If Feisal was to become king and not be seen as a British-imposed puppet, there was still much work to be done to achieve the desired result in a politically convenient way.

This became a major issue of discussion: How could it be made to look as if Feisal was the choice of the Iraqi people? The formula Churchill had in mind, which he tested in a telegram to Lloyd George on the 14th, was as follows:

> In response to enquiries from adherents of Emir Feisal, the British Government have stated that they will place no obstacles in the way of his candidature as Ruler of Iraq, and that if he is chosen he will have their support.

Churchill's exact wording was important for diplomatic reasons as well: Lord Curzon was now having to do his best to placate the French, whose opposition to Feisal's candidature had not diminished.

Churchill also concocted a bargain: Britain would offer to support France in German-related issues if the French agreed to let the British have Feisal.

Further subterfuge would be needed to make it look as if the British were playing no part in Feisal's candidature. First, Lawrence was to tell Feisal the results of the meeting on the quiet:

> On this, Feisal will at once proceed to Mecca [where his father Hussein was waiting for him], passing through Egypt on the way. We do not want any announcement, even in guarded terms, of [the above] formula if it can possibly be avoided until Feisal is at Mecca and Sir P. Cox [is back in] Baghdad about the middle of April.

Hussein was still proving difficult about his wish to extend the domains of his children into the main British mandate in Palestine, so Churchill no doubt hoped that Feisal's bringing good news of a Hashemite kingdom in Iraq would soften the blow.

The fact that Feisal's selection as king would be a "fix" can be seen in Churchill's next thought. The:

> method of choice will require careful study in order to avoid confused or meaningless expression of Mesopotamian opinion. Time is short, as Sir P. Cox must return, and all my plans depend on [a] clear settlement with him before we separate.

A "confused expression" might well mean the Mesopotamians—or Iraqis, as they were now increasingly being called—choosing the right person without overwhelming support, or, worse still, the wrong person, such as the ambitious Sayyid Talib. The urgency for Churchill is very clear: He wanted it all sewn up as soon as possible.

Nevertheless, Churchill had gone to Cairo with the specific mandate of saving money—and, at the forefront of his short-term political ambitions, with his desire to be Chancellor of the Exchequer. As he wrote to the Prime Minister, just to make doubly sure that Lloyd George got the message:

> I have no doubt personally [that] Feisal offers far away [the] best chance of saving our money. Please therefore endeavour to telegraph to me as soon as you possibly can [so that] I am free to make my plans on the basis of [the] formula.

In other words, choosing Feisal was the quickest way out of the financial hole the British government found itself in following the 1920 revolt, because of the need to keep British troops present. It was, though, far from being an Iraqi-centered solution—which would have entailed choosing the best person for Iraq, or, better still, letting the new Iraqis have a genuine say in how their new state was to be ruled.

The cost-cutting imperative continued in the afternoon, when the political and military committees met for a "combined" session.

Churchill began with the need to make the most drastic economies possible. All other decisions were to be seen in that light, since all cuts had to be made "without delay." General Haldane had suggested that even a modified garrison would cost around £25 million a year; Churchill wanted military spending to "come down to about two thirds of this figure."

Here the generals differed. To Haldane, it was only the lack of ships that delayed British troop withdrawals. But Congreve felt that the British were withdrawing far too fast, and Sir Percy Cox fully supported him. Removing the troops too quickly would "leave him [Haldane] in a very difficult position," since far more of them were needed than were allowed for in Haldane's plan.

These are exactly the same debates that have taken place in both Britain and the United States in the twenty-first century. What is the ultimate factor in making decisions: strategic need or saving money? If it is the tyranny of urgent financial pressure that is the driving force, can one be certain of making the best long-term decision?

Obviously, for Churchill in 1921, it was the money. In addressing the combined committee, "whilst agreeing that the situation was a somewhat difficult one," he:

[e]mphasised the fact that the British taxpayer could not be expected to continue to garrison the country at such high expense, and that rapid economies must be effected before the new financial year.

Churchill continued, saying he realized that the:

military commanders wished to refrain from placing a number of small detachments around the country involving long lines of communications, and risking the destruction of such forces in the event of hostile action, yet he thought it must be possible to find a medium whereby the General Officer Commanding might meet the High Commissioner by slightly increasing the numbers of stations from the three suggested [Mosul, Baghdad, and Basra]. At the same time it was essential that the training of the local forces be accelerated as much as possible.

Churchill's case was now unwittingly undermined by Trenchard, when he pointed out that the Royal Air Force would not be in a position to be fully operative in Iraq for at least a year. Since the RAF was pivotal to Churchill's long-term policing-on-the-cheap strategy for the new country, this was an unexpected blow.

Churchill then had the brainstorm that perhaps local people on the key communications routes could be subsidized by the British in return for being "responsible for guarding the railway." While it was an ingenious scheme, Sir Percy Cox was surely right when he warned them that "the time was scarcely ripe to place such a trust upon a populace which had so recently been in revolt against" the British. While this begs the question of whether British troops should have been there in the first place, the kind of financially motivated scuttle that Churchill was now proposing was hardly the right policy if law and order were to be maintained.

Nevertheless, Churchill continued to play the financial card, pointing out how expensive British troops were in Mesopotamia compared to neighboring Palestine, over five times more for the proposed Iraq force as for garrisoning the Palestinian mandate. He also covered himself politically by sending a telegram to the Prime Minister to gain higher authority for his planned cutbacks.

"Incredible waste," he told Lloyd George:

> can only be cured by driving large numbers of troops and followers out of
> the country and off our pay list. . . . I am met by the assertion that many
> thousands of men and followers could now begin to leave if shipping were
> available . . . . We have to carry everyone back sooner or later and keeping
> them waiting eating up our mutton is pure waste.

The two committees were therefore put to work on how to reduce
expenditure as much as possible. Senior officers could be replaced with
junior officers, for example, and if the 25,000 animals, costing nearly £2
million a year, could be sold off, that would save even more. (This was in the
age of cavalry. The Chartwell Papers contain reams of statistics that give
copious details on exactly how much each animal cost.)

In short, Churchill told them, once the military threat from a renascent
Turkey had passed and a local Arab army had been established, British troops
in Iraq could be reduced by at least 15,000 men.

There then was a discussion of what, in retrospect, was one of the Cairo
Conference's most unfortunate decisions—the question of Kurdistan. As
recent articles in the *New York Times* and London *Times* have argued very
persuasively, ever since the decision was made to create Iraq as a unitary state,
it has been a complete disaster for the people of that country.

In Cairo, Churchill was very open to the wishes of the Kurdish people
for a homeland of their own. The prospect of an independent Kurdish
state, acting as a buffer zone between a reborn Turkey and the newly independent Arab states, was an attractive one to Churchill and his "forty
thieves."

First of all, it was important that the Kurdish areas of the mandate be
kept safe from Turkish invasion, in case the new Turkish regime wanted to
re-conquer that oil-rich area as well as the Greek-inhabited parts of Mediterranean Turkey. As Churchill therefore told the political committee on the
15th, he thought, in the short term:

> [t]hat it might be possible to subsidise a Kurdish chief and his more
> influential subordinates and to grant provisional trading facilities in

consideration of an agreement that they would prevent the Turks from carrying out a policy in that area adverse to British interests.

Churchill was equally troubled about how an Arab ruler might treat his Kurdish subjects, a concern that proved well-founded during the Hashemite period of Iraq as well as under the considerably more brutal rule of Saddam Hussein. As he told the committee, with acutely accurate foresight, such a ruler:

> while outwardly accepting constitutional procedures and forming a Parliament, [might] at the same time despise democratic and constitutional procedures . . . [and] with the power of an Arab army behind him . . . ignore Kurdish sentiment and oppress the Kurdish minority.

This is exactly what has been happening to the Kurds for the past eighty years. While Churchill did favor a "friendly buffer state" between Turkey and the new Iraqi state, with a Kurdish army under British officers, he nonetheless conceded the need for a unitary state, as urged on the committee by Sir Percy Cox and Gertrude Bell.

Thus a Kurdish state was stillborn, with tragic consequences for the Kurds right up until the decision by Britain and the United States after the Gulf War in 1991 to have a locally ruled Kurdish enclave (minus the key city of Mosul). In early 2004, this whole topic remains a controversial issue. Wise commentators now propose the hitherto unthinkable position of breaking up Iraq into three separate states: Kurdish in the north, Sunni Arab in the middle, and Shiite Muslim in the south.

As people are only now realizing, Iraq was created out of three Ottoman *vilayets* that had previously been quite separate. The Kurds are Sunni, like the Arabs in the middle of the country, but ethnically they are Indo-European, like the Iranians. The Shiite majority in the south might be Arabs, but religiously they are of the same branch of Islam as Iran—Shiite—and therefore have loyalties that are quite distinct from those of the rest of Iraq's people.

All this could have been solved in Cairo. The Kurds could have enjoyed their own buffer state, and the rest of Mesopotamia could have been split into two kingdoms, as Lawrence had earlier proposed when he was trying to find kingdoms for Abdullah and Zaid, Abdullah's and Feisal's brother.

Churchill, ever mindful of the main reason for the conference, was continually telling his colleagues that the savings proposed to date were "quite insufficient." On the 16th, he telegraphed Lloyd George with the optimistic news that all the leading participants had "reached complete agreement on all the points, both political and military." If the ships arrived to take many of the troops back home, a savings of £5,500,000 could be realized. If an army was not needed and local forces were trained to protect the new state against a Turkish invasion, then the battalion strength could be reduced from twenty-three to twelve, thereby reducing the British government's bill to only £6 million a year—a savings of over £20 million.

As Churchill continued to find scope for further savings, he came once more into conflict with the military. Here, at least, he was on the side of the angels, since his desire to save money by training the local troops overrode the British officer's racist distrust of non-European soldiery.

Making these economies was eased by the unanimous view that airpower, rather than troops on the ground, should be the way of maintaining British military control in the region. In addition, Iraq was an ideal training area for the new Royal Air Force—nurtured since its birth and consistently supported by Churchill—and, as the committee concurred, RAF control in Iraq would provide the means of fulfilling the vital necessity of preparing and training an Air Force adequate to Britain's needs in war, the importance of testing the potentialities of the Air Force, the need for giving its superior officers and staffs the experience of independent command and responsibility, and the provision of an "All Red" [i.e., all-British] military and commercial air route to India.

Here again, British reasons—not Iraqi interests—were paramount. Churchill saw this as a golden opportunity to "carry out a far-sighted policy of Imperial aerial development in the future." Ever the enthusiast and with a keen grasp of strategy, he was well aware that, for example, getting from Cairo to Karachi, the nearest major airport in the Raj, would take eight to ten days less by air than it did by sea.

Churchill was also open to the commercial possibilities of air travel and, once more, to saving money as well. If the RAF was able to ensure "tranquillity . . . upon the route," then civilian services could use "the same aerodromes, sheds and pilots" that the RAF would be using "in time of war." All this "would lead to considerable economies." We should not forget that the major British airlines were state-owned monopolies until they were denationalized by Margaret Thatcher in the late 1980s.

The experts, led by Churchill, then had to discuss the thorny question of what was euphemistically called "subsidies and commitments"—or what we might, more strictly speaking, describe as bribes to local chiefs to keep them quiet or sympathetic to the British, preferably both. Even here Churchill wanted to save money: If a grant to a local chieftain meant peace in a region, that in turn meant British troops would not be needed to keep things under control.

Sir Percy Cox wanted the annual subsidy to Ibn Saud to be doubled, from £60,000 a year to £120,000. His reason was blatant appeasement; as he told Churchill and the others around the table, Ibn Saud "possessed considerable power to harm British policy." Elaborating on this theme, Sir Percy defended his view by saying that the reason for so acting "lay not so much in the actual services to be expected from him, but rather in the amount of harm he would be able to cause were his policy to become hostile."

Sir Percy's assessment of potential dangers was an understatement: Ibn Saud, with his Wahhabi—Islam-inspired Ikhwan warriors—was busy conquering as much of the Arabian peninsula as he could—but, significantly, not those regions under direct British rule such as Kuwait. He certainly also had his eyes on much of what was soon to become Iraq, but above all he coveted the territories of King Hussein of the Hijaz. Here lay the sacred cities of Mecca and Medina, and the lucrative control of the annual *Haj* pilgrimage traffic—the biggest revenue source in Arabia before the discovery of substantial oil reserves in one of the other regions that had just been conquered by Ibn Saud's shock troops.

Cox's appeasement policy drew strong dissent from Major Young, who pointed out that if Britain were to be fair, it would have to increase its annual grant to King Hussein as well as to Ibn Saud. Indeed, were the latter also to proclaim himself a king, he could then "claim membership of the League of Nations," and the independence that would give him would "tend to remove him from British control." This would be, Young argued, "undesirable in view of British interests in Arabia."

Young was to prove right; as Karsh and Karsh have pointed out, correctly this time, the real winner of 1921 was Ibn Saud. The British were mainly trying to appease him, except when it came to things like the borders of Kuwait, which Sir Percy Cox was to draw entirely in British interests, regardless of Ibn Saud's preferences. Thanks to Sir Percy, Ibn Saud was able to create a massive new Arab kingdom, conquering large swaths of territory without any opposition at all.

Britain's enabling the creation of an Arab kingdom with a uniquely medieval view of Islam (no other Muslim country has the draconian Hanbali/Wahhabi School of Islam as its official religion) was also a financial mistake. When oil was discovered in 1932 in what became Saudi Arabia, it was to the Americans Ibn Saud turned, not the British.

Even Gertrude Bell, the passionate advocate for the Hashemite cause, supported giving Ibn Saud a *douceur* (subsidy), since she was worried about the effect two more Hashemite kings—Feisal in Iraq, and possibly now Abdullah, too, in Jordan—would have on Ibn Saud's sensibilities. So Churchill agreed to a compromise: Ibn Saud's subsidy would increase to £100,000 a year, but it would be paid on a monthly basis. This was so that Britain "should then be able to bring more pressure to bear upon him to maintain the necessary tranquillity of the Nejd," the ancestral heartland of Ibn Saud's rapidly growing kingdom.

Young had insisted on parity for Hussein in the Hijaz, so once more Churchill suggested a compromise. He was happy to give Hussein an equal amount, provided that the king was willing "to maintain an attitude of goodwill towards the British Government" and also to "abstain from and entirely disassociate himself from anti-French propaganda."

The truth was that Hussein was feeling increasingly angry at what he regarded as British perfidy in Palestine and Syria. His son Feisal, ambitious for a throne of his own in Iraq, might not be willing any longer to upset the British applecart; but Hussein already had a kingdom in the Hijaz, and his son Abdullah was in Amman, ready to attack the French in Syria despite Feisal's recent and ignominious defeat there.

Since Churchill's advisers were split, he asked a subcommittee to finalize the decision on the subsidy issue. Among its members, who included T. E. Lawrence and Sir Percy Cox, was a young colonel who was later to become the linchpin of British policy in Iraq: This was Kinahan Cornwallis, who had directed the Arab Bureau in which Lawrence had served from 1916 to 1920. The subcommittee did what was expected and came up with the perfect compromise: £100,000 each for Hussein and Ibn Saud. As this book is about Iraq, I have not looked here in detail at the vexed issue of Palestine. But since the Cairo Conference spent much time on it and in effect created the states of Israel and Jordan, we have to consider it briefly. For while Churchill and his wife were able to spend much of the evening of the 16th dancing happily at a ball given by Lord Allenby, Churchill's part in the festivities was cut short just before midnight by the arrival of the British High Commissioner in Jerusalem, Sir Herbert Samuel. As a local paper put it, when Sir Herbert arrived, "Mr. Churchill at once went upstairs with him and they were seen no more."

Sir Herbert had been one of Churchill's long-standing colleagues in the pre-1914 Liberal government, so the two men knew each other well. The fact that Sir Herbert was one of Britain's most eminent Jews was a signal that Britain intended to take its Balfour Declaration promises seriously. The Chartwell Papers in Cambridge are filled with petitions to the new Colonial Secretary from both sides of the debate in Jerusalem. They came from eager Zionists delighted to be able to have a Jewish homeland at last, and anxious Arabs who realized what the long-term implications of the new settlements would be. Churchill, unlike many of his more prejudiced upper-class contemporaries, was strongly philo-Semitic, and this sentiment was to guide Britain's Palestine policy in the days ahead.

That night, Churchill and Samuel soon came to a disagreement, but it was not on the issue of Jewish immigration. Samuel strongly disagreed with Churchill's growing idea that a separate Transjordanian state should be created for Abdullah, who was in Amman waiting to plot his next move. When the Palestine Political and Military Committee met for the first time on 17 March, Samuel rapidly found himself isolated in his view, and when Churchill told him that the decision to create a separate Transjordanian state had already been made in London, albeit a view "arrived at after considerable discussion," Samuel was faced with an effective *fait accompli*. Nonetheless, he did his best. As he was able to remind Churchill and the others, the area had been one included in the specifically Palestinian part of the League of Nations mandate. If separated, it would soon be seen "as an independent Arab state." Should Abdullah become its ruler, he would not only use his new domain to attack the French in Syria, but he would also create a major source of anti-Zionist feeling "and thus prove a danger." With what we would now call massive understatement, there was, warned Sir Herbert, "some probability of controversy in Palestine for some years on the question of Zionism." His wildly optimistic projection of "some years" turned out, of course, to be decades—and still counting.

Churchill disagreed with Sir Herbert's prognosis. He wanted to use the same solution to the problem in Palestine as had been agreed on for Iraq: a Hashemite ruler, in this case Abdullah, the original Sharifian candidate for Iraq before Feisal had been so abruptly and conclusively ejected from Syria. It "would be courting trouble," Churchill felt, to support Feisal's candidature in Iraq but not Abdullah's in Transjordan, all the more so in light of the subsidy issue they had resolved the previous day, for by subsidizing Hussein in the Hijaz and then paying Ibn Saud not to attack it, "we could," Churchill averred, "obtain general peace and prosperity in Arabia." Abdullah ruling from Amman with full British support was thus a piece in a much bigger jigsaw puzzle. "It seemed inevitable," Churchill continued, "that in these circumstances we should adopt a policy elsewhere which would harmonise with our Mesopotamian policy."

Churchill's scheme was, in effect, to establish a series of pro-British client monarchies, all of whose rulers would owe Britain a debt of considerable gratitude simply for the fact that they were in power at all. As he told Sir Herbert and the other committee members, this way the whole Sharifian family—Hussein in the Hijaz, Feisal in Iraq, and Abdullah in Transjordan—would thereby be placed "under an obligation to His Majesty's Government in one sphere or another." Perhaps to soften the blow for Sir Herbert, Churchill added that "to guarantee that there would be no anti-Zionist disturbances" in the area under direct British control in Palestine, it was vital to support Abdullah with either money or troops. For "Abdullah's moral influence was of great importance."

T. E. Lawrence then entered into the argument on Churchill's side, opining that Abdullah could easily stop the local Arab leaders from stirring up anti-Zionist discontent. In what we can now call a ludicrously overoptimistic statement, Lawrence added that "in four or five years, under the influence of a just policy, the opposition to Zionism would have decreased, if it had not entirely disappeared." Again, the history of the past eighty years reveals the sad folly of such a view.

Lawrence then went on to give what was perhaps the key British reason for wanting Abdullah to rule the brand-new Transjordanian state from Amman:

> It was his view that it would be preferable to use Transjordania [the original British name for the area] as a safety valve, by appointing a ruler on whom he could bring pressure to bear, to check anti-Zionism. The ideal person would be a candidate who was not too powerful, and who was not an inhabitant of Transjordania, but who relied upon His Majesty's Government for the retention of his office . . . Sherif Abdullah, by reason of his position and his lineage, possessed very considerable power for good or harm over the tribesmen. This would not be the case with a local townsman who was the only other alternative.

This shows us clearly that the British were intending to use the Sharifian clan in the same way that the British Raj in India used the great array of maharajas, nawabs, and similar local client rulers to rule millions of Indians on the cheap (not to mention similar tribal chiefs in large parts of British Africa). The appearance of independence would be granted, but real control would remain British.

It soon became apparent, however, that Abdullah was presenting them with a *fait accompli:* He was already in Amman with his loyal troops. Nevertheless, one of the committee, Wyndham Deedes, the Chief Secretary for Palestine, resolutely opposed giving Abdullah anything. Then he was informed by one of Allenby's aides, the distinguished anthropologist Major Fitzroy Somerset, that it would be "impossible to get rid of Abdullah in the event of his not being appointed" or if Abdullah "refused to agree to the conditions of his appointment."

Here is an interesting difference between the British and the French: Whereas the French did not hesitate to use full force to get rid of Feisal when he refused to become their puppet in Syria, not long afterward, in identical circumstances, the British were arguing that it was impossible to get rid of his brother Abdullah.

Churchill decided to round off the discussion on a positive note. Since Britain was supporting Feisal in Mesopotamia and Hussein in the Hijaz, it could be hoped that Abdullah would set up a stable government in Amman. With "the help of a small force," he could use his influence "to prevent anti-French and anti-Zionist propaganda in Transjordania."

Worse was to follow for Sir Herbert and for Deedes. The military committee, under General Congreve, met later that day and decided that a Jewish army was out of the question. Since they had just agreed to an Arab force for Abdullah (later to be the famous Arab Legion under its British commander, Glubb Pasha), this was bad news. A police force was one thing, an army another. Churchill, consistently pro-Jewish and pro-Zionist, challenged this conclusion the next day. Unfortunately, the argument then got bogged down in a row between Congreve and Samuel over what kind of uniform a Jewish army would wear. The discussion went nowhere, and there was no official Jewish army in British-mandated Palestine until 1948, when the new Israeli Army was established.

As Sir Martin Gilbert ruefully puts it, in "three days, two new Arab states had been created, their sovereigns chosen, and part of the Zionist cause lost by default."

So was this, as Efraim and Inari Karsh would have us believe, a capitulation to the aggressive imperialist ambitions of the Hashemite dynasty? Or are Martin Gilbert and the more recent best-selling author David Fromkin right when they say that the transformation of the Middle East was a British creation—simply artificial lines in the sand?

There is no doubt that the Hashemites were ambitious. It was why Hussein was—foolishly, as it turned out—holding out against the British in his stubborn refusal to recognize the loss of Palestine and Syria to what he dreamed would be a Hashemite Arab Kingdom in the Middle East. (Foolish because, after Churchill left office and Ibn Saud invaded the Hijaz, the British government was disgruntled enough with Hussein not to stop the Saudi conquest.)

Similarly, Abdullah had the British in a very awkward spot in Amman; only by using the same kind of brute force the less scrupulous French had employed in Syria could he be dislodged. While many, such as Lawrence himself, preferred Feisal to Abdullah, we can say in retrospect that Abdullah was the cleverer of the two. His great-grandson, King Abdullah II, today sits on the Jordanian throne, and even though Jordan has nowhere near the natural resources of its theoretically wealthier neighbor, Iraq, it has not suffered the years of instability followed by tyranny, genocide, and oppression that the Iraqis have endured. Abdullah may not have gained a throne in Baghdad, but his descendants and their Jordanian subjects have been far luckier.

It is surely true to say that Abdullah was given Jordan as much because Britain had *already* adopted a pro-Hashemite policy as for the fact that he was already in place in Amman. Had the British not been sympathetic to his family and had they not already decided to back Feisal for the vacant Iraqi throne, it is unlikely that they would have been so tolerant of Abdullah. I think this was the real reason behind Britain's decision to not take the French option and launch an attack on Abdullah to remove him as the French had removed his brother.

Also, Abdullah was lucky that the predominant military mood was for empire on the cheap. When Sir Henry Wilson heard that Churchill proposed having British troops in Transjordan (as it now became), he was able to prevent it on the grounds of "expense and further commitment."

The final meeting of the combined military and political committee was on the 19th, with Churchill himself in the chair. In aid of his basic desire to get everything done as cheaply as possible, he made clear that the new Mesopotamian government must "pay a certain contribution" toward the cost of any British forces that remained, chiefly the RAF but some Army personnel as well. Not only that, but when the new Iraq did have an army of its own, it would "in itself, provide a considerable relief to the Imperial [i.e., British] garrison."

It was not all hard work, though; 20 March was a Sunday like the 13th, not a working day, so they would take some time off. Since Clementine Churchill was with her husband, we do not have Churchill's own account of how things went. But he, Clementine, Gertrude Bell, and T. E. Lawrence all decided to visit the pyramids. They were, like countless tourists before and since, photographed sitting on their respective camels in front of the Sphinx. Churchill's camel, like many of the local Egyptian nationalists protesting the

Colonial Secretary's presence, clearly disliked him, and threw him off. Luckily, Churchill escaped with only a bruised hand, and it was a sufficiently mild injury that it did not keep him from fulfilling his dream of painting. Evidently a more congenial camel was found, since he was able to ride back to the government guest house accompanied by a more expert cameleer, Lawrence himself.

Lawrence felt that their time in Cairo had been a success, telling his brother Bob that the nine days had been:

> one of the longest fortnights [*sic*] I have ever lived. . . . We have done a lot of work, which is almost finished. . . . We're a happy family: agreed upon everything important: and the trifles are laughed at.

Knowing that the Cabinet had to agree to everything, Churchill had composed a long telegram to Lloyd George prior to his talk with Samuel, putting what we would now call the best possible spin on all the decisions reached. Churchill had recently had a political setback: Andrew Bonar Law, the laconic Canadian former ironmaster and Leader of the Conservative Party, was stepping down because of ill health (an unnamed illness from which, in the autumn of 1922, he was to make an amazing recovery—in time to depose Lloyd George and Churchill and become Prime Minister himself).

The arrangement had been that the Conservative Leader would take the post of Lord Privy Seal, a sinecure but which in the Coalition Government meant in effect being Leader of the House of Commons. Law's successor as Leader of the Conservative Party was Sir Austen Chamberlain, Chancellor of the Exchequer, but formerly Secretary of State for India during the war, until he had had to resign for being politically responsible for the major British defeat at Kut. He was the son of the famous imperialist Joseph Chamberlain, and the older brother of the later Prime Minister Neville Chamberlain, Churchill's great political foe in the 1930s.

In the reshuffle, Austen Chamberlain now became Lord Privy Seal, which created a vacancy for the key political post of Chancellor of the Exchequer, the minister in charge of finances. This was the post Churchill would have loved to have himself. It would have been a clear step up the political ladder and due reward for the enormous amount of money he had saved as Colonial Secretary. Since no one then knew that the Liberal Party would be effectively finished as a major political force the following year, in 1922, Churchill still had strong political ambitions within Lloyd George's Coalition Liberals—perhaps in time of becoming Prime Minister himself.

But the unexpected vacancy found Churchill not in London, in a position actively to press his claim, but thousands of miles away in Cairo. This was a source of enormous merriment to Churchill's detractors and no doubt one of equal disappointment to Churchill. But his hopes of getting the job were surely unrealistic; not only did the position have to go to a Conservative member of the Coalition, but most Conservatives themselves still distrusted him as the turncoat who had deserted their party nearly twenty years before. Instead, it went to a man named Sir Robert Horne, who must rank as one of the most obscure people ever to hold the post, and whose political career was to end permanently with the fall of the Coalition in 1922. Ironically, Horne was also abroad when the summons came, in this case on vacation in France. Clearly, political considerations, rather than Churchill's absence in the Middle East, had been the deciding factor.

Churchill's telegram to Lloyd George, emphasizing the money he was saving and the fact that the troops could not all be withdrawn as quickly as he wanted, was, however, largely devoted to the way in which Feisal could be put on the throne at best advantage to the British. What this method could best be called was a softening-up operation to create a climate of opinion in Iraq, among those who mattered, that was favorable to Feisal.

Sir Percy Cox was to go back to Basra and announce an amnesty for those involved in the 1920 uprising against the British (with a few exceptions). Feisal was to go to Mecca as soon as possible, and, on 23 April, from there to:

> telegraph . . . his friends in Mesopotamia saying that the British Government had informed him, in response to their enquiries, that they would place no obstacle in the way of his candidature as ruler of Iraq, and that he would have their support if he were to be chosen; that he, after discussion with his father and brothers, had decided to offer [his] services [to] Iraq.

Here things became complicated, and Churchill needed Cabinet approval to make sure that relations between the new Iraqi government and Britain, as the mandate-holder, would stay on a proper footing:

> We think that Feisal, in order to counter anti-mandate propaganda in Mesopotamia, should make it clear that he was prepared to accept [the] terms of the mandate as laid before the League of Nations, but we are not of the opinion that he can do so unless I am authorised to guarantee that by so doing [the] possibility of subsequent readjustment of relations between the mandatory [Britain] and [the] properly constituted Government of Mesopotamia will not be precluded.

This would involve a treaty between the new Iraqi government and Britain, one which, thanks to Feisal's need to not be seen as a British stooge, was swiftly to prove far more complicated than Churchill and his experts in Cairo could have anticipated. Such a treaty would provide for the:

> Continuance of the support of the mandatory subject to adequate safeguarding and maintenance of [Britain's] special interests and privileged position in Iraq.

Feisal was then to contact both the Naqib of Baghdad and Sayyid Talib, as members of the Provisional Government in Baghdad, "saying that he hoped to have their support and personal co-operation in the future." As Sir Percy Cox well knew, but as Churchill may well not have been so aware, this was a very delicate thing to ask Feisal to do, for not only had the Naqib and Sayyid Talib been passed over in 1920 for the post of monarch, they were now keen to reopen the issue in a way that would derail British plans. The Naqib, who was nearly eighty, contemplated a deal whereby he would be the initial king, and then on his death, which could not long be away, Talib would succeed to the throne. (The Naqib's own sons were not thought of as being up to much, which actually had been one of the main objections to his candidature in 1920.)

Talib himself, from his power base in Basra as well as through his ministry in the capital, Baghdad, was eagerly agitating for power—an Iraqi king for the Iraqi people. It was not that he was anti-British *per se,* just that he wanted the power for himself and not for any Hashemite outsider.

All of this made the task of an effortless and unopposed candidature for Feisal more problematic, as intelligence reports by British agents in the field were beginning to show. In Cairo, Churchill seemed oblivious to the latest intrigues. He did, though, tell the Cabinet that he was also going to ask Abdullah to make it clear that the latter's earlier claim was now withdrawn in favor of Feisal—and here, one suspects, an offer of an alternative throne in Amman would not have been amiss. Churchill, in fact, seemed quite sanguine, on the basis of what his officials had assured him, that all would be clear sailing for Feisal:

> It is anticipated that Feisal's announcement [of his candidature], followed by arrival in [the] country, would result in such a definite expression of public feeling on his behalf as would render unnecessary for us to ask the [Iraqi] Congress to discuss [the] question of [the] ruler, and they would simply directly or indirectly confirm his nomination. This having been done, Feisal would dissolve [the] present Provisional Government, namely the Council of Ministers, and call [the] Naqib or someone to form [a] Cabinet.

Just to make sure that Lloyd George got the point, Churchill added:

> The foregoing recommendations have unanimously been adopted, and I urgently request you to obtain Cabinet sanction for them in time to allow me to concert final details with Cox before he leaves Cairo.

Churchill now had to deal with the vexed issue of Kurdistan, another of the unfortunate legacies for our own time of his period in office. The real problem was that Lloyd George and Churchill were actively at loggerheads over the Turkish situation, something now made far worse by the war between Turkey and Greece.

While the Treaty of Sèvres had drastically reduced the scope of the Ottoman borders, the campaign of the Turkish nationalist leader, Mustapha Kemal, was winning not just Turks to its side but many Kurds as well, especially in the name of Islamic solidarity against Western interference. The British, despite their best efforts, had been unable to discover a Kurdish Feisal or Abdullah, and so there was no obvious puppet ruler who could be found for a new pro-British, anti-Turkish Kurdish state. As a result, there was real difficulty in deciding what fell where in terms of a nascent Kurdistan. As David McDowall, author of *A Brief History of the Kurds,* correctly argues, the British had, for all intents and purposes, blown their last chance of a unitary Kurdish nation under British protection back in 1920, before Kemal had become active in his opposition to the many injustices of the Treaty of Sèvres. From our point of view, therefore, Churchill was already in a box from which no easy exit was possible.

Was the part of Kurdistan indisputably under British rule—"Southern Kurdistan," or the old Mosul *vilayet*—to be independent? Part of a new Kurdish state? Or a region attached artificially to the new Iraqi state Churchill and his officials had just created in Cairo? It was to a possible solution of this dilemma that Churchill now asked Lloyd George to agree.

He reminded the Prime Minister that Southern Kurdistan had not been deemed part of Mesopotamia because of its uncertain status in the Treaty of Sèvres, Article 62 in particular, which dealt with the Kurds. But Sir Percy Cox had now come up with an answer: He was going to deal directly with the local Kurdish chiefs. Furthermore, Churchill realized that a Kurdish state of the proper size was now no longer an alternative:

> Acting on the assumption [that] article 62 is no longer operative, and that accordingly there is no question of Southern Kurdistan at any future date opting for union with Northern Kurdistan, the Conference has considered what policy with regard to purely Kurdish districts should be pursued. Our conclusion was that if at this state any attempt was to be made to force them under [the] rule of the Arab Government they would undoubtedly resist, and a complication would thus be added to our withdrawal. We recommend, therefore, that they, together with the Iraq Government, should be informed that our intention under [the] mandate is to maintain existing arrangements until such time as [a] representative body of Kurdish States may opt for inclusion in Iraq. The advantage of this solution is that it will enable us to recruit Kurdish units under British

officers, and thus to accelerate [the] reduction of Imperial forces in certain areas. This policy will also tend to discount the endeavours of Turks to seduce Kurds in our territory.

So on the one hand, Churchill was still keen above all to save money and manpower; on the other, he recognized the need to treat the Kurds separately. However, as David McDowall points out, since there was now not going to be any "Northern Kurdistan" for the Kurds to join, and Islamic sentiment had taken the local Kurdish leaders over to Kemal's side, the Kurds under British oversight would be left very vulnerable once the new Iraqi state came into being.

Sadly for the Kurds, the worst-case scenario took place. Feisal's government did not like or wish to deal with a separate Kurdish entity on what it felt should be its territory. Caught between a renascent and very strong Turkey to the north and a zealously Arabic Iraq to the south, the Kurds of "Southern Kurdistan" ended up being part of Iraq, abandoned by their British allies.

Lloyd George was not slow to respond. He agreed entirely with Churchill's desire to save money, but in his reply there were two caveats in his major conclusions about Mesopotamia/Iraq. As Prime Minister, he had to think of the big picture—and this meant relations with France. As he reminded Churchill:

> We have repeatedly hinted to the French that if there is a strong desire for Feisal from Mesopotamia, and peace can be restored by establishing him as Ruler in Iraq, we should not feel justified in vetoing his candidature. Unless [the] initiative comes from Mesopotamia, however, our position with the French will be embarrassing, and we think it will be very difficult to reconcile [the] procedure you propose with the attitude we have adopted with the French Foreign Office in this matter.

He then made it clear that Sir Percy Cox and Gertrude Bell would have to let Churchill know whether this initiative could "be forthcoming."

Then there was the issue of the Kurds. Lloyd George was far more sanguine than Churchill on whether the Turks would invade British-ruled territory. Unfortunately, he based much of his optimism on a chat with the Turkish delegate in London, Bekir Sami Bey (later Bekir Kunduk), who positively oozed goodwill toward the British government. But since Lloyd George was ambivalent about the true strength of Kemal's forces, which he dismissed as "the extremists at Angora," not much store can be laid by the assurances he was given.

Lloyd George also had to admit that the British had "no certainty that [Britain's proposed] settlement will be accepted by [the] Turks." War between Greece and Turkey could break out again, with Britain unable to control either side. Lloyd George's next point was unlikely to find Churchill in agreement, in view of the latter's strong differences with the official policy. As the Prime Minister wrote:

> Should fighting occur it is difficult to judge what its reaction will be on the Mesopotamian front. We are, however, warning the Turks that if any hostile action is taken in Mesopotamia we shall consider ourselves at liberty to arm the Greeks.

This would have, for all intents and purposes, involved Britain in the war, something that Churchill wanted to do everything possible to avoid, and with good cause.

Churchill therefore had to write back to the Prime Minister, defending his actions in Cairo. His reply is helpful in that it shows us clearly how his mind was working and how he had been convinced of the merits of the Hashemite candidature. He emphasized that the procedure outlined in his earlier telegrams had been "devised by Cox, Miss Bell and Lawrence" and carried "with it unanimous opinion of all authorities here." He continued:

> We are as fully conscious as you are of [the] desire for securing a spontaneous movement for Feisal in Mesopotamia as a prelude to his being countenanced by us. Unless we have a mind of our own on the subject it is by no means certain that this will occur.

This admission by Churchill is extraordinarily revealing. For what he is really saying is that unless the British had decided in advance whom they wanted to win, it would be impossible to guarantee the result. So much for democracy and popular choice! Yet his problem was that in order to save money, it had to look as if the person the British chose—Feisal—was also the free choice of the Iraqi people. Otherwise, the British would be stuck in the country with all the expense of maintaining a full army in order to keep down a recalcitrant population. The only alternative to this would be to scuttle and leave the locals to themselves, with all the potential chaos— and Britain's shame over it—that would ensue.

The sentence that reveals the key to Churchill's thinking then follows:

> Situation is complicated by [a] variety of claimants to [the] Throne, several of whom are quite impossible, and none of whom affords a prospect of suitable Arab Government capable of relieving our military commitments.

Capable of relieving our military commitments. This is *the* key to how Churchill saw his priorities in Cairo: a solution with British priorities in mind.

Churchill did have to go through the motions of reminding the Prime Minister why other candidates had been rejected:

> As an instance, if chosen, Ibn Saud would plunge the whole country into religious pandemonium. Saiyid Talib, who is acutely intriguing for the job, is a man of bad character and untrustworthy. Naqib is tottering on the brink of [the] grave. That [the] Shereefian system offers far better prospects than these, we have no doubt whatsoever. It is, in fact, [the] only workable policy.

The good news from this was that Churchill did now fully realize that appointing a Wahhabi Muslim such as Ibn Saud would have dire effects on the majority Shiite population of Iraq. It would also have meant that since Saudi Arabia has more oil than any other single country in the world and Iraq's supplies of it are not far behind, a state that included the two oil-bearing areas, once those reserves had been discovered, would have had a massive stranglehold on the rest of the world. It would have created a Wahhabi Islamic superstate of enormous power, one that because of its large Shiite minority would have been profoundly unstable from the beginning.

One can also say that, in raising Ibn Saud as a possible—and deeply unsuitable—candidate for the throne, Churchill was creating a straw man who would be easy to dismiss and would inevitably make Feisal look and much better by comparison.

The Naqib, it turned out, was far from death's door: He lived another five years. Talib was no saint, but it is also possible that his unsuitability lay primarily in the fact that he had a strong basis of support within Iraq. He possessed a genuine constituency that, if he were elected, would automatically make him far less beholden to the British than would have been the case with a total outsider such as Feisal. Feisal, when on the throne, did not prove any more virtuous a character than Talib, so it is impossible to know if a dynasty from another family would have left Iraq a legacy any better than the one eventually left it by the Hashemites.

It is also clear that Churchill was convinced of Lawrence's claim that Feisal was far superior to his brother Abdullah:

> Among Shereefians we are equally agreed that Feisal is incomparably more suitable than Abdullah, who is weak and would not command [the] elements of support essential to [the] Shereefian system.

Again, whether this is true is open to question. It may be so that Abdullah was not as energetic as his brother, but in the long term he was to prove a far more capable ruler of Jordan, an even more artificial creation than Iraq, than his brother Feisal was to be of his kingdom. Jordan to this day has been a considerably more stable and much less violent state than its Iraqi neighbor. There is no way to know what Abdullah would have done with Iraq had he been chosen to rule there instead, but if he had managed it as successfully as he did Jordan, he could scarcely have bequeathed his Iraqi subjects such a sad future.

Churchill had also become convinced that it was right as well as prudent to give something to Feisal:

> Moreover, it would ensure failure of policy in both directions at once to

put [the] weak brother on [the] throne of Irak [*sic*] and leave [telegram wording garbled] excessively active brother loose and discontented to work off his grudges against the French by disturbing Transjordania.

This is odd, and it is a pity that the wording of the telegram is indistinct, for it was concern about what an angry Abdullah might do in Jordan that led to his being offered the throne of the part of Palestine that was to remain a purely Arab reserve, the land to the east of the Jordan river in the Palestinian mandate state.

Churchill now elaborated on how he proposed, as advised by Cox and Bell, to ensure Feisal's election without it looking like the fix it really was. Sir Percy Cox and Gertrude Bell had told him that his solution—that Feisal go to his father in Mecca and then send out telegrams—would be the best way forward. But Churchill, aware that this could not guarantee the right verdict, explained his thinking in more detail to the Prime Minister. The Cox/Bell method would deliver Feisal:

> but this will be partly because the mere fact that we have allowed him to return will universally be interpreted as if it were a coupon election candidature. ["Coupon" was the British political phrase for endorsement]. On the other hand, anything less than this course may lead to an incoherent verdict by a small majority in favor of an unsuitable candidate at elections scarcely worthy of the name in so scattered and primitive a community.

In other words, people as backward and unused to democracy as the people in Mesopotamia might give the wrong verdict! Once more, there are many parallels here to what followed the coalition victory in 2003. Churchill and Lloyd George were wrestling with the same issues the U.S. administration is facing in 2004: how to have a genuinely democratic Iraq that did not at the same time deliver the nightmare scenario of a clericalist and theocratic Shiite regime on the Iranian model.

All his proposals, Churchill told Lloyd George, hung together. As for Feisal's candidature, Churchill pointedly reminded the Prime Minister that "you were in favor of Feisal before I took this office." As a result, Churchill felt able to say:

> I could not help being disconcerted by . . . your telegram. . . . I do hope
> you will give me personally the support to which I am entitled in a task
> which I have not sought.

After sending the Prime Minister a separate telegram on the subsidies issue, Churchill wrote again to Lloyd George on the 21st on the matter of Mesopotamia, knowing that the crucial Cabinet meeting was to take place the next day. He wanted "reasonable latitude" from his colleagues on the candidature issue and fully admitted the "delicacy of [the] problem." There would, he conceded, "certainly be local opposition" to any Hashemite solution, especially by the local rivals. "But," he continued:

> we have no doubt whatsoever that the guarantee for stability of [the] government and [a] quick reduction of expense and responsibility would be [the] adoption of Feisal by a substantial preponderance of public opinion. In all the Arab world there is no other competing principle capable of maintaining an Arab state on modern lines than the Shereefian. On the other hand I am deeply conscious of [the] danger by a too . . . open advocacy of Feisal [that] we might defeat our own ends.

Churchill went on to suggest that Sir Percy Cox would be the best person to handle this when he returned, since:

> Much intrigue is rife in his absence, and we wish to have [the] liberty to do our best in unostentatious ways, having regard to all foregoing conditions, to secure [the] adoption of Feisal. Bear in mind also that Feisal must be given some assurance that we wish him well, and that he has a good chance before he will expose himself to the labours and embarrassment of candidature.

Churchill had come down in favor of a Hashemite solution and was hoping that Lloyd George would stick to his original ideas and do so as well. Here we come into the area of the big historical controversy: Why were the Hashemites chosen, and was it as a result of their intrigues that the Middle East is as it is today? On first impression, those who argue this case would seem to have a point: Churchill was telling Lloyd George that the Hashemite solution was the only one that would work.

As we have seen, Churchill wanted a cheap solution, and a Hashemite government was the cheapest and most quickly available solution to save the British government millions of pounds in expenditure, all the more so since the British troops that would be staying behind would be mainly Air Force, not Army. The United Kingdom could have a pro-British puppet regime in place without financial burdens on the Exchequer back home.

Once more, the modern phrase *empire lite* comes to mind, a form of having your cake and eating it too. This was to be a British solution for British goals. The long-term *Arab* outcome of what Churchill and his colleagues were trying to put together in Cairo and whether a Hashemite solution was best for the local people do not really seem to have been thought through at all.

Churchill's pleas to the Prime Minister, enhanced by his powers of eloquence, succeeded in winning Lloyd George's support, at least as far as Mesopotamia was concerned. On the same day the Cabinet concluded its meeting, Lloyd George telegrammed Churchill in Cairo. The members of the Cabinet (along with experts such as Sir Henry Wilson) had, he told Churchill, "devoted exhaustive consideration" to his proposals that morning:

> They were much impressed by [the] collective force of your recommendations and were in close agreement with the concluding paragraphs of your telegram of the 21st March. [Churchill had suggested there should be no hurry to tell the French of any decision.] It should not be difficult to reconcile [the] procedure suggested by you, which is generally accepted with due regard to our engagements and relations with the French; and it was thought that the order of events should be as follows:
>
> Sir P. Cox should return with as little delay as possible to Mesopotamia, and should set going the machinery which may result in [the] acceptance of Feisal's candidature and invitation to him to accept [the] position as the ruler of Irak. In the meantime, no announcement or communication to the French should be made. Feisal, however, will be told privately that there is no longer any need for him to remain in England, and that he should return without delay to Mecca to consult his

father, who appears from our latest reports to be in a more than usually unamiable frame of mind. Feisal will also be told that if, with his father's and brother's [i.e., Abdullah's] consent, he becomes a candidate for Mesopotamia and is accepted by the people of that country, we shall welcome their choice, subject, of course, to the double condition that he is prepared to accept [the] terms of the mandate as laid before [the] League of Nations, and that he will not utilise his position to intrigue against or attack the French.

(Hussein was resolutely opposed to the mandates since he was still holding out for a large kingdom that would include Palestine and Syria.)

Meanwhile, Feisal was hoping for a proper treaty between Britain and Iraq so as not to be seen by his future subjects in so dishonest and unpatriotic a position as that of an obvious puppet, an issue that, in Churchill's absence, had been considerably vexing the Foreign Office. On all this:

Your remark [Lloyd George and the Cabinet felt] in an earlier telegram . . . that [the] acceptance of the mandate by Feisal does not preclude subsequent adjustments of relations between [the] mandatory [i.e., Britain] and [the] Mesopotamian Government is concurred in, although it does not appear to be necessary at this stage to talk about a treaty.

If the above conditions are fulfilled, Feisal would then from Mecca make known at the right moment his desire to offer himself as [a] candidate, and should make his appeal to the Mesopotamian people. At this stage we could, if necessary, communicate with the French, who, whatever their suspicions or annoyance, would have no ground for protest against a course of action in strict accordance with our previous declarations. We trust that this procedure will commend itself to you and Sir P. Cox, and that you will act accordingly.

Since this is exactly what Sir Percy Cox and Churchill had just agreed to in Cairo, it surely would not have presented itself as a problem!

Unfortunately for Churchill, the Cabinet did not agree with his ideas about Abdullah and Jordan, Sir Henry Wilson having weighed in against Churchill at the meeting on the grounds of "expense & further commitments."

On the rather artificial Transjordanian state that Churchill was proposing, as the Cabinet correctly concluded, this was a "territory too small for a Kingdom." While they did not want to prejudice Churchill's imminent conversations with Abdullah in Jerusalem (Churchill was about to go there, mainly to see Sir Herbert Samuel but to see Abdullah as well), their own preference was for the region to be treated "as an Arab province or adjunct of Palestine."

As for the final issue, "Southern Kurdistan," the Cabinet felt:

> Your proposals were improved. But you must expect attempts from [the] Angora Government [the still unrecognized Kemalist nationalist regime] to seduce [the] Southern Kurds in co-operation with their northerly brethren with a view to incorporate [that region into the] Anatolian State.

Had the British Cabinet had their way on the Palestine/Transjordan issue, the entire history of the Middle East would have been drastically different. For what is now the Palestinian Authority area and also the Kingdom of Jordan would all have been part and parcel of the new state, with an incalculably altered outcome in 1948. Meanwhile, before setting out on his trip to Jerusalem, Churchill let Lloyd George know how grateful—and no doubt highly relieved—he was for their conclusions on Mesopotamia.

Although it is not directly part of our story, Churchill's visit to Abdullah and Sir Herbert Samuel ended up creating the hostility between the local Palestinians and the post-1948 Israeli state that we see today. As the Cabinet realized in responding to Churchill in Cairo, his plans for Abdullah, all part of the solution that was pro-Jewish west of the Jordan but forbade Jewish settlement to the east of the river, was "an Arab rather than a Palestinian solution."

Churchill, having backpedaled with Lloyd George, when the two met in Jerusalem, on supporting Abdullah for ruler of a new Transjordanian state, then became impressed with him. As a result, while he was there Churchill came down heavily in favor of the Zionists in the part of the mandate under direct British rule, which is very roughly (post-1967 border disputes notwithstanding) what the state of Israel and the Palestinian Authority are today. The temporary expedient of giving Abdullah and his wild anti-French

Syrian followers what they wanted ended up as a permanent solution. Abdullah accepted all of Churchill's conditions; as a consequence, what we now know as the Kingdom of Jordan came into being.

What was not dealt with was the non-Jewish, Arab part of the region west of the Jordan, which the more radical Jewish settlers deem part of a biblically correct Jewish state and where today's *intifada* is taking place. While Churchill could not have foreseen what would ensue, what to him was a temporary expediency precipitated hideous long-term military, political, and religious consequences. One can therefore say that, along with the creation of a unified Iraqi state, the creation of ambiguous entities in the Palestinian mandate was very much part of Churchill's folly.

Sir Percy Cox, Churchill informed the Prime Minister, was keen that Feisal should arrive "in Mesopotamia before [the] election takes place." All this, Churchill thought, "can presumably be arranged as a result of appeals and invitations to him from his powerful racial [Arab] supporters in the Iraq [*sic*]."

Churchill added that he was, however:

> not clear whether it is contemplated that someone in London should at once approach Feisal. I think it would be better if Lawrence, who has his entire confidence, send him the private telegram . . . strictly within [the] limits of which you have approved. This really is [a more noncommittal than] an official communication, and it will, coming from Lawrence, be quite sufficient. Feisal will then proceed to Mecca, and Lawrence, at some point on the route, will have to talk to him quietly.

Lawrence, being a longtime and passionate supporter of the Hashemite option, wrote a very different kind of unofficial telegram to Feisal, telling his old friend that:

> things have gone exactly as hoped. Please start for Mecca at once by [the] quickest possible route. . . . I will meet you on the way and explain the details. Say only that you are going to see your father, and on no account put anything in the press.

Churchill returned to the United Kingdom from his epic Middle Eastern trip in the second week of April. He and his "forty thieves" had—probably without fully realizing it—completely changed the map.

CHAPTER SIX

WINSTON'S BRIDGE

One would think that Churchill would have returned home from his Middle Eastern trip delighted that he had achieved so much. Sadly, this was far from the case. According to Austen Chamberlain, the new Conservative Leader, Churchill was "cross like a bear with a sore head." Even Lloyd George's mistress-cum-secretary, Frances Stevenson, observed how angry Churchill was, so certainly it would have been obvious to the Prime Minister himself. Churchill was indeed angry, because he had not been made Chancellor of the Exchequer; worse, the comparative nonentity appointed to that post, Sir Robert Horne, was quite openly admitting his own inadequacies for the task.

Churchill even contemplated resignation, and, as Stevenson noted, his relationship with Lloyd George, hitherto so strong, had sunk to a new low. Since Churchill owed his political comeback entirely to the Prime Minister's generosity after Gallipoli, this was not good news for the newly returned Colonial Secretary.

His main task on getting back to London was to prepare his defense of his Cairo policy, first to his colleagues and then to Parliament, focusing not so much on the Mesopotamian part of his decision as on Palestine and the creation of a safe Middle East air route.

His disillusionment can be seen most vividly in a very indiscreet interview he held with the editor of the *Daily Mail,* Thomas Marlowe, who
instantly leaked all of it to the paper's mercurial proprietor, the press baron
Lord Northcliffe. Churchill revealed that he was "fed up" with Lloyd
George. When it came to Mesopotamia, he told Marlowe that he was
preparing to speak in the House of Commons on the costs of maintaining
British personnel there. Money, and saving it, Marlow deduced, was at the
heart of Churchill's policy:

> He is [Marlowe told Northcliffe] going to take a very detached attitude on
> this subject. The estimates for this year will be thirty million pounds ster-
> ling . . . he hopes that next year's expenditure in Mesopotamia will be not
> more than ten millions and that this figure will not be exceeded for the
> next two or three years.

The following part of the interview is extraordinary, since it flatly con-
tradicts the facts, but it does very much reflect Churchill's brooding and
angry state of mind:

> Churchill is not responsible for Mesopotamia and Palestine either. So far as
> he is concerned they are inheritances. He did not initiate any of the liabili-
> ties there; the pledges were given and he is obliged to carry them out at the
> least possible cost. Mesopotamia and Palestine are twin babies in his care
> but he is not the father. He is reducing costs as drastically as possible. . . .

Churchill in Cairo and in his many rows with the War Office had
done everything possible to start with a clean slate and make the best possible job of Britain's Middle East position. As Colonial Secretary, he had
actively fought to become responsible for the whole Middle East area;
now he was pretending to the press that it was nothing to do with him.

Following the Prime Minister's decision to take the chair at the forthcoming Imperial Conference of British Empire leaders, Churchill was in a
rage. Marlowe, after listening to more venomous remarks about Lloyd
George and more gloomy reflections on the political situation in general,
asked Churchill the inevitable question. Marlowe's narration to Northcliffe:

At lunch Winston was asked by Mr. Marlowe what was his objection to us clearing out of Mesopotamia altogether. He [Churchill] replied that it was only because it would be disgraceful for us to do so. We have undertaken liabilities, turned out the Turks, and we cannot turn out backs on it all. All we can do is to reduce the cost of our liabilities to the lowest possible point.

This was very much to be Churchill's ongoing policy in Mesopotamia, and it reveals the major flaw in all that he was trying to do. It was not a proper Middle East settlement that he was after, certainly not so far as Mesopotamia/Iraq was concerned. It was a British solution to how to save money for the British Exchequer; it did not address the fate of the inhabitants of the areas over which Britain ruled. This can be seen above all in Churchill's complete acquiescence to the disgraceful decision of Sir Percy Cox to exile Sayyid Talib, the Naqib of Basra and Home Affairs Minister in the Provisional Government in Baghdad.

Talib had been a candidate for the throne, and while he was not anti-British, he wanted the peoples of Mesopotamia to have a say in who their new ruler would be. However unsavory he may have been as an individual, Talib was surely right to uphold the democratic rights of the people of the new state. But this was unacceptable to Cox, who therefore, on a trumped-up charge, had Talib arrested shortly after the Cairo Conference. On 17 April, he was exiled to Ceylon, a British colony sufficiently far away from the Middle East. This coup, aided and abetted by Gertrude Bell, was wholly undemocratic, but Churchill, back in London, did not challenge the decision. In Cairo, they had decided on Feisal, and that was the policy Churchill now supported.

Churchill won his case in the House of Commons in June, and he then wanted to get on with Feisal's enthronement. He therefore wrote to Sir Percy on 5 July, asking if it were necessary "to await [the] results of [the] elections" before proclaiming Feisal the "Emir of Iraq." His reason was that "there is much to be said in favor of striking while the iron is hot."

Sir Percy had the unenviable task of making sure that Feisal won while, as he was endlessly reminded by Churchill's officials, having to conduct the election in the manner dictated by Britain's League of Nations mandate. Telegrams to Sir Percy Cox, the High Commissioner, were going out under Churchill's name, though they were drafted mainly by Major Hubert Young of the Middle East Department and John Shuckburgh, the permanent official. Churchill soon tired of all this, writing to his old aide, Sir Archibald Sinclair:

> All this seems very complicated and I do not think we ought to bombard the High Commissioner with these elaborate instructions. . . . In the main . . . I think it much better to leave matters to Sir Percy Cox, who alone knows the local situation and who has the greatest possible interest in bringing out a satisfactory result.

The "result" referred to was of course Feisal's election. Churchill seemed to be very wary of the fact that everything had to be done according to the book, something that was not really in his temperament. He continued:

> There is also too much talk about "Mandates," "Mandatories" and things like that. All this obsolescent rigmarole is not worth telegraphing about. It is quite possible that in a year or two there will be no mandates and no League of Nations. Something quite different may have taken their place.

No official policy can account for Churchill's attitude or presumptions about the League of Nations. After all, Britain's sole legal basis for being in Iraq at all was the League of Nations mandate.

Given the endless telegrams to Sir Percy, ostensibly from Churchill himself, Churchill decided to telegraph the High Commissioner only if he diverged in any way from official British policy, which was, Churchill summarized in his draft:

(1) To get another large wave of troops out of the country and so to reduce the expenditure to the British tax payer
(2) To get Feisal on the throne as soon as possible
(3) To make whatever arrangements are the most likely to conduce to the above objects in regard to Basra (about which the only principle is that we do not put Kurds under Arabs).

Churchill then sent a telegram to Sir Percy in which he reminded him that the "main thing is to secure the early choice of Feisal."

Note that Churchill's commitment to save as much money as possible, however, was at the top of his summary, listed even before Feisal's election, important though that was.

Cost-cutting entailed battling with Sir Laming Worthington-Evans, the Secretary of State for War, whose obstinacy was forever causing Churchill irritation. The War Office persisted in wanting a larger force in the Middle East, if only to provide continued employment for British troops. They were now contemplating a new barracks in Iraq, a prospect that dismayed Churchill, who wanted political control of British forces in the region to be under his jurisdiction, not that of the War Office. It was another internal power struggle like the one he had had with the India Office and the Foreign Office back in January.

He wrote despairingly, and revealingly, to Worthington-Evans:

> If our policy is successful, we shall in a few years withdraw altogether our troops from the country and there will be nothing there except the Arab forces and possibly our Air establishment [the RAF]. It is intended to run Mesopotamia like an Indian native State and we are certainly not laying out plans of keeping a permanent British garrison there.

It is not just the cost-cutting imperative and the desire to seize political control that are telling here. It is the fact that he saw Feisal as no different, in essence, from some maharaja in the British Raj that is highly indicative of how Churchill saw the new state of Iraq.

Churchill had been Worthington-Evans's predecessor at the War Office, and the generals there did not like the idea of giving up control to him, however admirable he may have been personally. It was, to one of them, "preposterous," and a "sad case of the ex-gamekeeper turning poacher!" Angry letters now went back and forth between the Colonial Office and the War Office, with neither side prepared to surrender to the other. Even the news about the much-hoped-for transfer from Army to RAF forces in Iraq was bad: Lord Trenchard, head of the RAF, had to tell Churchill that the handover, originally planned for July, was now unlikely to take place before October.

However, General Haldane, Churchill's old South Africa nemesis, was able to give him the good news that:

> Feisal continues to maintain his popularity and, provided no fanatical pro-Turk assassinates him when he pays his visit to Mosul in the near future, his presence should make for peaceful conditions.

Churchill and Cox were now also on much better terms, though as a letter from Cox to Curzon reveals, it was because Churchill had come around to Cox's own point of view: that troop reduction without subsequent chaos could be achieved by appeasing Feisal. But more important from Churchill's viewpoint was the fact that Haldane was supporting him in his feud with the War Office. Haldane had become equally convinced that British troops were unnecessary. The RAF, the local Arab Army, and Indian troops could now do all the requisite duties. In terms of suppression, the RAF planes were "now really feared," and an Arab army could be ready by the following year. Even the climate helped Churchill's cause, since the temperatures, which were in summertime as high as 128°F, were, Haldane wrote, far too high for white men.

Trenchard had by now completed his proposals for the total handover of Iraq from the Army to the RAF, which meant that in writing to Lloyd George, Churchill would have two strings to his bow. (Presumably the hardy RAF pilots would be able to withstand temperatures of 128°F, but this is never stated. . . .)

So on 2 August Churchill put his thoughts in order for Sir Percy Cox prior to writing a much larger paper for discussion on the whole issue by his Cabinet colleagues.

The War Office proposals, Churchill told Sir Percy, would cost far too much, an "incredible figure," one that "there was no question whatever of my accepting." Provided that he was able to win over his Cabinet colleagues, Churchill now had a plan of how to proceed on the military front. He would replace General Haldane with General Ironside—something he had been trying unsuccessfully to do for months—and Ironside would hold the post for just one year. In October 1922, the "Air Force scheme will become operational, and an RAF officer will be placed in command of all [the] forces in

Mesopotamia." The RAF would "learn in the interim period [1921–1922] to feed and supply themselves." There could then be major cuts in the number of Army battalions in Iraq, as agreed at the Cairo Conference. Ironside would also, in this changeover period, be able to get the Arab Army together, and this "with the Air Force must form the basis on which King Feisal's authority is maintained."

Churchill realized that all this would be "hotly contested" by the War Office. The "economy campaign" sweeping the British government, named the "Geddes axe" after the Minister pushing it through, was pressing the War Office very hard, and they were:

> Desperately anxious to quarter at least 7 white battalions in Mesopotamia in order to avoid their possible disbandment. Any such solutions will be fatal to Mesopotamian interests.

Meanwhile, Lloyd George, with whom Churchill had conferred,

> while agreeing generally with the course I have proposed, is pressing me most strongly to go much further, ie to pay King Feisal [a] subsidy and withdraw all troops from the country. This I cannot consent to do.

(Churchill told his obstreperous colleague Worthington-Evans the same thing. Lloyd George "wanted to go much further and leave the Emir Feisal on a purely subsidy basis without troops of any kind [other than Air Force].") Churchill therefore went on to tell Sir Percy:

> I consider that [the] policy we framed at Cairo and which you have so ably carried thus far must be pursued perseveringly, and that adequate support for the Emir [i.e. Feisal] must be forthcoming, and that this must be provided within the limits of the 4 to 5 millions of the Cairo estimate.

(The War Office estimate would have cost at least £10 million to implement.) Churchill also told Cox that he would resign if he could not get his way at the Cabinet meeting, something he would tell his colleagues at their "forthcoming discussion." One could say that it was not necessarily Mesopotamia alone for which rejection of the War Office's extravagance would be fatal, but also Churchill's own ministerial career.

Churchill therefore spent the next three weeks fully engaged in preparing for the forthcoming Cabinet meeting, making sure that he had all possible facts at his disposal for an irresistible case. To him, it all revolved around two things: airpower, using the RAF instead of expensive British troops; and a local Arab army that would be Feisal's responsibility and not his.

In his "Policy and Finance in Mesopotamia 1922–23," Churchill totally rejected the War Office's garrison policy of 18,000 men. To force the fledgling Iraq to have so many troops "is to crush it, and if no other way can be found of holding the country, we had much better give up the Mandate at once." The RAF, his own preferred option, would be far better, and cheaper too. Much of the rest of the military part of the memorandum we have already seen.

As for the political side, Churchill felt that things "had greatly improved during the year," and that the political settlement was also going according to plan:

> The Emir Feisal is being generally acclaimed by the people, both townsmen and tribesmen, and Sir Percy Cox proposes to proclaim him King on the 15th [August]. I wish to make it perfectly clear that I have from the outset contemplated holding Mesopotamia as a whole in a Government and Ruler whom they have freely accepted, and who will be supported by the Air Force, and by British organised levies, and by 4 Imperial battalions. At a later stage I contemplate still further reductions, and look forward eventually to the country being in the condition of an independent Native State friendly to Great Britain, friendly to her commercial interests, and casting hardly any burden upon the Exchequer.

Once again, just to make extra sure that his financial point was made plain and that the War Office would be given no quarter, he added:

> But this prospect will be utterly ruined if we have cast upon us the

ponderous weight of a numerous British garrison with its elaborate and inevitably costly paraphernalia. . . . I cannot continue in the position of asking Parliament for estimates nine-tenths of which are made out for me by another Department.

After setting forth the timetable for the changeover that would begin in October, he concluded:

The government of the country will be conducted by an Arab administration under King Feisal, who will act in general accord with the advice tendered to him by the High Commissioner, Sir Percy Cox.

In case the nightmare scenario of a rebellion of the kind that had taken place in 1920 should be repeated, Churchill went on:

necessitating the evacuation of the country, all the Imperial personnel in Baghdad can be brought down the river by the armed vessels, for which special barges carrying high galleries capable of commanding the banks at low water, with machine guns and trench mortar fire, are being prepared by General Haldane. Thus we have every hope of carrying on at a moderate cost, and if the worst comes to the worst we shall retain the means of withdrawing from the country without the need of sending up an expedition. This is the best plan we have been able to make within the financial limits, which are inviolate.

Churchill had thus thought of everything down to the last tiny detail, and, as always, it was the financial bottom line that was "inviolate." Britain, he concluded, "simply cannot afford" the kind of expenditure that the War Office required.

Since the Prime Minister was about to go abroad, Churchill took the precaution of sending Lloyd George an advance copy of his plan on 7 August:

I am sorry not to see you before you go. There are several things I want to settle with you. Among them the Mesopotamian plans for next year are most urgent. I must be free from the WO & able to frame my own estimates & prescribe what troops if any we are to take from them. Otherwise I c[oul]d not possibly keep my promise to Parliament about reductions, nor [could] I present the estimates.

Churchill, in presenting so rosy a picture to his colleagues, was, sadly, deluding himself. First, bad news came from Sir Percy that riots and pro-Turkish demonstrations, along with possible Turkish activities, were taking place. This, Churchill told both Lloyd George and Lord Curzon, was "rather disquieting." The Greeks might be doing well against Kemal's forces—though we now know that this was only temporary—but Churchill was terrified of a Turkish nationalist–Bolshevik alliance. This would "encourage the anti-British elements on the Mesopotamian frontier." Furthermore, the:

Cairo programme of reduction in Mesopotamia is based on the assumption that there will be no armed attack from outside. Even the small Turco-Kurdish successes [that so worried Sir Percy] are likely to have a serious effect on a credulous, ignorant population, and a combined Turco-Bolshevik movement against Mesopotamia even though on a small scale and badly organised, would be disastrous. The Feisal policy is succeeding better than we hoped, but it needs a year or two of external peace if it is to be carried out, and I trust that everything you can do will be done to prevent an alliance which would infallibly wreck it.

On 15 August, Feisal was, as hoped, proclaimed King of Iraq by Sir Percy Cox. Much has been written, with what is probably a great deal of accuracy, about the highly questionable way in which the referendum was conducted. Many chiefs simply gave the British the answer they wanted, and since ordinary people had next to no say in the process, we cannot say that through a democratic process Feisal was the overwhelming and genuine choice of the new Iraqi people.

Britain ruled Iraq, as it must now be called, through the League of Nations. But a mandate, however generously interpreted, did not give true independence to the countries so designated. With most of the British and French mandates, including territories in Africa and Southeast Asia, this was not an issue—no one, the locals included, thought that independence was even an option. But in Iraq the British had opted for the Hashemite solution, with a single nominal native ruler for the whole mandate territory.

Feisal was, of course, the stooge of the British, and he knew it. But since it was so obvious, he knew that everyone else knew it too. That presented him with a major problem: credibility with his new subjects. In what was probably a vain attempt to prove that he was no puppet of the United Kingdom, he decided, not at all surprisingly, to show a modicum of independence and save face by making some major anti-British statements.

On 15 August he therefore announced that he would not accept the restrictions on Iraqi sovereignty implicit in the League of Nations mandate. Rather, he wanted a direct treaty relationship with the British, one that gave him, as the ruler, full sovereign powers. He wanted, in short, to be his own man.

It is surprising that Churchill, Cox, and the many others involved in getting Feisal on the throne all failed to see what was coming; there is no real hint of it in the voluminous correspondence on the establishment of Iraq. They must have believed that Feisal actually would be the pliant figurehead—but it was wishful thinking: Feisal had caught them napping.

Churchill's main Middle Eastern problem was now Palestine and Arab-Zionist relations. But he found time to write a note to Sir Percy in which he framed a direct appeal to Feisal himself. In the end he chose not to send it. As he wrote to the High Commissioner:

> I hope you will explain to Feisal that we wish him to manage the country with [your] assistance & advice. If he manages it so well that in a few years we can withdraw our forces, he will become a Sovereign with plenary powers subject only to treaty obligations with the Mandatory. But as long as we have to spend many millions a year to ensure the maintenance of order & to support his Government, we must expect him to rule in general conformity with the advice tendered to him by you.

As Churchill reminded Sir Percy, all this had already been made very clear to Feisal by Lawrence, and by Churchill when he had met with Feisal in London:

I told him then that the mandatory's wishes must weigh with him or who
ever was the ruler as long as the mandatory was required to supply money
& armed power. . . . We cannot accept the position of Feisal having a free
hand & sending in the bill to us. Feisal can be fully informed of the pro-
visions of this treaty in a few days, and can make his declaration in light
of it but in order to acquire validity this must be promulgated by the
Mandatory power & ratified by the Iraq Assembly.

Both points of view are clear: Feisal did not want to be seen to be a
stooge, and the British wanted direct control over Iraq.

While all this was going on, Britain was also negotiating along similar
lines with the Egyptian nationalists, the *Wafd*. In this instance, however,
there were some major differences. Egypt had had its own effective government since the 1880s, albeit under British guidance since then. The nominal
ruler, originally the khedive, then the sultan, and soon to be called the king,
was also an outsider; but in his case, he was a descendant of the Albanian
warlord, Mehmet Ali, who had taken control of Egypt decades earlier. Further, the High Commissioner in Cairo, Lord Allenby, the victorious wartime
leader, was in strong favor of Egypt's total independence. Egypt came under
the Foreign Office, so it was Lord Curzon who was dealing with the issues,
not Churchill as Colonial Secretary. Independence was granted the following
year, 1922, though things did not turn out quite as the Egyptian nationalists had wanted: Britain reserved the right to keep a large army in Egypt and,
with France, to retain sovereignty over the Suez Canal.

When it came to Iraq, Churchill did not see Feisal being granted anything like as much power as the ruler of Egypt. He also felt somewhat
betrayed by what he saw as Feisal's ingratitude and intransigence. In the
letter to Sir Percy that follows, is there also a note of regret?

It seems to me early days for Feisal to begin making difficulties. The
French Government have ceaselessly warned us that he will turn
against us at the moment he feels strong enough to do so & make the
same disastrous blunder that he made in Syria by allowing himself to fall
into the hands of the extremists. If so the consequences would be most
unfortunate for all concerned including himself.

In effect Churchill, in falling in with the Hashemite solution in order to save money and get the British troops out quickly, was now hoist with his own petard. Feisal had been proclaimed king—and in a referendum that was supposedly representative of the wishes of the Iraqi people. Nonetheless, Churchill did his best to put a brave face on it:

> But I have always taken the other view & believed that he [would] work in a loyal & honourable spirit with the British who have strained their position with their ally France in order to give him a second opportunity.

A summary of the potential mess Britain had got itself into could not have been better expressed. Churchill, still obviously trying to be optimistic, continued:

> His proper course is clear. He has but to show that he is building up a good & stable Government & is capable of maintaining himself. We should be only too pleased to transfer the burden more & more to his shoulders and reduce our expense. But while we have to pay the piper we must be effectively consulted as to the tune.

From Churchill's perspective, things were very clear. But his was the point of view of the Mandatory, Britain, not the mandated country, Iraq. Britain, in trying to create a halfway house—neither an outright colony nor a genuinely independent state—was to find the middle way of mandated semi-independence a very difficult one. A natural colonialist such as Churchill, who opposed independence even for India, was not the man to see the disadvantages of the middle way.

Churchill then drafted a direct appeal to Feisal, but again in the end did not send it, relying instead on Sir Percy Cox to have a few well-chosen words with the recalcitrant king. Churchill's draft, even though it was never sent, is nevertheless in its own way interesting:

> My friend while we have to pay so much for troops & instruments of war to sustain [your] Government we must expect that our solemn wishes shall count with you in grave matters. We have no end [but] to seek the

peace & good order of Iraq. We are quite willing without delay to make a treaty with you instead of the present mandatory system. But until there is a regular Government in Iraq there is no one with whom we can make a treaty. You have freely undertaken meanwhile to accept the mandatory system and to that word I hold you.

Churchill then pulled out a trump card, reminding Feisal of the considerable French antagonism toward him, from which the British had in effect rescued him by making him ruler of Iraq. It was a shrewd thing to do. Karsh and Karsh, in *Empires of the Sand,* a book not at all friendly to the Hashemite family, have legitimately pointed out that Feisal, in the space of a short time, had gone from a total failure at the hands of the French to the British-anointed king of a major country. This was not lost on Churchill, as is apparent in the following:

General Gouraud has just written a letter couched in terms of the utmost bitterness against you & your family in which he predicts that you will repeat in Baghdad the same mistake of falling into the hands of extremists as he charges you with in Damascus. I am confidently expecting you to arm me with the means of answering those who decry the good faith & stability of the Sherifian family by proving over a course of years that the British have been wise to trust them.

However, as Feisal would have known, the two sets of circumstances were very different. Following the Arab Revolt, Feisal had been able to liberate Damascus because Allenby had let him—rather than the Australian troops, whose real victory it was—enter the city as liberator. Feisal, in collaboration with the local nationalists, had then proclaimed himself King, and the British, not wanting to let the French gain too much of the Middle East, had allowed it. But once the French had been able to make good their claim to Syria, Feisal was effectively finished, as the French intended to rule far more directly there than the British planned to rule Iraq.

Now Feisal had been proclaimed King of Iraq with the full connivance of the British and ostensibly democratically; and though it was still open to Britain to throw him out—as the French had done in Syria—it would have been financially very costly. It would certainly have involved the loss of British lives and above all a huge loss of face for the United Kingdom. Feisal, while thus not in a strong position, was certainly in a far better one with Churchill than he had been with Gouraud in Syria.

In a sense, then, Churchill had to make the best of a bad job. After he dropped the idea of writing directly to Feisal, he put down a version of his thoughts in a telegram to Sir Percy. It would, Churchill thought, take some years for a fully independent Iraq to emerge (another eleven, as it turned out), but in the meanwhile he would get on with drafting a treaty, and Feisal and Cox could *then* draw up an appropriate joint declaration. The main thing for Sir Percy to do was to get on with Feisal's coronation.

In making the concession to Feisal so quickly in order not to upset "the harmonious march of events in Iraq," Churchill was, I think, caving in somewhat to Feisal's blackmail. But it is just as true to say that his main aim was not to lose face with the French; once more, an issue of European diplomacy decided the events in Iraq. As he told Sir Percy in a telegram copied to Lloyd George:

> I hope I need not infer from [your] telegram that he is going to play the same game as he played on the French in Damascus with disastrous result to himself. I cannot believe it, but the French & Gen. Gouraud lose no opportunity of predicting that he will become [the] tool of extremists & will only maintain himself by xenophobia. If you think it wise you [should] use this argument in a discreet manner. He surely doesn't want to give the French the joy of saying "We told you so."

If that had turned out to be the situation, the British would have lost face with the French, and then, as Churchill saw it, the British would have had no option but to scuttle; a war on the French model in Syria to get rid of Feisal was politically quite unacceptable. He said as much in his telegram:

> I am quite sure that if Feisal plays us false [and] a policy founded on him breaks down [that] the Br[itish] Gov[ernmen]t will leave him to his fate & withdraw immediately all aid & military force.

Since this would be disastrous, Churchill cautiously added:

> All the above is personal & secret but you may use it as you think fit. Tele-
> graph what you will do but do not delay necessary action. I have got con-
> fidence in you, & unless it were definitely decided to evacuate the country
> when I expect we [should] differ, I will back you up through thick & thin.

Cox replied the next day. Feisal was resolutely refusing to give in,
insisting that Britain's only status in Iraq was to be one of "goodwill and
mutual confidence." The powers implicit in the mandate system were unacceptable. As Sir Percy told Churchill:

> Generally speaking, he [Feisal] feels his accession must be marked by some
> definite sounds of outward change. If [the] impression is given that he is
> to be merely a puppet in [the] hands of [the] British his influence will be
> weak and he will not be able to recover it.

From Feisal's standpoint this was entirely reasonable, since he wanted
to be seen to be his own King of his own people. Furthermore,
Churchill's calling the nationalists "extremists" was a very colonialist way
of looking at them; they were nationalists who wanted to be able to rule
their own country. The fact that this was gross ingratitude to the British,
who had put him there in the first place, was clearly unimportant to
Feisal.

When the Cabinet met to decide its policy on the Middle East, much
of the discussion was on Palestine, with a strong feeling among some that the
troubled mandate there should be offered to the United States, if possible.
But on Mesopotamia there was now a group wanting to pull out altogether,
including Sir Robert Horne, Churchill's nemesis at the Treasury, and, more
sadly from Churchill's viewpoint, his old and long-standing friend F. E.
Smith, now Lord Birkenhead and also Lord Chancellor. Thankfully,
Churchill eventually got his way, with the Cabinet deciding to adopt his
scheme of handing over all British forces in Iraq to the Air Force beginning
October 1922.

But while Churchill was able to prevail, his colleagues knew full well that all was not in hand in Iraq. As a result, a special Cabinet Committee was established with Churchill in the chair and as committee members, two of Churchill's old sparring partners, Lord Curzon and Edwin Montagu, along with the eminent historian and President of the Board of Education, H. A. L. Fisher. Various legal advisers also attended, and the Committee met for the first time on 19 August in Churchill's office.

Churchill began with his best tactic—accentuating the positive. He told his colleagues that:

> he had just received information from Mesopotamia [*sic*] now officially Iraq] that Feisal had been elected by an overwhelming vote and he was most anxious to make the best use of this favorable opportunity to place Feisal on the throne and obtain from him a promise of satisfactory relations for the future.

In the light of Feisal's obduracy, this is really what we would now call "spin," and Churchill continued to put events in the best possible light:

> The High Commissioner [he told the Committee] strongly recommended this course of action, but it appeared that the Draft Treaty was too rigid a document which might not find favor with King Feisal; the League of Nations might also take exception to its terms on the grounds that it did not convey a sufficient measure of autonomy.

Suitable draft wording, therefore, had to be found for Feisal's imminent coronation, and Churchill suggested "His Majesty's Government have decided to recognise me as sovereign of the State of Iraq." But this careful phrasing did not meet with the Committee's approval (alas, the account does not tell us who objected).

There were also growing international ramifications to what Britain could and could not do, as the discussion soon made clear:

> Although the Mandate for Mesopotamia had been conferred on Great Britain, the League of Nations had not yet confirmed its terms; in addition the United States had certain objections to raise in connection with

[the] Mandates and they would be still less likely to agree to a Treaty [being] substituted for a Mandate not confirmed by the League.

Here, although the Committee did not refer to it as such, we see the first reference to the complex question of oil. While some of the British were very aware of the potential of Iraqi oil, this was by no means the case with all of them, including the powerful Foreign Secretary, Lord Curzon. But the Americans, with much more experience in oil prospecting, were very aware indeed of the potential for future oil wealth under the sands of Iraq and were making full representations accordingly. As Churchill put it to Sir Percy the following day, the High Commissioner should make clear to Feisal that his Provisional Government:

> must proceed in [a] lawful & regular manner in regard to their treaty obligations under the Covenant of the L[eague] of N[ations] & special undertakings like the Anglo French oil treaty. US are making difficulty under pressure of oil interests & if they join with the French against the Feisal regime we shall have serious difficulties on [the] Council of [the] L[eague] of N[ations]. These difficulties might well become insurmountable unless we follow absolutely correct procedure.

Churchill then relayed this comment from the Committee on the previous day:

> It was also pointed out that it was doubtful if a Mandatory Power could elect a King for its mandated Territory and His Majesty's Government had not allowed such action in the case of Syria: if we now announced Feisal as King of Mesopotamia the French would undoubtedly object.

In fact, the French *were* objecting—and it had been they, not the British, who had ended Feisal's hopes of being King of Syria.

In the midst of all this, Churchill was becoming increasingly "anxious for his sick child," Marigold, then just two and a half years old. One could equally apply the term "sick child" to Iraq, too, as things were turning out to be far more complicated than Churchill, with all his initial optimism, could have predicted.

Churchill and the assembled Ministers reported this further discussion:

> Feisal's objections to ascending the throne with an undefined status were
> then referred to and the danger of his refusing the throne at the last
> minute unless he fully understood his exact position vis à vis the British
> Government. It was pointed out how much he owed the British Govern-
> ment and that he must be made to recognise the difficulties of that Gov-
> ernment in making a Treaty with him when the League of Nations had
> not confirmed the terms of the Mandate.

We could, though, also point out that it was precisely *because* Feisal
knew how much he owed the British that he was being awkward; it was the
fact that he *was* a figurehead that caused him to raise objections to his precarious position as British-anointed King. He did indeed, as their puppet,
have a very "undefined status."

The Committee had to make some quick conclusions: The suggestion
was then made that Feisal's accession take place as arranged and the treaty be
drafted thereafter. It was considered that this might be accomplished if a
telegram were immediately dispatched assuring Feisal that His Majesty's
Government desired to see him become a real sovereign but could only
invest him with such powers through the League of Nations, after which he
would be recognized as King by the entire world.

This, while ostensibly a face-saver for Feisal, in reality was surely one for
the British as well, since his demands had also put them in a very precarious
position. We can see this in the opening of the telegram that Churchill sub-
sequently sent to Sir Percy:

> You sh[ould] tell Feisal from me that I have not changed in any way to his
> disadvantage. Only change has been that whereas we formerly contemplated
> substituting [the] Treaty for existing relation [i.e., the Mandate] at some
> indefinite date in the future we are now prepared to do it as soon as possible.

In other words, Feisal had won.

Marigold Churchill died on 23 August. Winston and Clementine were
in profound grief, and they were inundated with letters of consolation, even

from political foes. As one old friend, Sir Abe Bailey, told Churchill, "you seem to be getting your share of trouble & family losses."

September found Churchill engaged in matters other than the problem of Iraq. By the end of the month, however, he did become concerned again when earlier Greek successes against the Kemalist forces began to be reversed. This worried him because of the vulnerability of Mosul. As he informed his Cabinet colleagues on the 26th:

> Mustapha Kemal, unable to develop any strong offensive towards the West, will have only one outlet for any forces at his disposal, namely, Mosul. Here, for the very smallest expense of troops and ammunition, he can cause us enormous embarrassment. . . . A few thousand troops sent into the Mosul Vilayet will compel us to choose between stopping the evacuation of the Army or even bringing back new troops and embarking on field operations at the cost of at least 5 or 6 millions on the one hand, or giving up the Mosul Vilayet on the other. The Arab Army and the [tribal] levies are not yet ready to take any effective part in a defence against external attack. I have never been an enthusiast for Mesopotamia, still less for Mosul; but I should be sorry if just when things are beginning to go well internally in these regions we were forced to throw aside all our work and admit failure.

Britain was now paying a price for not having set an effective Kurdish policy immediately after World War One. If, when the circumstances had been more in the Allies' favor and the United States was still actively engaged in the region, Britain and the other victorious powers had instituted a real Kurdish state, the Mosul *vilayet* would not have been of concern to Churchill in late 1921. But as it was, the best moment had passed, and Churchill was stuck with the results of his predecessors' inaction.

As for caring less for Mosul, however, here Churchill was responsible. The Kurds were no more a natural part of an Arab Iraq than they were of a nationalist Turkey; and back at the Cairo Conference, Churchill recognized that ideally the Kurds should not come under Arab rule—something he was entitled to say under the existing treaties and mandate regulations. It is a shame that his desire to cut costs overrode his sympathy for the plight of the Kurdish people, but fortunately the invasion he feared never came.

General Haldane, whose command had been extended until October 1922, when the RAF was to take over, reported that "the tribes are quiet." Sir Percy, given to seeing the worst, this time thought that even Kemal would not try to detach Feisal from the British, so Churchill was able to breathe again. Instead, he once again indulged himself in interfering in other government departments, writing a long memorandum on unemployment for the Cabinet and in the process, unfortunately, leaving Lloyd George perplexed and irritated.

Churchill mind was brought back to Iraq with a jolt, however, when he was reminded by his distinguished colleague, the former Conservative Prime Minister A. J. Balfour, that the Iraq Treaty had to be agreed upon by the League of Nations Council before it could be signed. The French, Balfour reminded him, would be "opposed to everything which increases the importance of King Feisal." Churchill should, Balfour told him, consult first with other countries, including League members France, Italy, and Germany, "and possibly with America," to see what to do next.

Churchill recognized that all this would be difficult from the League's point of view, but he disagreed with Balfour's approach. Britain would have to keep withdrawing its troops from Iraq; Parliament was not prepared to pay for troops to hang around—nor would Churchill request them to:

> We shall have to make a treaty with Feisal [he told Balfour] to strengthen his position on the throne and ensure so far as possible the permanence of his loyalty. If this fails and another rebellion breaks out we shall have to quit the country with the white people and leave it to complete anarchy. I hope, however, it will not fail, and I am encouraged by the progress of events during the last year. The garrison is being reduced from 50 battalions to 4, and nearly 20 millions are being saved in military expenditure, and yet order is maintained, broadly speaking, throughout the whole of these vast regions, including Mosul and large portions of Kurdestan. This has been done in spite of the fact that we have suffered from continuous Turkish intrigues in revenge for the anti-Turkish policy of the Government. . . . It must be clearly understood . . . that the practical steps that we will take will be in full harmony with the principles of the Mandate, and in so far as they appear to depart from the

Mandate they will do so only in the sense of reaching the desired conclusion of self-government of the people of Iraq at a period much earlier
than has ever been contemplated.

All this was taking place against the background of increased Turkish
successes against Greece and continued disturbances in Palestine. Not only
that, but Churchill was now actively involved in the negotiations which
led to Irish independence in 1922. Among the IRA negotiators was
Michael Collins, with whom Churchill got on well. Collins's murder at the
hands of rejectionist IRA men led by Eamon De Valera was to prove a
great tragedy that effectively undid much of the good he and Churchill
had been able to achieve during the talks. All this is the context in which
Churchill was also having to deal with the endless negotiations now being
carried out by Sir Percy Cox with King Feisal to obtain a mutually satisfactory Iraq Treaty.

The situation then became even more acute. The French had begun
actively helping Kemal against the Greeks and stirring things up against the
British. As Churchill pointed out to his Cabinet colleagues at the end of
October, the French:

are, of course, very angry about Feisal, and would be delighted to see Iraq
thrown into such a state of disorder that Feisal and the British policy associated with him would fall altogether.

All this was part and parcel of the legacy of Lloyd George's continued
support for the Greeks against the Turks and, one can fairly add, of
Churchill's paramount desire to save as much money as possible in Iraq.
Lord Curzon added to the mounting crisis by expressing concern that Feisal
might be treacherously negotiating with Mustapha Kemal.

Churchill had no problem with letting Feisal negotiate with the Turks,
who were, after all, on his borders, "subject to certain limitations as to the
scope of the negotiations." Curzon was not happy, though, seeing this as
unpardonable interference on Churchill's part. Churchill, needless to say,
vigorously defended himself to Curzon, and the impasse between the two
men continued. Churchill cannot have been the easiest of colleagues;

nonetheless, on 11 November, he authorized Sir Percy Cox not to allow "Feisal to negotiate with Kemal," since they might interfere with "other and larger [negotiations] . . . already in train."

Since Hubert Young had fought alongside Feisal during the Arab Revolt, Churchill sent him to Baghdad to help Sir Percy Cox with the treaty negotiations. Young made it abundantly clear to Feisal that the King "would enormously increase our own difficulties if he failed to realise that we are, at least to a certain extent, responsible to the League for our treatment of Iraq." Unfortunately, this did not seem to make much difference, as Feisal remained obdurate.

Meanwhile, Churchill was still trying to save money. A Colonial Office discussion in late October came to the cheerful—and almost certainly mistaken—conclusion that the RAF alone could repel any invasion of Iraq that might be attempted. Britain would, for at least the next ten to fifteen years, have to retain ultimate control for internal disorder and external defense, until the "independent Islamic state of Iraq can stand alone." But as a quid pro quo for Feisal, defense of the new kingdom would initially rest with Feisal "in the first instance, without prejudice to the ultimate responsibility" of the United Kingdom.

Perhaps because Churchill was being asked to concede so much without getting anything in return, he was becoming increasingly fed up with Feisal. When presented with yet another set of Feisal's demands, he dispatched a note to two of his officials on 24 November as to what he would really like to say to Sir Percy Cox, who was in the unenviable position of being go-between. It is very revealing of how angry and frustrated Churchill had become:

> I am getting tired of all these lengthy telegrams about Feisal and his state of mind. There is too much of it. Six months ago we were paying his hotel bill in London and now I am forced to read day after day 800-word messages on questions of his status and his relations with foreign powers. Has he not got some wives to keep him quiet? He seems to be in a state of perpetual ferment, and Cox is much too ready to pass it on here. Whenever Feisal starts talking about Arab aspirations, his sovereign status, and his relations with the French, etc., Cox ought to go into the financial

aspect with him and show him that the country on to whose throne he
has been hoisted is a monstrous burden to the British Exchequer, and that
he himself is heavily subsidised. Let him learn so to develop his country
that he can pay his own way, and then will be the time for him to take
an interest in all these constitutional and foreign questions.

The next day, Churchill sent a note to the same two officials, Sir James
Masterton-Smith and John Shuckburgh (who had been drafting his correspondence to Feisal). "What is all this talk," he asked them, "about 9 millions for Mesopotamia next year?"

There is absolutely no question of anything over 7. Not one farthing
more than 7 will be asked for by me, together with [two and a half] for
Palestine. Everything has got to be cut down to this level by any means
that you like and at any risk or cost.

In other words, Churchill was in a pickle, and one of his own making.
The fact that he concedes openly that he had foisted Feisal on Iraq shows
that he was realizing the consequences of his actions in Cairo the previous
March.

The message he sent to Sir Percy for Feisal was thus far more muted.
The King:

has only just been installed and instead of constantly seeking to have his
position defined he should devote himself to developing good government tranquillity and prosperity within Iraq. In a few years all these points
will doubtless be satisfactorily settled, but meanwhile why instead of fret-
ting and fussing can he not live quietly for a few days together without
feverish agititation about status. The enormous cost and burden Iraq has
been and still is to us is the important point to notice. I am now con-
fronted with some 3 millions civil deficit at 31st March 1921. I suppose
Feisal will expect me to extract these charges from the British Parliament
although they ought to fall on the Iraqi taxpayer. Moreover we are asked
on present estimates to find at least nine millions sterling next year to
pay for British and local forces and railways. While this state of affairs

continues [the] first task for Feisal is clearly to save money and promote
internal tranquillity. His talk about extending Arab control . . . is merely
fantastic, seeing that he cannot pay for his Arab army for home defence.
If he will show us his capacity to relieve us from our heavy expense we
shall be delighted to give him satisfactory definitions about his independence and his responsibility. All the while he takes our money he will have
to take our directions. In my opinion you ought to cool him off with considerations of this kind expressed no doubt in your own admirable
manner. As regards the French we will deal with them from here. Above
all do not let him work himself up against them.

Even in this much modified version, without reference to any of Feisal's
wives, Churchill did not, alas, realize that when it came to what the priorities
should be, he and Feisal were living on different planets. It is natural that
Churchill, in cost-cutting mode and with ambitions to be Chancellor of the
Exchequer, should have money at the forefront of his mind. But why should
Feisal, even though he owed his throne to British intrigues, have been expected
to make the Treasury's need for expenditure cuts his own royal priority? His priority was, rather, to establish his own *bona fides* as their King on a people whom
he had hitherto scarcely known, so that his rule could be effectively established
once the British had gone. He was playing for the long term, not next month's
or next year's budgetary arrangements in the House of Commons.

Much of Churchill's concern now shifted to Palestine, the Zionist
issue, and the negotiations with Ireland. But he did not forget Iraq. So
keen was he to save money that even the irascible Sir Henry Wilson, himself opposed to unnecessary military adventures, dismissed Churchill's aim
of reducing expenditure from £9 million a year down to £7 million as
"simply ridiculous."

Churchill would surely have made a good certified public accountant,
as he was able to spot the smallest expenditures and ask why they were necessary. Take this letter from him on 13 December to Sir Percy Cox and
General Haldane:

Latest War Office return gives the number of Indian followers in Iraq on
November 14th as 21,632. This is a shocking figure. Please inform me

what is its explanation and what steps you are taking to repatriate and discharge all these people who are living on the British taxpayer. There are 4000 more Indian followers than there are Indian soldiers. In addition there are 1,897 Indian labour and 4,056 local labour.

But it is his Departmental minute of 16 December 1921 that has lived on in infamy, since it has been quoted in many recent books about him and on several television programs of the past few years. This is the issue of using gas bombs.

Churchill had been asked by the Royal Air Force what his policy was on such matters, as had Sir Percy Cox. Churchill's aide, Colonel Richard Meinertzhagen, suggested that poison gas was unwise, because:

If the people against whom we use it consider it a barbarous method of warfare, doubtless they will retaliate with equally barbarous methods. As I have said before, the Moors of the Riff [in Morocco] are killing one Spaniard for every bomb dropped from an aeroplane. Again, say what we may, the gas is lethal. It may permanently damage eyesight, and even kill children and sickly persons, more especially as the people against whom we intend to use it have no medical knowledge with which to supply antidotes.

Morally and pragmatically, the Colonel's logic is surely impeccable. But Churchill, unfortunately for his twenty-first-century reputation, saw it very differently. He told his Department on 16 December:

I am ready to authorise the construction of such bombs at once; the question of their use to be decided when the occasion arises.

In my view they are a scientific experiment for sparing life w[hic]h sh[oul]d not be prevented by the prejudices of those who do not think clearly.

The fullest details of the recent American experiments [should] be supplied.

Churchill was quite consistent in his views, but they do reveal a lack of understanding as to what such gas could do. For example, a few weeks earlier he had written a memorandum on the use of poison gas against Palestinian demonstrators:

> I can't understand why it sh[oul]d be thought legitimate to kill people with bullets & barbarism to make them sneeze.

Poison gas, of course, does make people do far more than sneeze, as he clearly failed to grasp.

Sadly, we can only conclude that, along with his support in World War Two of the massive carpet-bombing of civilian cities in Germany, this is a moral black mark against Churchill that he cannot erase.

Churchill was able to relax as the New Year came, spending most of it in the luxury of a friend's villa in the South of France. Meanwhile, though, other issues were brewing that he would have to deal with when he returned to London. At least one of his major worries—the Irish question—had been peacefully resolved (albeit with consequences we are still facing in the twenty-first century).

Lloyd George was now contemplating evacuation from Iraq altogether; at the same time, the Secretary of State for War was showing Churchill "obstruction of the most insuperable character." The issue had to be dealt with by yet another ministerial committee, which met on 9 February. Lloyd George's problem was a mix of the financial and the political; so-called "Anti-Waste" right-wing Conservative candidates were doing well in by-elections and sometimes actually winning seats. Britain's numerous foreign obligations were a good place to start saving money. As Churchill wrote to Sir Percy Cox on 1 February 1922:

> A fierce economy campaign is on foot here and a very heavy attack is likely to be made upon forthcoming expenditure in Iraq. the Prime Minister has asked me whether Feisal would not be able to carry on without British assistance if we made a treaty with him as a completely independent Sovereign and gave him, say, a million a year. Alternative suggestions about retiring to Basra are also being made. I should like to know your view of what would happen if we were forced by want

of money to withdraw from the country in the next two or three months. Do remember that things have gone very much better in Persia [where Britain had had troops to prevent a Soviet invasion] since we cleared out.

Once more, the British need to save money and Hashemite ambitions, tied in neatly. But as always, Iraqi decisions were being made according to the exigencies of British needs without regard for local events.

Churchill was aware, as he wrote to Sir Percy a few days later, that the resolution of much of the issue depended on whether British troops would be needed to defend Mosul against a Turkish invasion—Churchill's concern about this issue continued—and that depended on the result of the war between Greece and Turkey. Churchill was frustrated, but of one thing he was sure:

> I do not wish the garrison of Mosul to be further diminished. . . . I shall press this upon the Cabinet unless War Office consent. Meanwhile you should hurry up the arrival of the Iraq Army and maintain a firm posture. We must of course be ready to act according to circumstances. There must in any case be no hiatus between the arrival of the Iraq Army and [the] withdrawal of Imperial forces. No doubt this situation will impose anxiety upon me, but in all the circumstances I think the risk should be accepted. . . . I realise fully the hard task which I am setting you and the anxiety which you no doubt will suffer. I still consider, however, that we are right to persevere in securing a good solution.

The Cabinet Committee finally met on the 9th, and Churchill prevailed: His scheme for the Air Force to look after Iraqi defenses was adopted. But as he did not hesitate to remind his colleagues, all depended on the negotiations with the Turks, and this issue was still fully unresolved.

Churchill, meanwhile, was determined to keep expenditure safely within his £7.5 million maximum. In late 1921 he turned down £150,000 for a hospital in Iraq as unnecessary, as British troops were leaving, and when, early in 1922, Sir Percy asked for £60,000 for Iraqi railways just to keep them running, Churchill's terse response was "No. Not a penny." But Sir Percy could, Churchill told him, assure Feisal that "I am doing all I can to procure a peaceful settlement with Turkey, as well as to secure a prompt settlement of the Treaty with Iraq."

Churchill was also having to persuade T. E. Lawrence not to resign. As Lawrence wrote to his brother:

> I asked Winston to let me go, and he was not very willing: indeed he didn't want it. I told him I was open to hold on a little till his first difficulties were over (there are new things happening just now), but not in a formal appointment . . . I don't think ever again to govern anything.

The "new thing"—the treaty negotiations between Britain and Iraq—were still dragging slowly on. The sticking point was now an objection by Curzon and the Foreign Office to letting Iraq have its own diplomats abroad—the "right of foreign representation." Churchill told his colleagues that he had no problems with what Feisal wanted. He "laid stress on the importance of raising an Arab army capable of defending Mesopotamia" and reminded the Cabinet that Feisal did not want to be "a mere puppet monarch."

Fortunately, the former Prime Minister and Foreign Secretary, A. J. Balfour, supported Churchill. But Balfour, who represented Britain ministerially at League of Nations headquarters in Geneva, nonetheless pointed out that the French would "abominate" giving Feisal such powers, since France had not the slightest intention of allowing the Syrians similar foreign representation.

Lloyd George temporized. On the one hand, he asked his colleagues "most warmly to congratulate" Churchill on having turned "a mere collection of tribes" into a nation. But on the other hand he asked Churchill to send Cox a telegram to say that the:

> Cabinet felt the greatest reluctance in agreeing to the separate diplomatic and consular representation of Iraq until the State had become an accomplished fact and had made good.

Since the Cabinet backed Lloyd George, Churchill lost.

In fact, the treaty negotiations were about to take a turn for the worse. Churchill told Sir Percy in a letter on the 23rd that he now objected to the use of the word Mandate altogether. "The people," he informed Sir Percy "have acquired a repugnance towards the term 'Mandate,' its terms and interpretations. . . ." Feisal wanted nothing less from Britain than "a definite statement providing for a sincere and friendly alliance."

This was a mess, since it was the League mandate that legitimated Britain's presence in Iraq altogether. Worse still, the Colonial Office heard on 6 March that Feisal had given a "kind of ultimatum . . . and threatens in effect to drop the treaty negotiations altogether if the point is not conceded to him." (It seems that in Arabic, "mandate" and "protectorate" were the same word, and "protectorate" had bad connotations of colonial rule—of exactly the kind Allenby was trying to end in Egypt at that very same time.)

The Iraq Committee met at the Colonial Office on the 14th. Churchill, Balfour, H. A. L. Fisher, and T. E. Lawrence were all present, and they decided to try to "force the reluctant Feisal to accept [the] Treaty & Mandate." Churchill tried again to get Feisal a proper Iraqi diplomatic corps and was again overruled by Lloyd George. Once again, Churchill was stuck between the recalcitrance of Feisal on the one hand and the immobility of his British colleagues on the other.

He did, though, have one piece of good news: Lord Curzon had begun negotiations with the Turks over the disastrous Treaty of Sèvres. As Churchill told his colleagues at a Cabinet meeting on 20 March (with characteristic hyperbole as well as an evident feeling of relief), "the signature" of that treaty "had been one of the most unfortunate events in the history of the world." Churchill made plain why the talks had to succeed:

> He had always said that he could not hold Mesopotamia without peace on
> its borders. If there were no peace, it was very likely that there would arise
> a pressure on Mesopotamia, which would drive us out. The Turks recog-
> nised the British Empire as their great enemy. At one time they would
> have taken anything from us, but we had rejected them and now they had
> in their hands an easy means to inflict humiliation upon us and to com-
> plete the destruction of our policy in Mesopotamia.

Later in the discussion, Churchill "pointed out that if the worst came to the worst, the British might have to evacuate Mesopotamia." But now his ghosts came back to haunt him. The British were still in occupation of Gallipoli—the site of Churchill's downfall during the war. Whereas he was prepared, *in extremis,* to agree with Lloyd George to scuttle Iraq, he did not feel the same about Gallipoli. As he ominously informed the Cabinet, he "would rather have a continuance of a state of war, even involving the evacuation of Mesopotamia, than to return the mastery of the Straits to the Turks."

Churchill's main concerns continued to be Ireland and the vexed issue of whether to recognize the Soviet regime in Russia. This was something that Lloyd George was keen to do at the forthcoming summit at Genoa and which made that resolute anti-Bolshevik, Churchill, more than unhappy. Once again, he threatened to resign. His opposition on this issue can also fairly be said to be one of the significant markers that transformed Churchill the prewar radical Liberal into what was, after 1924, to be Churchill the Conservative MP.

He did not forget Iraq, though, as the negotiations endlessly plodded on, still without resolution. He found time on 31 March to write his colleagues a memorandum on a possible way forward. Feisal clearly had a "misunderstanding" with the British, according to Churchill, that he proposed to resolve:

> I consider that the best means of clearing up this misunderstanding will be to send Colonel Lawrence to Baghdad in order that he may make the whole situation plain to the King by oral explanation. I also set great store on Colonel Lawrence's personal influence with Feisal, which, as my colleagues are aware, dates back to the time of the Arab rising during the great war.

As Churchill knew, all this would come to nothing if no progress were made on the diplomatic corps issue; "even Colonel Lawrence's influence" would be useless without concessions.

While Churchill was surely right to say that a trip by Lawrence could have made a huge psychological difference to Feisal and helped the cause, he forgot that Sir Percy would have seen the arrival of the highly unorthodox Lawrence as a personal affront—proof of his own failure. Not surprisingly,

Sir Percy refused to countenance Lawrence's involvement. Rather tersely, he told Churchill on 4 April that:

> in so far as [the] treaty is concerned Lawrence would not cut any ice, while in respect of other matters his presence—granted most loyal intentions on his part—would merely be a source of weakness to me.

Churchill thus had to give in, and Lawrence did not go. Curzon then added to Churchill's troubles by telling the Prime Minister that Churchill's compromise with Feisal was unacceptable and might indeed "cause us a good deal of trouble in the future." Churchill, now mainly occupied with the civil war in Ireland and its consequences, reluctantly wrote to Sir Percy on 19 April:

> The British Government have no power to abrogate or terminate the Mandate which they hold from the League of Nations, except by resigning once and for all their special position in the country. The other great Powers on the Council of the League of Nations would not agree to Britain having a special position in Iraq unless controlled by the Mandate. America, though not a member of the League, would also refuse consent. There is no possibility, therefore, of Britain freeing herself from the Mandate other than by washing her hands altogether of responsibilities towards Iraq.

Churchill then came up with an ingenious way of looking at the League of Nations mandate system:

> The meaning of the Mandate and its whole purpose was to restrain Britain and not to restrain Iraq. The Mandate regulates and restricts the action of the mandatory Power, and is intended solely to safeguard the interests of Iraq. The other great Powers would never allow Britain to have special treaty relations with Iraq while escaping from the Mandate. If we were to offer to the League of Nations to release us from the Mandate, they would refuse; and the only course open to us would be either to bow to their decision or to quit the country altogether.

Then he went on to outline what he thought would be the good news:

> Of course, when Iraq becomes strong enough in our opinion to stand
> alone, we shall be in a position to state that our task has been fulfilled, and
> that Iraq is in fact as well as in status an independent sovereign State. But
> this cannot be said with any respect for truth and fact while we are forced
> year after year to spend very large sums of money on helping the Iraq
> Government to defend itself and maintain order.

The fact that it was "in our opinion"—that of Britain, the colonial
power—of course rankled with Feisal; again, it was something that
Churchill, who was unsuccessfully opposing Allenby over total independence for Egypt, completely failed to see.

Churchill then had to break the bad news, using the League of Nations
and its regulations as what we could call the bad cop, as compared with himself, the good cop:

> We therefore are unable at the present time to alter in any way the posi-
> tion which has been reached in the negotiations for the Treaty. If there is
> to be a Treaty it must be signed on this basis and no other. If the King or
> his Cabinet or the Assembly cannot agree to a Treaty on this basis, then it
> will be impossible to frame a form of agreement regulating the relations
> of Britain and Iraq. These are facts which do not depend on the wish of
> the British Government but on powers and laws to which they must bow.
>
> The King will therefore see that if the Treaty, which was his idea and
> not ours, cannot be agreed, there is nothing for us but to go forward on
> the present indeterminate basis until Iraq is strong enough to stand
> alone. There is really no use searching in vain for vain formulas which
> disguise the fact that Britain has to obey the League of Nations, and
> that Iraq must accept our guidance whilst it requires our aid.

In one true sense, Churchill was a good cop; France would never even
have begun to allow such freedom for her Syrian and Lebanese subjects. So
while Churchill was indisputably acting like a colonialist, he was at least
trying to get for Iraq a much more liberal colonial regime than would have

been entertained by any of the other mandatories, the "Great Powers," to use the old nineteenth-century phrase Churchill employs in putting the issue straight to Feisal, coming as near to blackmail as he could allow himself to get:

> Does he [Feisal] desire us to quit Iraq forthwith? We have installed him and his Government in power, and the country is at present in an orderly state. We could begin the evacuation immediately after the bout of hot weather and all British troops and civilians could be out of the country before the end of the Christian year. If this is the King's wish, he should say so, with the knowledge that the responsibility for what follows will rest upon him. I will then bring his wish to the notice of the Cabinet, who alone can take the final decision. The British nation would rejoice to be relieved from a burdensome charge devoid of the slightest advantage to them but which they have carried out thus far from a sense of duty to the people of Iraq, whose Turkish Government they overturned in the war, and out of loyalty to the King, whom they believed wished to continue for himself and the Sherefian family the friendly relationship established in the Great War.

Feisal did not budge, and it soon became apparent that he was in close touch with the Iraqi groups that were actively agitating against a treaty on British terms. So too was the venerable Naqib of Baghdad, the notional Prime Minister in the acting government. Not surprisingly, Churchill wrote a few days later to his regular Cabinet sparring partner, Lord Curzon, that:

> Feisal is most unreasonable, and the Naqib stupidly obdurate. . . . I do not propose to encourage Feisal's return to England. He asked for the Treaty. It has been so shaped as to give him the fullest measure of satisfaction. If now he declines to sign, I propose to leave matters in an undefined and indeterminate condition and see what happens next. I would rather get through these dangerous months before presenting what I expect will be the inevitable ultimatum.

He also shared his woes with Feisal's old friend from the Arab Revolt, Major Hubert Young, whose services had been so helpful at the Cairo Conference. Churchill was evidently eager, if not to say desperate, to find a way out:

I cannot understand why it is not possible to come to an agreement. What is the outstanding clash on the Treaty? Be ready to show it to me. . . . I do not see why it is necessary for us to refer to the Mandate in the preamble of the Treaty. The Mandate does not depend upon the Treaty but has a wholly different and persisting authority. Nor do I see any reason why we should not say that when Iraq is ready to stand by itself we shall have discharged the conditions of our Mandate.

The next few months saw Churchill completely dominated by the Irish crisis, which included the assassination of his military nemesis, Sir Henry Wilson, by IRA gunmen on 22 June 1922.

But on 4 July, Churchill had a blow: Lawrence offered his resignation. Lawrence wrote to John Shuckburgh that:

it seems to me that the time has come when I can fairly offer my resignation from the Middle East Department. You will remember that I was an emergency appointment, made because Churchill meant to introduce changes in our policy, and because he thought my help would be useful during the expected stormy period.

After Cox, following the Cairo Conference, had vetoed Lawrence's trip to see Feisal in Baghdad, it is not certain how useful he had been to Churchill; but if Lawrence was aware of a connection, he made no mention of it to Shuckburgh. He continued:

Well, that was eighteen months ago; but since we have "changed direction," we have not, I think, a British casualty in Palestine or Arabia or the Arab provinces of Irak [sic]. Political questions there are still, of course, and wide open, there always will be, but their expression and conduct has been growing more constitutional. For long there has not been an outbreak of any kind. . . .

As a consequence, therefore:

While things run along the present settled and routine lines I can see no

justification for the Department's continuing my employment—and little
for me to do if it is continued. So if Mr. Churchill permits, I shall be very
glad to leave so prosperous a ship. I need hardly say that I'm always at his
disposal if ever there is a crisis, or any job, small or big, for which he can
convince me that I am necessary.

Since the cautious, rule-abiding, more orthodox civil servants had in
effect frozen Lawrence out, his resignation is understandable, however much
a blow it may have been to that equally unorthodox, buccaneering
Churchill. Lawrence himself was soon to start on the strangest part of his
career, pretending to be someone called Shaw in order to join the RAF in the
ordinary ranks. He also began writing the book described earlier, which we
now know to be a strangely twisted and distinctly truth-bending set of memoirs: *The Seven Pillars of Wisdom.*

Churchill was very sorry to see him go, writing to him that:

I very much regret your decision to quit our small group at the Middle
East Department of the Colonial Office. Your help in all matters and
guidance in many has been invaluable to me and to your colleagues. I
should have been glad if you would have stayed with us longer. I hope you
are not unduly sanguine in your belief that our difficulties are largely sur-
mounted. Still, I know I can count upon you at any time that a need
arises, and in the meanwhile I am glad to know that you will accept at
least the honorary position of Adviser on Arab Affairs.

Churchill was to go to Lawrence's funeral some years later; as Air-
craftsman Shaw, Lawrence had a fatal motorcycle accident on what, my wife
and I discovered, is still a dangerous stretch of road.

As for Lawrence, he wrote in November 1922, after Churchill and
Lloyd George had been ejected from office, that if Britain was to "get out of
the Middle East Mandates with credit, it will be by Winston's bridge."

The Colonial Office officials dealing with the treaty issue were now
realizing the enormity of their decision to put Feisal on the throne. One of
them, Reader Bullard, moaned about the "serious defects in Feisal's character
which the last year has revealed." When, he lamented:

it was decided to send Feisal to Iraq, the decision was taken on the assumption that he would play straight with us. It was always a forlorn hope.

Even Sir Percy Cox, to whom, thanks to his advice, Feisal owed his position on the throne, vented his spleen, describing his protégé as "crooked and insincere."

Churchill wanted Feisal in London, but the king refused to come without the guarantee of a solution, which, owing to Feisal's refusal to give in, was obviously unlikely.

The civil servants were so confounded by the impasse that they even asked Lawrence, now departed from service, for his advice. Lawrence was for giving Feisal an ultimatum: Sign "within a specified time (say a week or so) [or] we will drop the Treaty and carry on without it."

But Churchill rejected his old friend's suggestion. The treaty, he said:

was Feisal's plan, not ours. We consented to it in order to meet his views. If he obstructs the Treaty & will not sign it, it is for him to suggest a method of avoiding the deadlock. At any rate I see not the slightest reason for hurry on our part.

The Cabinet was unlikely to meet until September, and Churchill was happy to let matters rest until then. Feisal was, Churchill told the Prime Minister, "playing a very low & treacherous game with us . . . Feisal seems determined to justify every word Gouraud ever said about him."

Churchill was on vacation in Biarritz, back in his favorite haunt, the South of France, when he contemplated sending a telegram to Feisal, which in the end he did not do because the King was supposedly ill. It is perhaps just as well, since it would not have helped the negotiations one bit. But it does reveal to us the extent to which Churchill had in all likelihood come to realize the folly of his adoption of the Sherifian/Hashemite option for Iraq:

I have learned with profound regret of the course in wh[ich] Your Majesty is resolved to persevere. It can only lead to the downfall of those hopes of cooperation between the British Gov[ernmen]t and the Sherifian family in pursuance of which we have with so much labor & expense facilitated

[Your Majesty's] accession to the throne of Iraq. Having laboured so long to serve your interests & to create for [you] a stable throne & a prosperous country I cannot view without sorrow the return wh[ich] the exertions & sacrifices of Britain have received.

Churchill then hoped to ram home his point by forcing Feisal to remember his fate at the hands of the French:

The prophecies of the French & of General Gouraud wh[ich] I have so often repulsed are apparently to be fulfilled to the letter. [Feisal] has no doubt measured v[er]y carefully the consequences which must follow a complete failure of cooperation between us before even a single year has passed. I will present the whole issue to the Cabinet when it resumes its meetings in September. I cannot anticipate what their decision will be, but I desire to place before the Cabinet [Your Majesty's] solemn answer to the following question: In the event of [Britain] deciding to withdraw from Iraq before the expense of another year is incurred, are King Feisal & his Gov[ernmen]t prepared to assume sole & unaided responsibility for the Gov[ernmen]t of the country exclusive of the Basra Vilayet, & from what date?

Sir Percy Cox was all for calling Feisal's bluff, but that did not seem to make Britain's negotiating position any easier.

Events that were swiftly to lead to the overthrow of the Lloyd George coalition government by angry Conservative backbenchers were now coming to a head. These were principally the massive and very successful Turkish counteroffensives under Mustapha Kemal that were to drive the Greeks out of Asia Minor, thereby ending in some areas thousands of years of Greek habitation. The attack itself began on 26 August, and both France and Italy, Britain's old wartime allies, actually supplied the Turkish nationalist forces with arms and equipment. By the 31st, Turkish troops had reached the sea.

Churchill was not at a loss to see what potentially dire implications this had for Iraq. Just before the final Turkish push, he told a group of Cabinet ministers—all now back in London—on 28 August that a decision on Iraq needed to be made. When it came to Feisal:

No argument had been of any effect with him. He [Feisal] had recently taken up the Extremists [*sic*] who now regarded him as their patron . . . [Churchill had] authorised the High Commissioner to inform Feisal that [he, the King] was responsible for preventing violence which would have the most disastrous consequences for Iraq.

Most Iraqi ministers had either resigned or threatened to do so, so there was now no real effective government in the country. Feisal was actively helping what Churchill referred to as "the Extremists." We might prefer to call them Arab-nationalists; either way, the situation there had become dire.

In fact, Feisal's "illness" might well have been diplomatic, not that Churchill and his colleagues in London and Baghdad realized it (or if they did, there is no official record of it). For, as Churchill told the Cabinet, the King's indisposition enabled Sir Percy Cox, as the High Commissioner, to take over effective government power in the absence of any form of Iraqi administration, "to maintain security."

Cox had now clearly seen what had been obvious for some time to the French. He told Churchill, who passed on his views to the Cabinet, that Feisal was "quite unfitted for his position and was directly responsible for unrest in Iraq, and for bad administration."

One could, though, look at this differently, as some historians have done, and simply say that Feisal was acting as a normal nationalist, a patriot, doing all possible to get rid of the colonial power. But it would also be fair to say that he was doing so in a weaselly way, hiding behind illness to let Sir Percy make the nasty decisions and then miraculously "recovering" in time to take back control.

The Cabinet decided on a tough policy. If it became necessary to withdraw from Iraq, "Feisal should not be allowed to remain there." Churchill was asked to support Sir Percy's takeover of power, and told that a final decision should be made by the middle of the month.

By the time Churchill wrote to Lloyd George on 1 September, the Turks were in the Aegean. Things were now going not at all as Churchill had wished, and he was realizing—far too late—the folly of his earlier decisions. Even so, we can see in his letter a mix of high strategy on the one hand and, on the other, the need to save even the smallest amounts of money for the British taxpayer:

> I am deeply concerned about Iraq. The task you have given me is becoming really impossible. Our forces are reduced now to very slender proportions. The Turkish menace has got worse; Feisal is playing the fool, if not the knave; his incompetent Arab officials are disturbing some of the provinces and failing to collect the revenue; we overpaid £200,000 on last year's account which it is almost certain Iraq will not be able to pay this year, thus entailing a Supplementary Estimate in regard to a matter never sanctioned by Parliament; a further deficit, in spite of large economies, is nearly certain this year on the civil expenses owing to the drop in revenue.

It had been Churchill himself who was responsible for the drastic force reductions in Iraq. Now all his nightmares about a revanchist Turkey seeking to regain its lost territory were coming true. Lloyd George was, as always, insistent on supporting the Greeks; they had lost their war with the Turkish nationalists, and now there was a real possibility, if the Prime Minister had his way, of war between Turkey and the United Kingdom. All this worried Churchill, too—as did the extra £200,000 in expenses!

He continued:

> I have to maintain British troops at Mosul all through the year in conse-quence of the Angora quarrel [Kemal's HQ was at what is now the Turkish capital, Ankara]: this has upset the programme of reliefs and will certainly lend to further expenditure beyond the provision. I cannot at the moment withdraw these troops without practically inviting the Turks to come in. The small column which is operating in the Rania district inside our bor-ders against the Turkish raiders and Kurdish sympathisers is a source of constant anxiety to me.

Churchill then highlighted the political issue: The British people simply did not want to go to war (a factor of considerable resonance to many twenty-first-century Britons, who can vividly recall the debates and marches against going to war with Iraq in 2003):

I do not see what political strength there is to face a disaster of any kind and certainly I cannot believe that in any circumstances any large reinforcements would be sent from here or from India. There is scarcely a single newspaper—Tory, Liberal or Labour—which is not consistently hostile to our remaining in this country.

Somewhat bitterly, I think, Churchill noted:

The enormous reductions which have been effected have brought no goodwill, and any alternative Government that might be formed here—Labour, Die-hard or Wee Free [i.e., non-Coalition Conservative or Liberal]—would gain popularity by ordering instant evacuation. Moreover in my heart I do not see what we are getting out of it. Owing to difficulties with America, no progress has been made in developing the oil. Altogether I am getting to the end of my resources.

It is hard to be anything but deeply sympathetic with Churchill at this point. It is not often that the folly of a politician's actions becomes so apparent to him so soon, yet this was unquestionably the case with Churchill when the most dreaded consequences of his decisions were coming to pass. As Churchill continued telling the Prime Minister:

I think we should now put definitely, not only to Feisal but also to the Constituent Assembly, the position that unless they actually beg us to stay on our own terms in regard to efficient control, we shall actually evacuate beyond the close of the financial year. I would put this issue in the most brutal way, and if they are not prepared to urge us to stay and to co-operate in every manner I would actually clear out. That at any rate would be a solution. Whether we should clear out of the country altogether or hold onto [sic] a portion of the Basra vilayet is a minor issue requiring a special study.

Churchill did try to give himself, and the Prime Minister, a feasible optimistic scenario. But even that had a potentially dangerous pitfall:

It is quite possible, however, that face to face with this ultimatum, the

King, and still more the Constituent Assembly, will implore us to remain.
If they do, shall we not be obliged to remain? If we remain, shall we not
be answerable for defending their frontier? How are we to do this if the
Turk comes in? We have no force whatsoever that can resist any serious
inroad. The War Office, of course, have played for safety throughout and
are ready to say "I told you so" at the first misfortune.

Since it had been Churchill who had so zealously refused to contemplate the War Office's repeated request to maintain high-expense British
troops in Iraq, the new state of affairs must have been an especially bitter pill
for him to swallow. Yet, politically, had he had any alternative to reducing
great numbers of troops? Withdrawal would have resulted in a terrible loss
of face. Perhaps now could have been the time to detach the Kurdish
regions from the Arab parts of Iraq, something that, under the treaty,
Britain was theoretically allowed to do. Alas, Churchill did not take up this
option, and the opportunity passed. Instead, he let his sense of despair take
over. He concluded his missive to the Prime Minister by saying:

> Surveying all of the above, I think I must ask you for definite guidance at
> this stage as to what you wish and what you are prepared to do. The vic-
> tories of the Turks will increase our difficulties throughout the
> Mohammedan world. At present we are paying eight millions a year for
> the privilege of living on an ungrateful volcano out of which we are in no
> circumstances to get anything worth having.

Presumably, Churchill had forgotten about the future possibilities of oil;
but as these were still speculative, he may simply have not thought the petroleum potential of Iraq worth fighting for. Things were not going well for
Churchill. He had been disappointed over the decision at the Genoa Conference to award the Bolshevik regime *de jure* recognition, a decision that seems
obvious today but which was greeted with dismay by the resolute anticommunist. He was also despondent about how the Turks had hammered the Greeks
so successfully that the international situation was now very dangerous. At this
point, finding himself vindicated for forcefully advocating a deal with Turkey
three years earlier only made him feel worse. As he told Lord Curzon:

> The Greeks have been led to their ruin and the Turks erected again into a
> formidable power by a policy against which I have always protested and
> with which I know you have very little sympathy.

There are times when being right is painful, and this was one of them.

So in the end it was Lloyd George who came down in favor of staying
in Iraq, and Churchill who was open to a scuttle. Lloyd George wrote a
lengthy reply to Churchill just a few days later, on 5 September. It is an odd
letter from a Prime Minister to a subordinate, in that it attacks decisions
made years earlier by a Liberal government of which both Lloyd George and
Churchill had been leading members. But it gives a good indication of why
Britain finally, alas, decided to stay in Iraq.

Lloyd George agreed with Churchill that Iraq needed the Cabinet's
close attention, but the Prime Minister's whole Turkish policy was about to
unravel. The Turks were massacring the Greeks in Smyrna and engaging in
what we would now call massive-scale ethnic cleansing of the Anatolian
Greek population. So it is not surprising that no member of the Cabinet was
really focused on Iraq.

Churchill's request, though, prompted the Prime Minister to reminisce:
"The whole problem has risen out of the decision to attack the Turks in
Mesopotamia," he wrote, looking back to 1914 and 1915. Many American
and British commentators have echoed these sentiments of Lloyd George's
in more recent times:

> Strategically, I think, the whole decision was faulty. To be effective we had
> to leave our base on the sea for hundreds of miles in a torrid country
> utterly unfit for white fighting [i.e., fighting by European troops]. We
> ought to have concentrated on Gallipoli and Palestine or Alexandretta
> [now the Turkish town of Iskenderun, on the Mediterranean]. The Taurus
> [mountain range] was then unpierced. The decision was taken when I was
> hardly on the fringe of the War Cabinet. You were in it. Having provoked
> a war with the Turk we had to fight him somewhere, but the swamps of
> the Tigris were a badly chosen battle-ground.

While Lloyd George was right to say that Gallipoli would have been a better landing ground, he is of course being monstrously unfair to Churchill, whose strategic genius had foreseen an attack at Gallipoli as *the* place where the Turks could easily be knocked out of the war. Lloyd George, who during that period had been Chancellor of the Exchequer and then Minister of Munitions, was hardly a "fringe" member of the Cabinet either, but rather one of its most important members. In any case, decisions made years back could not now be undone, as Lloyd George went on to remind Churchill:

> Whatever, however, the merits or demerits of the original decision to fight in Mesopotamia, it certainly is responsible for our difficulties now; and tracking the story back to that decision, I do not see how any of our subsequent troubles could have been avoided.

Lloyd George then defended his policy after becoming Prime Minister in 1916:

> It was quite clear to me when I became Prime Minister that we could not afford to relax our campaign against the Turks in that region. Such a decision, after the withdrawal from Gallipoli, and the surrender of a British army at Kut, would have weakened our position throughout the Mohammedan world.

Lloyd George then went on to make a morally salient point that linked British obligations to the Arabs to the declaration in Woodrow Wilson's Fourteen Points that promised self-determination for the former peoples of the Ottoman Empire:

> Having beaten the Turks both in Iraq and Palestine, we could not at the Armistice have repudiated all our undertakings towards the Arabs. We were responsible for liberating them from Turkish sovereignty, and we were absolutely bound to assist them in setting up Arab governments, if we were not prepared to govern them ourselves.

Lloyd George was right to remind Churchill of Britain's obligations, but as Prime Minister he was also responsible for the way in which Churchill had decided to operate the mandate system—by creating several highly artificial states under outside-imposed rulers. This is, sadly, yet another case of a politician evading responsibility at the sign of trouble.

As for the "present situation," he continued, it was "very disappointing" that:

> Feisal has responded so badly to your excellent efforts to make him self-supporting with a minimum of British protection; but I do not think that an effective case can be made against us on that score, if we stand together and meet criticism courageously.

This is an obvious attempt to get Churchill to stop rocking the boat. It is also unfair, since it was British policy as a whole that was responsible for Feisal being there in the first place. Indeed, a very effective case could be made against the British government of which Lloyd George was the leader.

Lloyd George then made the key point about Iraq, one that is so obvious to us now but which was surprisingly absent from Churchill's considerations—the question of oil:

> If we have failed in Iraq, it is because we have taken no effective steps during our years of occupation to prospect the possibilities of the country. As you know, I was anxious that the Anglo-Persian [Oil Company (now BP), in which Churchill had been responsible for giving the British government a major share] should bore to ascertain the value of the oil deposits. We have, however, done virtually nothing in that respect. If we leave, we may find in a year or two that we have handed over to the French and the Americans some of the richest oilfields in the world—just to purchase on [*sic*] derisive shout from our enemies. On general principles, I am against a policy of scuttle, in Iraq as elsewhere, and should like you to put the alternatives [before the Cabinet].

So while Britain did not go to *Mesopotamia* to obtain oil, one could say that the British stayed to obtain the oil of *Iraq*.

Churchill replied to Lloyd George immediately and very defensively. He reminded him that both of them were equally responsible for all the decisions made during the war, and that the primary impetus to invade Mesopotamia via Basra had come from Lord Crewe, the Secretary of State for India. He could have mentioned Gallipoli as well, but clearly chose not to. "However," he continued, "when victory was achieved" and when:

> Turkey was prostrate it seems to me that we were undoubtedly free to decline the Mandate for Iraq and to quit the country as rapidly as our troops could have been withdrawn. We were also free to make a treaty with Turkey which would have secured a real peace on the general basis of the victories which we had won over the Turks.

(Here he is really getting at Lloyd George, whose responsibility for the overly-harsh Treaty of Sèvres was considerable.) Churchill continued his letter in a similar vein:

> Such a peace could certainly have provided either for the creation of a quasi-independent Iraq under Turkish suzerainty, or alternatively if we had decided to take the mandate we could have ensured staying there undisturbed and unmolested by the Turks. However, events have taken a different course and I have done my best and will continue to do my best to cope with them.

Churchill then outlined what he had asked Sir Percy Cox to do in the dangerous climate of the time. One column of troops had been withdrawn:

> At the same time the whole of the Suleimaniyeh province will have to be abandoned as the result of an incursion by a few hundred Turks. I did not feel that I could run the risk of a minor military disaster at the same time as we were making a *coup d'état* and facing a crisis in Baghdad itself.

It is significant that Churchill was so open with Lloyd George about what he and Sir Percy had done, effectively seizing power in Baghdad despite all democratic protestations to the contrary. Iraq may have had the semblance of a democracy, but it was the colonial/mandatory power, Britain, that was really pulling the strings of power behind the scenes.

Churchill thus went on to inform the Prime Minister:

> This crisis has been successfully dealt with by Cox, who is now going to
> come to a very clear understanding with Feisal and to make it plain to him
> that he will have to rule as a constitutional Sovereign in the future and
> that he must be guided by the advice of his Ministers and of the British
> High Commissioner in all important matters.

Churchill hoped against hope that there would be peace in Iraq, something that would make his life much easier. He had come to regret his decision to opt for retreat, although his official biographer, Sir Martin Gilbert,
thinks that by fall of 1922, he did actually want to go. Churchill may, therefore, have been insincere in concluding to the Prime Minister that:

> Like you, I am very much against the policy of a scuttle and after your
> clear expression of opinion you may be sure that I shall do all in my power
> to avoid it.

The Cabinet met the next day, on 7 September. Churchill does not
seem to have spoken directly of Iraq but of the growing crisis created by the
destruction of the Greek army at Turkish hands. Both he and Lloyd George
were able to agree that it would be a disaster if the Gallipoli peninsula, which
was guarded by a small British force, were to fall into Turkish nationalist
hands. Mustapha Kemal was determined to seize all Turkish territory, fully
including Gallipoli, the scene of his earlier victory over the British. As was
becoming obvious to many Conservatives in and out of the government, the
only way to stop this from happening would be a war between Britain and
Turkey. Intrigues were already taking place, including one involving Lord
Curzon, who was about to defect to Bonar Law, the former Conservative
leader, who was now making an amazing recovery from the ill health that
had kept him out of politics the year before.

To Curzon, "Feisal" was "a bad hat." Churchill duly defended himself
and his record:

> Before bringing the Iraq position to the Cabinet I should be glad to have

a talk with you, in order that we may if possible speak with one voice. You must remember that my task has been to make bricks without straw and to blow bubbles without soap; and that at any rate our commitments [in Iraq] are enormously reduced and that we are riding only at single anchor.

In a wonderfully Churchillian flourish, he concluded that the "wealth of metaphor may be reconciled if goodwill is used at each stage."

Churchill's concerns were now primarily with Chanak, the location of the small British force in the Dardanelles. War was distinctly possible. But he did not forget the endless and still-unresolved issue of Iraq and the treaty.

On 11 September, Feisal's former comrade in arms, Major Hubert Young, told Churchill that Feisal was now willing for the United Kingdom to support Iraqi membership in the League of Nations once the elusive treaty was signed. Sir Percy felt that this signified at least some kind of recognition of the mandate. But not everyone was so optimistic. As Sir Archibald Sinclair, Churchill's former aide, wrote to him on the 13th:

You must be full of tender anxiety for your tender Arab plant in Iraq with this furious storm raging on—and threatening to spread from—the Asia Minor horizon.

Fortunately for the British, their commander at Chanak, General Charles Harington, was determined to avoid war. The new French government was equally adamant that it would not support any British move against its old wartime enemy, the Turks. Finally, on 1 October, news came that Harington was not prepared to fight. At the same time, Mustapha Kemal agreed to negotiate. There would not be a war. But for Churchill and Lloyd George a political crisis was about to begin, as the Conservatives were appalled at how close to war with Turkey Britain had come.

Just as Churchill's political world was about to collapse, good news finally came from Iraq: on 1 October, the Royal Air Force had taken control of the British forces there. Since the Secretary of State for Air was Frederick Guest, a cousin of Churchill's, this meant that there would no longer be endless tussles with the obstreperous Sir Laming Worthington-Evans at the War Office.

Then, on 5 October, Feisal finally decided to accept the treaty. Just as exciting for Churchill, the Foreign Office agreed with what the Colonial Office wanted. After "months of negotiations," Churchill told the Cabinet, progress had finally been made:

> This draft Treaty conformed in all respects to the requirements of the League of Nations, and also fully complied with the pledge which had been given to King Feisal that in the case of Iraq Great Britain would substitute a Treaty relationship for a mandatory relationship. Throughout the idea of the Cabinet had been to establish Iraq as an independent Arab State bound to Great Britain during the mandatory period by Treaty relations.

In other words, the mandate was not being given up, simply reestablished on a different legal basis:

> The Arabs were themselves opposed to the ordinary mandatory relationship, but it had been pointed out to them . . . [that] their objections could be satisfactorily met inasmuch as if and when Iraq was admitted to the League of Nations the necessity for any mandate would cease. When a stable government had been established in the country, when the frontiers had been defined, when an organic law had been passed and certain military and financial arrangements had been definitely executed, then Great Britain would be prepared to advocate the admission of Iraq to the League of Nations.

Churchill did not give the Cabinet a timetable for the plan; there was none. He went on, giving more details of the good news:

> King Feisal had accepted this solution, and his acceptance had no doubt been influenced by his illness and the energetic action taken by the High Commissioner in suppressing the extremists.

How far Feisal's illness was genuine and to what extent it was diplomatic— getting him out of a nasty hole with the Arab-nationalists, or "extremists"—

has to remain a matter of conjecture. It certainly did relieve him of having to make the major decision himself. But Churchill does not refer to the illness—said to have been appendicitis—as anything other than real, so perhaps we should give Feisal the benefit of the doubt. What Churchill did share with his colleagues was the following:

> It had been made clear that in this particular matter [signing the treaty] the Government would not deal with Feisal alone, but that he must arrange for the formation of a Ministry and act on the advice of his Ministers, and that the Ministers themselves must give full assurances that they would accept and work the Treaty. The High Commissioner had succeeded in meeting these requirements, and all that was now necessary was to authorise him to sign the Treaty.

Here Churchill skated over many a Baghdad intrigue. Cox had partly solved the problem by exiling as many of the nationalist leaders as possible from the capital to the city of Henjam. Nevertheless, even the venerable Naqib of Baghdad, the head of the provisional government, tendered his resignation and was persuaded to put together a new Ministry only with the utmost reluctance.

Churchill then put the good news into context for his colleagues: The talks with the Kemalist forces at Mudania were still a source of concern, and no one could be absolutely certain of success in the negotiations or of avoiding a war.

> The moment for this action seemed opportune. Trouble with the Turk was the time for friendship with the Arab, and inasmuch as the Treaty was extremely favorable to Arab aspirations the publication of its terms would undoubtedly have an excellent effect and would enable Feisal to unite the Arabs against any Turkish attack.

This troubled Churchill's colleague, Major Young, who felt that he was being bounced into the treaty. With Turco-British negotiations still delicate, Young told Churchill that the:

latest news of the Mudania Conference and the Turkish reply . . . are very serious and the risk of collision in the Dardanelles appears to be increasing. It is vital that allied solidarity should be preserved at this moment and that nothing should be done which is likely to prejudice it. We have yielded to Sir P. Cox's insistence on the necessity for [the] immediate signature of the Treaty, but he has never answered our question as to the effect on the position in Iraq of the recent Turkish developments. I feel very strongly that the inter-allied position should be explained to him and that the arguments in favor of suspending action for the moment should be placed clearly before him . . . he must satisfy himself that the position is fully understood in Iraq and that signature does not commit us to more than an understanding to do our best to preserve the present frontier. . . . He should explain quite clearly to Feisal that the term "Iraq" means only that territory which is ultimately detached from Turkey, either as a result of the present peace negotiations, if they materialize . . . or as the result of a final settlement that may be made, possibly after a second war with Turkey. It should also be pointed out to Feisal that signature of the Treaty at the present moment may just provide the provocation which will render a collision inevitable.

Thankfully, war did not happen. But it is hard to avoid the feeling that Young was right: signature was premature. As Churchill was adding his final touches to the treaty, Conservatives were actively plotting to overthrow the Coalition government and replace it with one that was exclusively Conservative. Yet Churchill seems to have been motivated to persist primarily in cost-cutting and the need to be friendly to the Arabs, as is clear from what he told the Cabinet:

The Treaty did not commit Great Britain to giving any further definite military or financial assistance; it merely provided for the making of supplementary agreements dealing with military and financial arrangements. If warlike operations could be avoided it seemed probable that next year the cost to the British Exchequer of Mesopotamia would be reduced to £4,000,000 as compared with £8,000,000 in the present year and £32,000,000 two years ago.

This was the *empire lite* decision: to have the benefits of empire without having to meet the full cost.

The Cabinet discussion that followed is revealing, in that it makes one wonder why on earth, in view of all Feisal's evident failings, the British had chosen him at all, or persisted in supporting him after his lack of qualities had become apparent. While some of what follows is rife with the white Western racist superiority of the time, it is not at all inaccurate in its summation of the kind of ruler Feisal would be:

> The view was expressed that, while the successful conclusion of the negotiations was a matter of great satisfaction, there might be some doubt as to the possibility of King Feisal being able to maintain a civilised and stable Government in Iraq. The genius which the Arabs had displayed in the Middle Ages for administration had apparently disappeared. Moreover, the personality of Feisal, who was weak and intriguing, did not inspire confidence. Nevertheless, there could be no doubt that the course of action suggested was the right one to adopt.

The Arabs, the Cabinet remembered, had been conquered centuries ago, in the Middle Ages, by the Ottomans or, in the case of some parts of the Arab world, had been under British, Italian, or French rule for some while. How much had the desire to reduce expenditure—from £32 million to an eighth of that, £4 million—been the key factor in deciding that the treaty should be signed? Likewise, did the threat of war with Turkey, particularly as the Turks still coveted Mosul, also play a role?

The treaty was finally signed on 10 October. But it was not to do Churchill much good. Nine days later, on the 19th, Conservatives met together in their political club in London, the Carlton. They decided to overthrow the Coalition government for an exclusively Conservative replacement under Andrew Bonar Law, who had clearly recovered from whatever had ailed him the previous year. By the end of the day, Churchill had lost office, and the last-ever Liberal Prime Minister, David Lloyd George, had resigned.

There was now to be a General Election. Then Churchill had to be rushed to a hospital. Feisal's appendix problem could have been either fabricated or genuine, but Churchill definitely had appendicitis and was unable to spend the first part of the election campaign fighting to defend his seat in Dundee. Clementine did her best in his absence, but she was not the orator her husband was capable of being.

So Churchill, having lost his job and his appendix, then lost his seat in Parliament as well. It was a sad turn of events for so dynamic and active a man.

CHAPTER SEVEN

FROM FEISAL TO SADDAM

Aaccording to the leading Arabist historian, David Pryce-Jones, in an article in 2004, you can trace a direct line from King Feisal in the 1920s through to Saddam Hussein, deposed in 2003. Depending on your viewpoint, this maybe unfair to Feisal, who, whatever his faults, was no psychopath in the Saddam class. But there is a basis for such an accusation, however great the difference between the first ruler of Iraq and the most recent.

A brief digression: One of the problems of writing the history of more recent times is that it is very difficult to maintain objectivity. The nearer to your own time you come, the easier it becomes to let your prejudices reign; not only that, it is hard to see the overall picture. As the writer John Lewis Gaddis shows in his books on the Cold War, now that it has ended, we can write about the whole of it and see its different aspects in proper perspective. We also know who won, even if not everyone is agreed on why the Soviets lost. But as Gaddis points out, a history of the Cold War written in, say, 1963, when it was in full swing and the outcome was completely unpredictable, would have to be radically different from those published, say, in 2001, ten years after it was over.

To use Gaddis's analogy, the same could also be said for a history of

World War Two written, for example, in 1941, the year that Churchill, as Prime Minister, had to send troops to Iraq to get rid of a pro-Nazi government that had been briefly in power. A history composed in, say, July 1941 would be rather depressing—Britain hanging on by its fingernails to North Africa, much of Western and Central Europe in Axis hands, and the Soviet Union looking likely to fall to the massive Nazi onslaught, Barbarossa. Not only that, but the United States, however sympathetic to the Allies Roosevelt may have been privately, was still neutral and out of the conflict. It would, in short, have to have drawn a very somber picture.

Ever since the first Gulf War in 1991, many histories of Iraq have been published, many of them excellent and listed in the bibliography. They were, however, written when Saddam Hussein was still very much in power, as he had been for the past twenty years and more. So, as with accounts of World War Two written before 1945 or of the Cold War pre-1991, they do not possess the knowledge we now have that gives us a dramatically different perspective. Now, post-2003, we know that Saddam is ruler no more and that whatever happens to Iraq, his return to power is not on the agenda.

I wrote this book in an interim phase of Iraq's history, after the liberation but before the outcome of the democratic experiment is fully known. In this post-Saddam but pre-whatever-comes-next period, I can therefore look at Iraqi history from a new perspective.

While we now see the Middle East as a tinderbox, it is with the advantage of over fifty years of hindsight. That what Churchill and the others created was to turn out to be a disaster could not have been immediately apparent to them. We could argue that the true extent of the mess did not manifest itself fully until 1948, when the war over the creation of Israel, followed by the Suez fiasco of 1956, finally ended European power and influence in the region. We could also say that we are still living in the post-1948 Middle East world, with the wars and causes of wars of that period still unresolved. To that extent, we are the equivalent of the historians of 1941 or 1963 who were writing in the midst of a conflict, before it was over, the outcome unknown.

If we look specifically at the numerous excellent histories of Iraq that were written up until 2003, we find that many of them are about "how Iraqi history led to Saddam Hussein," with major emphasis on the years of his despotic rule. Now at least we can look at Iraq through another lens; but given Iraq's uncertain future, what we see is not completely clear.

To add to the difficulties of the task, much of the history of Iraq from 1921 to 2003 is incredibly complex. Up until 1936, it had been, in theory, a parliamentary state, but one in which the actual parliament had no effective influence. During the monarchical period, from 1921 to 1958, there were fifty-eight changes of government, which means that many governments did not remain in power for even as much as a year. Beyond that, some of the time, the people who held high office were not those who held the real power and pulled the strings from behind the scenes.

What follows is a bird's-eye panoramic view of post-1921 Iraqi history, looking at what I think are its main themes and concentrating on the legacy of Winston Churchill in particular. This is a minefield! After reading many fascinating accounts of Iraqi history, what is most obvious to me is that historians disagree passionately about it.

Most of this book is based on archival documents—that is, records of what key people such as Churchill actually said and wrote. In this chapter, however, what I have written is based on the work of other historians. I have had to take the facts on trust and develop my ideas from primary research done by others. Given that historians disagree with one another, this could be dangerous. However, since I studied the Churchill archives myself, I was able to use hard evidence to reach my own conclusions. You can call what follows my post-Saddam perspective, but since Iraq is very much in a state of flux as I write this, please take that into account. With these *caveats* in mind, we look at the history of Iraq from 1922 to 2004.

Fifty-eight governments in thirty-seven years is a sure sign of chronic, unresolved instability, and that was exactly the case with Iraq under the monarchy from 1921 until its violent overthrow in 1958. It would be unfair to blame Churchill alone for all this; many other British colonial officials, diplomats, soldiers, and politicians must share the responsibility. Yet it is surely true to say that Britain as a whole, as the paramount colonial power, was indeed to blame for much of what happened in the Middle East during this thirty-seven-year time frame, as David Fromkin's *A Peace to End All Peace* so ably shows. Palestine and the post-1948 Palestinian-Israeli struggle are equally part of the unfortunate British legacy to the region. Jordan was lucky in its Hashemite rulers, especially in the decades-long rule of King Hussein, but even that relatively stable country has not escaped the turmoil of war and revolution.

In Iraq, Feisal attempted to get out of the treaty with Britain because he saw that the key issue for many of his subjects would be his *legitimacy* as their ruler. This, however, was something that Churchill and many other Europeans simply did not understand—that Feisal was an outsider, a prince from the Arabian peninsula who had spent much of his life living in Turkish Constantinople and had been imposed on the peoples of Iraq by British decree. Feisal had an excellent reason for not wanting to be seen as a British stooge; but since he relied on the Royal Air Force and British goodwill for his survival, he really did not have much of an option. In this sense, none of the rulers of the Hashemite period had any real legitimacy, except for the brief period in 1941 which marks Churchill's fleeting return to involvement in the Middle East.

Historians differ as to what they think of Feisal and his rule, which lasted until 1933. To some he was an Arab hero, doing the best he could in unpromising circumstances. Several of the more recent books see it this way: for example, Thabit Abdullah's *A Brief History of Iraq,* Charles Tripp's *A History of Iraq,* and Geoff Simons's *Iraq: From Sumer to Post-Saddam,* which has a foreword by the left-wing antiwar British politician, Tony Benn. To others, notably Elie Kedourie in his famous *The Chatham House Version,* Feisal was a totally incompetent disaster from start to finish. Finding a consensus on Feisal's twelve-year rule is thus well-nigh impossible—and the more I read, the harder I found it to sympathize with either side!

Using the same basic facts as they appear in all the books in the preceding paragraph, as well as some of the more recent books on Iraq under Saddam Hussein (all listed in the bibliography), I give my interpretation of what happened, with the aim of putting together a synthesis of my own.

What happened next, after Feisal's death, is also very controversial. Once again, much seems to depend on whether one thinks the British presence and background influence in Iraq were a good thing or not. If they were a bad thing—and nowadays most of us would be against imperialism—then there is a danger that anyone anti-British automatically becomes a hero. Unfortunately, many of the anti-British players in Iraq at the time, such as King Ghazi Rashid Ali, were sympathetic to Britain's enemy, Nazi Germany. So I feel we cannot really say that they should be regarded as heroes for being anti-British, because they were also pro-Nazi, and that, surely, was not good!

As more recent history also demonstrates, opinions often collide on a minefield of deeply held political and social views. In 2003, for example, the British left was split. On one side there was the pro–human-rights left, for whom Saddam Hussein's suppression of the Kurds and Shiite Muslim "Marsh Arabs" in the south was so terrible that Saddam had to go. Then there was the anti-American left, for whom any enemy of the United States was a friend of theirs and who thus opposed intervention.

Many recent books, including those cited earlier, tend to look at the issue of whether or not Kuwait should really be part of Iraq, for example, in the light of the authors' feelings about imperialism rather than on the historical merits of the case. This is anachronistic thinking—reading one's present views into the past. While strong views on present-day politics are perfectly legitimate, I am not sure that anachronism makes for good history.

Let us look at the post-1936 history of Iraq in as dispassionate a way as possible.

In 1936 Feisal's successor, King Ghazi, the young playboy ruler, allowed the installation of a military coup. For the next five years there was not even the pretense of constitutional rule, since military might, not elections, determined who held the power. Here again it gets confusing, with groups called "the circle of seven" and "the Golden Square" (a clique of four particularly influential officers). King Ghazi himself was killed in mysterious circumstances, and the regent for the young King Feisal II, along with the everambitious and pro-British politician, Nuri al-Said, played games of bewildering complexity.

This period of military power also boded ill for the future, in that it persuaded many people that a coup or some kind of military-backed regime was the best way forward. From 1958 until 2003 this was to be the kind of rule Iraq had, without even a pretense of democracy. The 1936 coup, therefore, set a terrible precedent that was to plague Iraq thereafter.

By 1941 a former royal official, Rashid Ali, was the Prime Minister. Looked at from the perspective of a nationalist Arab politician, in 1941 it was more than likely that Britain would lose the Second World War. The British had just been ignominiously expelled from Greece, their last toehold on continental Europe, and were not performing terribly well against Axis forces in North Africa. The U.S.S.R. was, pre-Barbarossa, a neutral state giving active help to Nazi Germany, and there was no prospect of the United States entering the war on Britain's side. Not surprisingly, Rashid Ali did not want to be stuck on the losing side.

To compress a long and fascinating story, Rashid Ali therefore made links with the Nazis, as did many other nationalist Arab leaders of the time, such as the Mufti of Jerusalem, a leading Palestinian Sunni religious figure. Churchill fully realized the enormous strategic threat to Britain that this posed. He therefore diverted troops to Iraq, and within a few weeks British forces had ejected the Rashid Ali regime. For the remaining years of the monarchy, no overtly anti-British government held office in Iraq. As a result, the legitimacy problem never went away.

This legitimacy problem was considerably worsened by the foolish and unsuccessful decision by Britain in 1956 to ally with France and Israel against nationalist Egypt when its ruler, Colonel Gamal Abdel Nasser, decided to nationalize the Suez Canal. This, in the eyes of all Arab-nation-alists, put Britain firmly on the side of their Israeli enemy. All Britain's efforts—including the signature of the Baghdad Pact with countries such as Iraq and Turkey—to create a pro-Western Arab zone under British influence were now torn apart. So, too, were the Hashemites in 1958; in an exceptionally bloody revolution, the dynasty was not just overthrown but also butchered, along with thousands of its supporters. The issue of legitimacy had proved fatal to the long-term survival of Britain's Hashemite protegés. (Historians such as Charles Tripp and Geoff Simons have contrasted this with the significantly less violent revolution in Egypt in 1953, in which far fewer people were killed and the King was allowed to go into exile.)

Furthermore, during the entire period of the monarchy, British policy did not allow for full democracy in Iraq; many of the politicians were tribal leaders or officials who had survived from the days of the old Ottoman Empire. Nearly all of them were Sunni, although Sunni Arabs constituted no more than around 20 or 25 percent of the total population. Not until the late 1940s did the 60-plus percent Shiite majority population enjoy real access to power, and even then it was sporadic at best.

The Sunni-Shia issue was one of the reasons that Feisal and other leading Sunni Arabs wanted the Kurds within Iraq's borders; the Kurds were not Arab but they were in the main Sunni Muslim in their spiritual allegiance. While the final decision to incorporate the Mosul *vilayet* into Iraq was made after Churchill's time, one can equally say that he failed to ensure sufficient safeguards for the Kurdish minority while he still had the chance. The "Kurdish problem" of Iraq has never been solved, and the region has been unstable from that day to this. Not until 1991, with the Kurdish autonomous area in the "no-fly zone" after the Gulf War, did the Kurds begin to have the kind of effective regional self-government they should have been enjoying since the 1920s.

One does have to concede that Sunni dominance in Iraq preceded the British. This is historically correct: The Ottomans were Sunni, and Shiite sympathies were always associated with Iran, over the border. But while this is true, the British did nothing to ameliorate the imbalance. Indeed, by their choice of a Sunni, Feisal, they perpetuated it. While Feisal would make the occasional act of obeisance to his Shiite subjects, he ruled, in effect, through a narrow Sunni Muslim clique, many of whom, like the future kingpin Nuri al-Said, had been soldiers fighting alongside him in the Arab Revolt. Most of the key posts in the army were also filled by Sunni Muslims, and this continued to be the case right through the rule of Saddam himself, a Sunni Muslim from near Tikrit, a town at the heart of the so-called "Sunni Triangle." We know from the archives that Churchill asked his advisers about the differences between Sunni and Shia, and that all the key British officials were well aware of them. Yet it made no difference to which ruler they chose for the new state. Nor did the indirect method of democracy selected for the parliament, one that strongly favored tribal leaders, help in removing the imbalance.

All subsequent rulers of Iraq were Sunni Arabs. Saddam Hussein simply took this Sunni predominance a step farther, by selecting Sunni Arabs from his own tribal group around Tikrit. (General Abdul Karim Qasim, the ruler from 1958 to 1963, was half-Shia on his mother's side to but, in this case, a rare Kurdish Shia, so not from the 60 to 65 percent Shiite Arab majority.)

This has meant that the majority of the Iraqi people have been permanently excluded from any say in how their own country has been run.

Some historians such as Thabit Abdullah feel that the borders of Iraq are natural, not totally artificial. The borders we now have were finally drawn up after Churchill was in office, when the Kurds were, after all, incorporated into Iraq and without any of the safeguards he felt they should have. The result is that the Kurds, a single people, are now split between Iraq, Iran, Syria, and Turkey, in all of which they are or have been oppressed. When in 2004 a major atrocity took place in Kurdish Iraq, many Kurds blamed Arab (and possibly Al Qaeda) extremists. This shows that the thirteen years from 1991 to 2004 of immunity from such acts is over, and that once more the Kurds will be a minority in an Arab state.

Many of the other Middle East borders were also drawn up after Churchill's time, notably by Sir Percy Cox, who, before his own retirement, drew up the borders of southern Iraq, Saudi Arabia, and Kuwait, allocating much of the land Kuwait wanted to Ibn Saud, who incorporated it into his growing empire. Saudi Arabia's present borders are in effect those of conquest—the warring campaigns of Ibn Saud and his hard-line Wahhabi Muslim shock troops. They are in many ways as artificial as the rest of the boundaries of the Middle East. But for timely British intervention, for example, Ibn Saud would have conquered Jordan in the 1920s and possibly other areas under British protection, such as Yemen, Oman, and what we now call the United Arab Emirates, then called the Trucial States.

Here, as on most things, however, I agree with David Fromkin, who in his introduction to *A Peace to End All Peace* lays stress on two key elements of the post-1918 settlement. These are the complete artificiality of the borders, and the overwhelming role of the West in putting them together. On the latter he disagrees with Karsh and Karsh, in their controversial but superbly researched *Empires of the Sand*. They attribute an equal role to the ambitions of the local dynasties, Hashemite and Saudi. But as I hope my narrative has made clear, the Europeans had a strong degree of choice: Britain could have ignored Hashemite imperial longings and thrown them out, as the French had thrown Feisal out of Syria in 1920; but indirect rule, an old British colonial favorite from Africa to India and Southeast Asia, was Britain's choice. It could have opted for direct rule.

Instead, it chose the cheapest solution: a local ruler backed by the full power of the Royal Air Force.

Had the violent coup of 1958 not happened, the two Hashemite states, Jordan and Iraq, could have merged, as Nuri al-Said planned that they should. This would have created a far more viable entity, as comparatively tiny Jordan would have been absorbed into a much bigger overall state. But by 1958, for such schemes—designed to counteract the brief United Arab Republic of Egypt and Syria—it was too late. When General Qasim took power in Iraq, the British acted to protect Jordan, and the unification idea was dropped.

Qasim did try, however, in 1961 to claim what he felt was a lost Iraqi province, Kuwait. Once more the British intervened, and the Iraqi dictator was forced to withdraw. As we all know, Saddam Hussein was to make the same mistake in 1990, only to be ejected a few months later. Since prior to 1918 all these areas were parts of a much larger empire, and the Saudis in 1922 had also claimed Kuwait and succeeded in being given large swaths of Kuwaiti-claimed desert by the British, one cannot really say that the claims of 1961 and 1990 had any real legal validity at all. Once again, the inherently artificial nature of the boundaries created major problems—as has also happened in Africa, where synthetic Western-imposed borders have caused no end of suffering and perpetual civil wars.

To be fair to the British, though, it was not only in Africa and the Middle East that artificial states came into being. The same can also be said of many of the post-1918 states in Europe, none of which any longer exist. Czechoslovakia was dismembered in 1938 and 1939, losing the Ruthene part of the country permanently in 1945 to the U.S.S.R. (and now the Ukraine), and split, thankfully peacefully, in 1993. As for Yugoslavia, we know all too well the hideous and bloodthirsty death throes of that artificial state. Also split up during World War Two, with a vicious civil war taking place as well as German and Italian occupation, Yugoslavia managed to hold together after 1945 only because of the strong man rule of Josip Broz Tito, the leader of the resistance movement during the war. After his death, it fell apart again, and hundreds of thousands of innocent civilians were slaughtered, raped, or drastically dislocated in the civil wars of the 1990s.

After 1948, similarly, Iraq held together only by virtue of dictatorial rule and repression of a kind seen only in the other Ba'athist-controlled state, Syria. The military dictatorship of Qasim lasted only five years; then, after various Ba'athist and then military coups, the country settled down in 1968 to thirty-five years of vicious and frequently genocidal Ba'athist rule. Under Saddam Hussein, who ruled from 1979 to 2003, the country also became involved in war, not just with Kuwait but also in a singularly sanguinary conflict with Iran, in which hundreds of thousands died on both sides. Since after the overthrow of the Shah, Iran was a Shiite theocracy, the West foolishly armed Saddam on the basis that our enemy's enemy is our friend. Once again, Western interference was propping up an unsavory regime—this time one far more vicious than anything Feisal could have contrive, had he even wanted to try.

Worse still, in 1991 when at Western urging, many Iraqis rebelled against Saddam's monstrous rule, thousands more were massacred by a vengeful Saddam, and the rebels were given no effective help by the winning Western coalition. It was perhaps not surprising that it took some while for many of the Shiites, remembering the carnage of 1991, to believe that this time, in 2003, the West really meant business, that they were there to get rid of Saddam once and for all.

Only now is the Shiite majority of Iraq—after centuries of first Ottoman Sunni rule, then Western-imposed Sunni rulers, followed by Sunni military dictatorship—able to be part of a country in which they can have a major say. But this now takes us into the realm of speculation, and that will be my main aim in the Afterword that follows.

A VERY SPECULATIVE AFTERWORD

Murphy's Law—anything that can go wrong, will—applies as much to political analysis as it does to life in general. In late 1989, an esteemed annual international publication confidently predicted that the Romanian Communist dictator, Nicolae Ceausescu, would survive the trend to democracy in the rest of Central and Eastern Europe. A few days after I read that issue, Ceausescu and his wife had not only been deposed, they had been shot by their own people.

Similarly, at an off-the-record briefing in late 2001, I was told that if war broke out between the United States and Iraq, street fighting in Baghdad would result in thousands of *American* casualties. While American lives were—and continue to be—lost in Iraq, that particular prediction was wrong, as the Iraqi capital fell like a house of cards.

As I write this, there is heated debate in Washington, D.C., on who exactly knew what prior to September 11, 2001. Once again, hindsight has proved a wonderful thing.

Finally, in the brief period between my writing the first draft of this Afterword and the final version you are now reading, hundreds of Spaniards were massacred in Madrid, resulting in a change of government in Spain; and large numbers of Shiite Muslims were murdered by Sunni Muslim extremists in both Iraq and Pakistan.

So in writing about Iraq in early 2004, I am on perilous ground. Between the time this book goes to press and the time you read it, anything could happen—and, tragically, well might.

We know that Saddam Hussein has gone and will not be coming back. We can also guess that this time the Shiite majority in Iraq will no longer allow anyone to prevent them from finally achieving power. But beyond that it is dangerous to guess. Furthermore, the planned withdrawal of coalition forces in June lies just ahead, and the results of the 2004 presidential election in the United States, with all the implications they may or may not have for Iraq, will not be known for several months to come.

Ayatollah Muhammad Bakr al-Hakim, who led the major Shiite political organization in Iraq during the Baathist regime, was murdered soon after the regime fell. His brother, Abdul Aziz al-Hakim, is now in a leadership position. Grand Ayatollah Ali al-Sistani has emerged as a powerful presence, the source of the majority Shiite population's legitimacy. As I write this in late March, he has warned that the shared leadership the United States envisions—Kurd, Sunni, and Shia—could lead to a breakup of Iraq. Meanwhile, people like me in the West tend to think this would be a good idea, since much of the violence in Iraq clearly stems from Sunni extremists reluctant to be under the rule of a Shiite majority.

So while many may be pontificating on what will happen after the notional handover of power on June 30, 2004, I remain very cautious in my speculation.

History does, though, give us some clues as to what we might be able to expect.

First, any new Iraqi regime will have the same major problem of *legitimacy* that so hampered the Hashemite period of Iraq from 1921 to 1938. We saw that Feisal and his successors were never really able to shake off their perceived lack of legitimacy in the eyes of their subjects. Ironically—as the debate over the 1922 treaty demonstrated—being seen to oppose the dominant Western power, as Feisal tried to do surreptitiously that year, has been the tactic of choice. It could mean that the only way in which a post-Saddam democracy could be seen to be authentic would be for a newly independent Iraqi government to make policy decisions *against* the United States—say, over Palestine. This would, for many in the West, defeat the whole purpose of getting rid of Saddam in the first place—to install a pro-Western, maybe even pro-Israeli Arab government. Reactions in Washington would therefore be very similar to those in London in the 1920s, where cries claiming ingratitude were heard loud and clear.

But genuine democracy—of a kind the British failed to give Iraq—means the absolute right of the people to make even the *wrong* choice. This may well be, from the Western point of view, what will happen in Iraq. I would not want to speculate on what a majority Shiite government might be like. It could have non-Shiites in it, as a move toward nonpartisan national unity. But Iraq could in time end up with a theocratic regime not entirely dissimilar to the one in Iran. This would have enormous potential human rights consequences for the Sunni Arab and Sunni Kurdish minorities, not to mention the large Christian minority, which is very worried about the prospect of living under a government based on Islamic principles and laws.

We also need to ask if a state as originally artificial as Iraq can continue to exist in its present form in the long run without either a monarch or a despotic military government to hold it together. What will happen if the Kurds, and the Sunni Arabs wish to withdraw from what will be a majority Shiite state?

This issue, of course, begs the question of how people in Iraq today see themselves. One of the surely legitimate criticisms made by Karsh and Karsh is that the new regimes created by the British and French in the 1920s went beyond the boundaries of natural tribal loyalties. This was true of Iraq, but also of the French creation, Lebanon. Here the precedent is not good: Lebanon imploded in the 1970s in a religious civil war, one that was in effect ended only by the imposition of *de facto* Syrian army rule. Lebanon, notionally independent, is in reality a Syrian protectorate.

Again, in between drafts of this Afterword came news of massacres and mosque-burning in Kosovo, with violence between Kosovar Albanians and Serbs. This too is the legacy of the 1918 to 1923 peace settlement and breakup of the old Ottoman Empire. NATO occupation in 1999 was supposed to solve the problem; but, with the exception of Bosnia, which has achieved a good measure of stability, most of the region is four years later clearly as volatile as ever.

Since Iraq is much bigger than Lebanon or Kosovo, less integrated, and more populous (approximately 25 million), any civil war that might occur would therefore be far worse. And now that Iraq is the second-biggest producer of oil after Saudi Arabia, disputes over who controlled the oil resources, in case of a split, could also lead to terrible fighting.

Perhaps the most important imponderable is how Muslim sectarian differences will play out now that the Shiites are no longer a suppressed majority. Will they look to Iran? If they do, will they choose the more moderate path of the reformers or the overtly theocratic way of the ayatollahs?

From the point of view of the West, the 2004 elections in Iran are not encouraging.

The unlikeliest outcome for Iraq would be a split like the so-called "Velvet Divorce" of Czechoslovakia in 1993 into two separate states. But if a genuine sense of Iraqi nationality does arise, along with democracy, then religious differences may end up being seen as less important than loyalty to a newly democratic state, however artificial Iraq's original boundaries may have been. In this scenario religious and ethnic differences, while still important, would be overridden. Shiites would still be Shiites and Kurds would be Kurds, but being Iraqi would be seen as much more integral to identity than anything else. In this case the prognosis for Iraq could be good, since the state would be able to continue without the need for a strongman to keep it from flying apart. The Lebanese and Yugoslav precedents are not good, but there is no reason why Iraq should not be able to silence the doom-mongers and stay together without bloodshed.

It does seem obvious, however, from postliberation events, that there are many among the Sunni community who fear a Shia-dominated Iraq. Worse still, those influenced by the Wahhabi, Saudi-financed form of Islam which Al Qaeda represents do not regard Shia Muslims as genuine members of the Islamic community at all. Furthermore, the Shia, who seem to be the most organized, do not believe in genuine separation of what we in the West call Church and State. Quite how Sunni Arabs and (Sunni) Kurds would fit into such a clericalist-ruled state remains to be seen.

Under Ba'athist rule, all civil society was abolished or forcibly co-opted by the state, so people's actual, genuine allegiances were to either their religion or their tribe, forms of identity that often overlapped. As Efraim and Inari Karsh cogently argue in their book, these are very much local loyalties to groups far smaller than an Iraqi nation-state would be.

We saw what happened in the former Yugoslavia when strong central rule ended with the death of President Tito: the country split into its ethnic and religious component parts, such as Slovenia and Croatia, for example, which then split internally along ethnic and religious lines. The consequence was hundreds of thousands of deaths in Bosnia and Kosovo.

I would love to be proved wrong, but I fear that this is exactly what might happen within the next few years in Iraq. Not only that, but in the same way that there are Albanians in both Kosovo and in Albania proper, there are Kurds not just in Iraq, but in great numbers in Turkey, Iran, and Syria as well. If the Kurdish problem really blows up, there could potentially be conflict on a truly massive and international scale. We in the West would have a strong moral imperative to step in, just as we did successfully in Bosnia in 1995 and in Kosovo in 1999. Self-determination is a great principle but, as the peacemakers of 1918 discovered, it is a double-edged sword, one that could cost the West dearly—in casualties as well as cash.

Also, we ought not to forget about oil, since the Americans of 2004, unlike Churchill, are fully aware of Iraq's vast oil reserves. One can hope that oil will be used to the good and for an effective reconstruction of the country. In an optimistic scenario, a democratic Iraq with the world's second-largest oil reserves would be a powerful beacon of democracy. In a pessimistic alternative, the issue of who gets to control the oil could precipitate civil war. The Arab components of the state would not want most of the oil to fall into Kurdish hands, and since many of the inhabitants of the oil-bearing regions are ethnic Turks (Turkmens or Turcomans), if fighting were to begin, Turkey would also want to have a say. Oil, a blessing, could as easily become a curse.

The oil issue would also make a difference in whether British and American firms get a major part to play in Iraq's reconstruction process. If all goes well, a revived Iraq will remember its friends in the West. If not, the Russians, who held many of the old concessions under Saddam Hussein, could well end up the main beneficiaries of change in Iraq. One thing can be said in favor of the Russians: Because of their own problems in Chechnya, they are as against Islamic extremism as the West is and they would be as unhappy with an extremist Shiite regime in Iraq as we would. On the other hand, as a major oil producer themselves, they would be the first to suggest Russian oil as an alternative to supplies from a Shiite-controlled Iraq.

When it comes to looking at religious issues in general, I think we can say that one of Britain's biggest mistakes in the 1920s, and one that the Coalition is repeating now, was assuming that *nationalism is stronger than religion.* Although Churchill was clearly told the differences between Sunni and Shia, in the end it did not make any difference to what he intended to do: place a Sunni on the throne of predominantly Shia Iraq. King Feisal's

Arab-nationalist credentials may have seemed impeccable, and he was also a proven descendant of the Prophet Muhammad. But in the end, as Iraq's subsequent history tells us, the fact that Feisal was a Sunni Muslim turned out to be more important than his undoubted Arab nationalism.

These potential scenarios all show how difficult it is to predict what will happen next. I can at least be grateful that by the time a contract was signed for this book, Saddam Hussein had been both deposed and apprehended; otherwise it would have become outdated horribly quickly. Much may have changed by the time you read this—I hope for the better. The people of Iraq, whether or not they stay together, deserve the future we in the West denied them in 1921.

Christopher Catherwood
March 2004

BIBLIOGRAPHY

Most of this book has been based upon manuscript sources, the Chartwell Papers at the Churchill Archive Centre at Churchill College Cambridge. I have also in the past used the Chamberlain Papers at the University of Birmingham. Other papers are as quoted in Gilbert's two invaluable *Churchill Companion Volumes* listed below, notably the Lloyd George Papers. I have also used many official documents—those not in the Churchill Archive are in the National Archive in Kew, a suburb of London (the Cabinet Papers and Minutes and the Colonial Office files).

Books

Here are some of the many books worth reading on the subject, and which I have used to write this one.

Abdullah, Thabit. *A Brief History of Iraq* (London: Pearson/Longman, 2003).

Aburish, Said. *Saddam Hussein: The Politics of Revenge* (London: Bloomsbury, 2000).

Asher, Michael. *Lawrence: The Uncrowned King of Arabia* (London: Viking, 1998).

Best, Graham. *Churchill: A Study in Greatness* (London: London and Hambledon, 2001).

Daily Telegraph. *War on Saddam* (London: Robinson, 2003).

Dodge, Tony. *Inventing Iraq* (London: C Hurst & Co., 2003).

Fromkin, David. *A Peace to End All Peace* (New York: Henry Holt, 1989 and Owl Books edition, 2001).

Gilbert, Sir Martin. *Winston S. Churchill vol. IV 1916–1922* (London: Heinemann, 1975).

Gilbert, Sir Martin (ed.), *Companion vol. IV Part 2: July 1919–March 1921* (London: Heinemann, 1977).

Gilbert, Sir Martin (ed.), *Companion vol. IV: Part 3: April 1921–November 1922* (London: Heinemann, 1977).

Goodwin, Jason. *Lords of the Horizons: A History of the Ottoman Empire* (London: Chatto and Windus, 1998).

Hourani, Albert. *A History of the Arab Peoples* (Cambridge. MA: Belknap/Harvard University Press, 1991).

Jenkins, Roy. *Churchill* (London: Macmillan, 2001)

Kaplan, Lawrence, and Kristol, William, *The War over Iraq* (San Francisco: Encounter Books, 2003).

Karsh, Efraim, Karsh, and Inari. *Empires of the Sand* (Cambridge, MA: Harvard University Press, 1999).

Keay, John. *Sowing the Wind: The Seeds of Conflict in the Middle East* (London: John Murray, 2003).

Kedourie, Elie. *The Chatham House Version and Other Middle-Eastern Studies* (London: Weidenfeld and Nicolson, 1970).

Keegan, John. *Churchill* (London: Weidenfeld and Nicolson and New York: Viking Penguin, 2002).

Kleiman, Aaron. *Foundations of British Policy in the Arab World: The Cairo Conference of 1921* (Baltimore: Johns Hopkins University Press, 1970).

Lewis, Bernard. *The Middle East* (London: Weidenfeld and Nicolson, 1995).

Lewis, Bernard. *The Multiple Identities of the Middle East* (London: Weidenfeld and Nicoloson, 1998).

MacMillan, Margaret. *Peacemakers* (London: John Murray, 2001). Published in the USA as *Paris 1919.*

McCarthy, Justin. *The Ottoman Peoples and the End of Empire* (London: Arnold, 2001.

Mango, Andrew. *Ataturk* (London: John Murray, 1999).

McDowall, David. *A Brief History of the Kurds* (London: IB Tauris, 1997).

Palmer, Alan. *The Decline and Fall of the Ottoman Empire* (London: John Murray, 1992).

Sachar, Howard. *The Emergence of the Middle East* (New York: Alfred A. Knopf, 1969).

Simons, Geoff *Iraq: From Sumer to Post-Saddam,* 3rd edition (Basingstoke and New York: Palgrave, 2004).

Simpson, John. *Wars Against Saddam: The Hard Road to Baghdad* (London: Macmillan, 2003)

Sluglett, Peter. *Britain in Iraq 1914–1932* (Oxford and London: The Middle East Centre of St Anthony's College Oxford/Ithica Press, 1976).

Sluglett, Peter. and Farouk-Sluglett, Marion, *Iraq since 1958* (London: IB Tauris, 1990).

Tarbush, Mohammad. *The Role of the Military in Politics: A Case Study of Iraq to 1941* (London: KPI, 1982).

Tripp, Charles. *A History of Iraq* (Cambridge UK: Cambridge University Press, 2000; paperback 2002).

Winstone, H. V. F. *Gertrude Bell* (London: Constable, 1993).

Articles

I must have read thousands of these. Of those easily available, I found articles by Fouad Ajami in *US News and World Report*, Thomas Friedman in the *New York Times*, Seymour Hersh in the *New Yorker*, John Keegan in the *Daily Telegraph*, Bernard Lewis in *Foreign Affairs*, and Fareed Zakaria in *Newsweek* all by far the most helpful. What follows is a small selection of other articles I have found useful. Note: of those I found through Gale Group Info Trac online (through the University of Richmond) I can cite only the journal date, as the service does not give page numbers.

Ajami, Fouad. "Iraq and the Arabs' Future." *Foreign Affairs* 82:1 January–February 2003.

Baram, Amatzia. "Neo Tribalism in Iraq: Saddam Hussein's Tribal Policies 1991–1996." *International Journal of Middle Eastern Studies* 29:1, February 1997: 1–31.

Commins, David. "Religious Reformers and Arabists in Damascus 1885–1914." *International Journal of Middle Eastern Studies* 18:4 November 1986: 405–425.

Eppel, Michael. "The Fahdil Al-Jamali Government in Iraq." *Journal of Contemporary History* 34:3, July 1999: 417–442.

Karsh, Efraim. "Military Power and Foreign Policy Goals: The Iran–Iraq War Revisited." *International Affairs* 64:1 Winter 1987–1988: 83-95.

Khalidi, Rashid. "Arab Nationalism: Historical Problems in the Literature." *American Historical Review* 96:5 December 1991: 1363–1373.

Longrigg, S.H. "New Groupings among the Arab States." *International Affairs* 34:3 July 1958: 305–317.

Lustick, Ian S. "The Absence of Middle East Great Powers." *International Organisation* 51:4, Autumn 1997: 653–683.

Nakash, Yizhak. "The Conversion of Iraq's Tribes to Shiism." *International Journal of Middle Eastern Studies* 26:3, August 1994: 443–463.

Neff, Donald. "The US, Iraq, Israel and Iran: Backdrop to War." *Journal of Palestine Studies* 20:4 Summer 1991 23–4 1.

Peretz, Martin. "The Pan-Arab Fantasy: The Man Who Would Be Nasser." *New Republic* 203:10, September 3, 1990.

Pfaff, Richard. "The Function of Arab Nationalism." *Comparative Politics* 2:2 January 1970: 147–167.

Pryce-Jones, David. "Remember Suez: Nasser and the Canal; Saddam and Today." *National Review* 55:1 March 10, 2003.

Shatz, Adam. "The Native Informant." *The Nation* 276:15 April 28 2003.

Sluglett, Peter, and Farouk-Sluglett, Marion. "The Historiography of Modern Iraq." *American Historical Review* 96: 5 December 1991 1408–1421.

Smith, Charles. "The Invention of a Tradition." *Journal of Palestine Studies* 22:2 Winter 1993: 48–61—*key reading on the McMahon–Hussein/Husayn correspondence.*

United States Institute of Peace Special Report No. 98, January 2003. *Would an Invasion of Iraq Be a "Just War"?*

United States Institute of Peace Special Report No. 104, April 2003 *Establishing the Rule of Law in Iraq.*

Yapp, M.E. "Two Great British Historians of the Modern Middle East." *Bulletin of the School of Oriental and African Studies* 58:1, 1995: 40–49.

NOTES

Chapter 1: From Abraham to Allenby

1. The secondary sources I have used as the historical basis for this chapter are all listed in the bibliography at the end of the book. In particular, the books by Geoff Simons and by the late and deeply missed Sir Robert Rhodes James proved invaluable in writing this chapter.

36. Lloyd George was nicknamed "the Goat" on account of his insatiable sexual appetite—he was a notorious womanizer—and by the time he moved into 10 Downing Street as Prime Minister, he had a full-time mistress, Frances Stevenson, whom he installed there officially as his secretary. Like John F. Kennedy later on, he was fortunate in that the press barons of his time did not report his shenanigans. Such a public and very libidinous career would be unthinkable today.

37. Not everyone was taken in by Lloyd George; his eye doctor and fellow Welshman in London, Tomas Phillips, knew the full truth, as did Phillips's beautiful medical student daughter, Bethan, who was one of the few women who did not get to know Lloyd George as well as he would have liked. She was to marry a fellow doctor, Martyn Lloyd-Jones, later a famous preacher, who at this time spent much of his spare time in the Public Gallery of the House of Commons watching his heroes, Lloyd George and Churchill, in debate. Martyn and Bethan are my maternal grandparents, so while I cannot say, as the famous ditty has it, "Lloyd George knew my father, father knew Lloyd George," many of my family certainly did, and they followed in the greatest detail the events described in this book.

40. Here, in passing, is an interesting interpretation of what Britain was trying to do in 1917: capture the Arab world *and* grant the Jews a

homeland, all at the same time. While Lloyd George was heavily influenced by the same kind of Christian pro-Zionist thinking that prevails in much of the United States today, that was hardly the case with his philosophical, worldly, and essentially secular Foreign Secretary Lord Balfour. It was Balfour's infamous Declaration to Lord Rothschild in 1917 that proclaimed the fulfillment of the Zionist dream. But a large Jewish presence in Palestine, granted by Britain, would make it far more difficult for France to rule over the area after Allied victory, even though most of Palestine was allocated to France under Sykes-Picot. So one can fairly argue that it was in part Britain's desire to undo the damage done to British interests by Sykes-Picot that led to the creation of a British-sponsored Jewish homeland, with all the many consequences that that decision has had since.

Chapter 2: The Arab Revolt and the Great Betrayal

43. There are many discrepancies between reality and fiction in a recent blockbuster, *Braveheart,* for example. The real William Wallace never met Isabel of France and was executed years before the birth of the future King Edward III.

46. The most notorious of Lawrence's inventions is his story of sneaking into an enemy-held city and being captured, then raped by a sadistic Ottoman official. In all likelihood, this scene is total fiction. So, too, is the story of how he went back through a sandstorm to rescue a lost member of a raiding party; at least one of his biographers, Michael Asher, now believes this to be either considerable exaggeration or pure invention. Lawrence was always having to prove himself against inner demons or giving imaginary vent to masochistic and probably homoerotic fantasies, and biographers such as Michael Asher feel that Lawrence's psyche probably prompted him to invent the mythical scenes in the book rather than try to record actual events.

47. The newspaper we choose to read is often based on our political beliefs, whether it is the *Guardian* or the *Daily Telegraph,* or the *New York Times* or the *Wall Street Journal.* Even in television news, whether we watch CNN

or Fox News (or whatever the equivalent is in our own country), tells us that facts are more than just facts; they are matters of opinion.

54. In this chapter there is only one direct quotation from one of the many works written on this controversial area: Fromkin, *A Peace to End All Peace,* p. 219. But I have used Fromkin's book extensively for background detail, especially pp. 218–228. I have used Karsh and Karsh, *Empires,* as well, particularly pp. 185–221. Michael Asher's biography, *Lawrence,* was also invaluable.

55. This is exactly what Turkey did in 1939, carefully not joining the winning side until early 1945, when it was beyond doubt that the Allies would beat Hitler. (This was despite five years of pleading by Britain—and later the United States—that Turkey join them, done by none other than the wartime Prime Minister, Winston Churchill.) The Turks could equally have made the same choice in 1914, or at least they could have waited until they were sure that one side was bound to win—instead, they made exactly the mistake that the Italian dictator Mussolini made in siding with Hitler in 1940.

Chapter 3: How Two Men in London Changed the World

63. I have used many of the books listed in the bibliography for this chapter, in addition to those with page references cited here. The books cited are therefore my principal source but not necessarily my only published source of the information in this chapter. In addition, I have made extensive use of the Churchill Archives, those that are pre-1945 now known as the Chartwell Papers.

63. "Well, what are we . . . about Mosul": MacMillan, *Peacemakers,* pp. 392–393, Margaret MacMillan's fascinating and insightful unraveling of this complex issue.

64. Mosul *vilayet*: McDowall, *A Brief History,* pp. 115–146, superb and detailed background on this entire area.

64. Sykes-Picot: Fromkin, *Peace to End,* pp. 189–196, a most useful and invaluable account.

66. Mosul's oil potential: *Keary, Sowing the Wind,* pp. 122–129, what I think is the best summary of all the business of Iraq's oil history.

65. Colonial expansion lobby: *Peacemakers,* pp. 395–397.

66. "Kurdistan": *Modern History,* pp. 115–146.

66. David McDowall's book *A Brief History of the Kurds* details Britain's many unsuccessful attempts to create a Kurdish homeland and examines how Britain dealt with the 1920 rebellion in the Kurdish-speaking areas.

66. Here I agree with . . . *Middle East":* Keay, *Sowing the Wind, pp.* 124–129.

66. "sole oil . . . 1927": Keay, *Sowing the Wind,* p. 129.

67. "oil is the . . . security": quoted in Sluglett, *Britain in Iraq,* p. 107, one of the best possible scholarly accounts of the details of British policy from 1914 to 1932.

67. "The daily press . . . and the USA": *Ibid.,* p. 107.

67. "It is not . . . promising": *Ibid.,* p. 106.

68. "under permanent British control": *Ibid.,* p. 108.

68. "There is some . . . Company": *Ibid.,* p. 109.

68. "was not until . . . Iraq": Keay, *Sowing the Wind,* pp. 124–129.

68. Smyrna: Gilbert, *Winston S. Churchill, Vol. IV,* p. 472.

69. After World War Two, the United States, thankfully, stayed engaged with the rest of the globe, and part of Churchill's genius was to realize that it was now unquestionably the world's leading power. But this was not the case after World War One, and there were still many who believed that Britain ruled the waves then. Churchill was realistic about imperial overreach even in 1919—unless it was a case of fighting the Bolsheviks—and this dominated his thinking and formed his policy. In the more brutal postwar world, the British Empire would have to cut its cloak according to its cloth—and there was not a lot of cloth. Keay, *Sowing the Wind,* p. 129.

69. "The responsibilities . . . to maintain": Churchill to Lloyd George: (CAB 24/106, National Archive, Kew).

70. "we have maintained . . . unsupportable": Churchill to Balfour, 12 August 1919 (Chartwell Papers, 16/10).

70. Murmansk: There is an enormous amount of correspondence on this in the Churchill Archives, all helpfully spelled out by Sir Martin Gilbert's official biography. Here I have quoted from just one letter: Churchill to Sir Henry Wilson, 29 August 1919 (Chartwell 16/17).

70. "There can be . . . by Great Britain": Churchill to General George McMunn, 31 August 1919 (Chartwell 16/17).

71. "so obsessed . . . expenditure": Lloyd George to Churchill, 22 September 1919 (Chartwell 16/11).

71. "unkind" and "unjust" . . ."criticisms": Churchill to Lloyd George, 22 September 1919 (Chartwell 16/11). This letter was written on Turf Club notepaper!

72. "I asked . . . Mesopotamia": Churchill to General McMunn, 25 September 1919 (WO 32/5227, National Archives).

73. "greatest Mahommedan. . . ." "India . . . gravest kind": Churchill Cabinet Memorandum (Chartwell 16/18).

74. save money: for example, Churchill to Austen Chamberlain, Chancellor of the Exchequer, 30 October 1919 (Chartwell 16/18).

76. Churchill saw: Churchill Cabinet note, 6 January 1920 (Chartwell 16/51).

77. Army estimates: All quotations from Churchill Cabinet Memorandum, 7 February 1920 (Chartwell 16/54).

75. "In Mesopotamia . . . in the future": General Radcliffe to Sir Henry Wilson, 9 February 1920 (WO 32/5227, National Archive).

75. I have followed the account of Churchill's concerns in Fromkin, *Peace to End,* pp. 433–437.

76. In view of later controversies in which Britain, along with France, is supposed to have betrayed Arab-nationalist aspirations after 1918, it is significant that Lloyd George privately approved Feisal's actions. But as British troops were withdrawing from the Syrian mandate area, and as French controlled Algerian forces were now arriving, there was not much Britain could actually do to support Feisal's aspirations.

76. On 1 April . . . "which is not ruinous": quotations from Churchill to Haldane, 1 April 1920, Gilbert, *IV/2*, pp. 1063–1064.

76–78. "attention . . . effected . . . the result . . . Colonial Office . . . mounting up": all taken from Churchill Cabinet Memorandum in CAB 24/106 (National Archive).

78. fatal decision: Fromkin, *Peace to End*, p. 410–411, but my own interpretation.

79. instinctive Zionism: Gilbert, *Churchill IV*, pp. 485–486 and 568–569.

80. "This hostility . . . run together": *Ibid.*, pp. 488–489.

80. Gilbert's assessment of Churchill at this time is vindicated by copious evidence from Churchill's own papers. But what he does not expand on is an interesting irony of Churchill's career: that in the 1920s, finance was forcing Churchill into a policy of appeasement ("unless Turkey were *appeased*". [my italics]), though he later staunchly opposed appeasement of Nazi Germany. Ironic, too, that Churchill's rationale in the 1920s was exactly the same as that of his arch political foe, Neville Chamberlain, in the 1930s—money.

81. summer of 1920: Tripp, *A History of Iraq*, pp. 40–45.

81. "Next are we . . . made good": Churchill to Lloyd George, 13 June 1920 (Chartwell 16/47).

81–82. "withdraw everywhere . . . in Mesopotamia": Churchill Cabinet Memorandum, 15 June 1920 (Chartwell 16/54).

82. "the despatch . . . good lesson": Wilson diary, 15 July 1920, from Gilbert, *IV/2*, p. 1143.

82. "wild wire": 16 July, *ibid.*

82–83. When General Coningham's . . . soldiers: Gilbert, *Churchill IV,* p. 291.

83. Not until 30 July . . . rebels: Wilson diary, in Gilbert, *IV/2,* p. 1152.

83. A. T. Wilson . . . rescue: See Keay, *Sowing the Wind,* p. 151, for an account that is most sympathetic to Wilson and what he was trying to achieve in Iraq.

83. "I have not . . . real one": Churchill to Lloyd George, 5 August 1920, in Gilbert *IV/2,* p. 1161.

83. Sir Percy . . . to Baghdad: Wilson diary, in Gilbert, *IV/2,* p. 1164.

84. Cabinet Finance Committee: For the many quotations from this document on 6 August 1920, see CAB 27/71 (National Archive).

84. "With regard . . . end November": Churchill to Lloyd George, 26 August 1920 (Chartwell 2/110).

85. "The Cabinet have decided . . . better situation": Churchill to Haldane, 26 August 1920 (Chartwell 16/34).

85. "I think . . . upon them": Churchill to Trenchard, 29 August 1920 (Chartwell 16/52).

85. more recent commentators: for example, the eminent BBC journalist John Simpson in some of his broadcasts during the 2003 conflict.

86. "we are . . . single soldier": Churchill to Curzon, 31 August 1920, quoted in Gilbert, *IV/2,* p. 1197.

86. "Churchill . . . did not send": All quotations from this long, fascinating, and unsent letter are from Churchill to Lloyd George (not sent), 31 August 1920 (Chartwell 16/48).

89. As one historian . . . 1915: notably Sir Martin Gilbert: Gilbert, *Churchill IV,* p. 497.

89. Wilson's failure: Fromkin, *Peace to End,* p. 398; again, my own interpretation.

90. "very unpleasant": Churchill to Lloyd George, 10 November 1920 (Chartwell 16/50).

90. "An opportunity . . . so many years": Churchill Cabinet Memorandum, 23 November 1920 (Chartwell 16/53).

91. "sorry how far" . . . "sea supremacy" . . . "in the war": all quotations from Churchill to Lloyd George, 4 December 1920 (Chartwell 2/111).

91. on 13 December . . . British control: Gilbert, *Churchill IV*, p. 504.

92. on the 15th: all quotations from Gilbert, *Churchill IV*, pp. 504–505, quoting in turn from *Hansard*, the official record of House of Commons debates.

93–94. "Our own military" . . . "Mohammedan feeling": Churchill Cabinet Memorandum, 16 December 1920 (Chartwell 16/53).

94. On 31 December . . . Churchill: Cabinet minutes of that day, (CAB 23/23, National Archive).

Chapter 4: Churchill and the Forty Thieves

95. Overall note: Sir Martin Gilbert's *Churchill*, volume IV, pp. 507–530, looks at much of the same material I have, though my conclusions on the identical archive material are often different.

95. "difficult & embarrassing": Churchill to Lord Curzon, 8 January 1921 (Curzon Papers).

95–96. "It is impossible" . . . "our efforts": Churchill to Sir Percy Cox, 8 January 1921 (Chartwell 17/16).

96. "know the position" . . . "in the Cabinet": Curzon to Churchill, 9 January 1921 (Chartwell 17/2).

96–97. "Do you think" . . . "should be framed": Churchill to Cox, 12 January 1921 (Chartwell 17/16).

97. "a strong feeling" . . . "mock turtle": Churchill to Curzon, 12 January 1921 (Chartwell 17/26).

97. "pretty much . . . territories": Churchill to Lloyd George, Curzon, and Lords Harding and D'Abernon, 12 January 1921 (Chartwell 16/71).

98. "I need . . . Ireland": Churchill to Archbishop of Tuam, 14 December 1920 (Chartwell 2/111).

98. The irony of Churchill's earlier policy is all the greater because his arguments in the 1920s were the same as Neville Chamberlain's a decade later: Britain's defense and foreign policy had to be based firmly on what was financially feasible.

98. "greatest Mohammedan" . . . "Greeks": Churchill Cabinet Memorandum (Chartwell 16/53).

99. "and a reconciled . . . Middle East": Churchill to Lord Derby, 21 December 1920 (Chartwell 2/111).

99–100. "the same boat" . . . " the war": WSC to Lloyd George, Curzon, etc., *ibid.* (Chartwell 17/71).

99–100. "all one" . . . "Arabian triangle": Churchill to Lloyd George, 12 January 1921 (Chartwell 17/2). When Churchill became Prime Minister in 1940, this was a lesson he took very much to heart, making himself his own Minister of Defence and thus politically in charge of all British defense policy.

1060. Morin: Major G. J. P. Geiger to Sir Archibald Sinclair, 13 January 1921 (Chartwell 16/75).

100. "utter impossibility" . . . "expenditure": Churchill to Lloyd George, 14 January 1921 (Chartwell 17/2).

101. "want more . . . not less": see Cox to Churchill, 13 January 1921, and Churchill to Cox, 16 January 1921(Chartwell 17/16).

101. begging letters: Churchill to Lloyd George, 14 January 1921 (Chartwell 17/2).

101. stop him resigning: Cox to Churchill, 13 January 1921 (Chartwell 17/16).

101. "right to . . . spot": Churchill to Cox, 16 January 1921 (Chartwell 17/16).

101. "out to" . . . "for him": Curzon to Churchill, 17, January 1921 (Chartwell 17/2).

101–102. Lawrence got in touch . . . "speed of settlement": Lawrence to Edward Marsh, 17 January 1921 (all quotations in Chartwell 17/14).

102. Churchill now discovered: Edwin Montagu to Churchill, 18 January 1921 (Chartwell 2/114).

102. "a bottomless pit" . . . "extravagant": Sir Arthur Hirtzel (India Office) to Churchill, 19 January 1921 (Chartwell 17/2).

103. "Please telegraph . . . useful": Churchill to Haldane, 19 January 1921 (Chartwell 17/16).

103. "violently anti-Turk" . . . "Greek stunt": quoted from Montagu to Churchill, 18 January 1921 (Chartwell 2-114).

103–104. "I will never" . . . "window": Sir Henry Wilson to Congreve, 20 January 1921, Gilbert, *IV/2*, p. 1317.

104. Churchill told Wilson: *Ibid.*, p. 1319.

104. he wanted maps: Churchill memo to Hirtzel, 23 January 1921 (Chartwell 17/17).

112. "his own caprice": Churchill memo to Hirtzel, 23 January 1921 (Chartwell 17/14).

105. "I had not appreciated" . . . "will suffice": Churchill memo to Hirtzel, 23 January 1921 (Chartwell 17/14).

107. "the man is a fool": Wilson diary, Gilbert, *IV/2*, p. 1327.

107. "attitude . . . long experience": Churchill to Sir Laming Worthington-Evans, Secretary of State for War, 27 January 1921 (Chartwell 17/13).

107. "native" . . . "by expense": Churchill to Haldane, 28 January 1921 (Chartwell 17/16).

107. verbal war . . . Prime Minister: Churchill to Lloyd George, 25 January 1921 (Chartwell 2/114).

107. As Roy Jenkins . . . mercurial: Jenkins, *Churchill,* pp. 345–348, 352.

108. one of his officials . . . "Mesopotamia.": Churchill to Hirtzel, 23 January 1921 (Chartwell 17/14).

1108–109. As Churchill wrote . . . "present year.": all quotations from Churchill to Lloyd George, 25 January 1921 (Chartwell 17/2).

109. "agreeable . . . as usual": Churchill to Clementine Churchill, 6 February 1921, Gilbert, *IV/2,* p. 1333.

109. "forty thieves": because there were forty full-time British officials asked to be present in Cairo.

109. "First, the new . . . administered": Churchill to Cox, 7 February 1921 (Chartwell 17/1).

110. "great deal . . . money": Churchill to Haldane, 7 February 1921 (Chartwell 17/16).

110. "got to pay . . . Baghdad?": Churchill to Hirtzel, 8 February 1921 (Chartwell 16/73).

110. subsidy: Churchill to Hirtzel and Young, 8 February 1921 (Chartwell 17/15).

110–111. "I know full . . . Curzon": Lord Rawlinson to Churchill, 10 February 1921 (Chartwell 17/2).

111. key staff appointments: Churchill to Sir James Masterton Smith, Ministry of Labour, 13 February 1921 (Chartwell 17/15).

111. "Are you sure . . . weighed this": Masterton-Smith to Churchill, 14 February 1921 (Chartwell 17/15).

111. "long wrangle . . . interest": H. A. L. Fisher diary (Fisher Papers), 14 February 1921.

112. "Asiatic Foreign Secretary": Lord Curzon to Lady Curzon, 14 February 1921, Curzon Papers.

112. "what they would . . . of the mandate": Churchill Cabinet Minutes, 10 February 1921 (Chartwell 16/73).

113. some of the officials: Keay, *Sowing the Wind,* pp. 130–133.

113. "friendly state" . . . "destroyed": Cabinet Minutes, 14 February 1921, CAB 23/24, National Archive.

113. "put on . . . collar": Churchill to Clementine Churchill, 16 February 1921, Gilbert, *IV/2,* pp. 1354–1356.

113. Churchill covered his bases: Churchill to Curzon, 16 February 1921 (Chartwell 17/2).

113. "Lawrence . . . intrigue": Curzon to Churchill, 16 February 1921 (Chartwell 17/2).

114. "all chance . . . destroyed": *Ibid.*

114. Soviet threat: Churchill memorandum to Curzon, Worthington-Evans, and Montagu, 18 February 1921 (Chartwell 17/15).

114. "terribly wasteful": Churchill to Sir Herbert Creedy, 18 February 1921 (Chartwell 17/15).

114. special dockets: Churchill to Sir George Fiddes, 17 February 1921 (Chartwell 17/1).

115. "getting rather . . . with them": Churchill to Clementine Churchill, 21 February 1921, Gilbert, *IV/2,* pp. 1367–1368.

115. "given great . . . naturally": Lord Allenby to Curzon, 21 February 1921 (Curzon Papers).

115–116. "six days . . . positions to be held": Churchill memorandum to Shuckburgh, 18 February 1921 (Chartwell 17/18).

116. "but South Persia . . . effort": Churchill to Curzon, Worthington-Evans, and Montagu, *ibid.*

128. "Divisions . . . terribly wasteful": Churchill to Creedy, (Chartwell 17/15).

117–18. "that our Eastern" . . . "genius and work": Churchill to Lloyd George, 22 February 1921 (Chartwell 22/5).

121. "In undertaking" . . . "greatly hampered": all quotations from Churchill to Sir George Ritchie, 23 February 1921 (Chartwell 5/24). The parts in [square brackets] were omitted by Churchill in the final draft that he sent to Sir George. But as they reveal his thinking, I have left them in. My comments are in {curly braces}.

125. "Winston is quite . . . things he does": Wilson diary, 19 February 1921, Gilbert, *IV/2*, p. 1366.

121–24. As always, the French . . . "point of view": All quotations from this meeting on 24 February 1921 in Chartwell 17/15. As in a similar dispute over Iraq eighty years later, the French stood in complete opposition to what Britain wanted to do.

125. "It is . . . all important . . . part of it": Churchill to Lloyd George, 28 February 1921 (Chartwell 17/18).

125. As some historians: McDowall, *A Brief History*, pp. 151–159.

126. "knowledge and experience . . . Arab question.": Churchill to Allenby, 28 February 1921 (Chartwell 17/18).

Chapter 5: Changing the Map: The Cairo Conference of 1921

Note to readers: As with the other chapters, I have used several books in writing this chapter, in addition to the many documents at Churchill College. Probably the best academic books are those by Sluglett and Sachar (listed in the bibliography), but these are, alas, probably only available at specialist libraries. Therefore, in these notes, I have cited the primary accessible sources.

127. "a marble . . . is here.": T. E. Lawrence to Bob Lawrence, 20 March 1921, quoted in Gilbert, IV/2, p. 1405.

127. Jessie Raven: I am grateful to her grandson, Denis Alexander, for his memories; those given here are from Gilbert, *Churchill IV*.

128. "when things . . . the garden": Gilbert, *Churchill IV*, p. 557.

128. airmen had good news: *Ibid.*, pp. 544–545.

128. two committees . . . the military: *Ibid.*, pp. 544–557, in Sir Martin's chapter on the Cairo Conference. Unfortunately, the minutes are not in the Chartwell Papers, so my quotations from them are those made by Sir Martin Gilbert for the official biography. To photocopy the Colonial Office and Foreign Office copies in the National Archive would have been prohibitively expensive (they are hundreds of pages long), but those with time and money can see them in the CO and FO 371 archives at the National Archive in Kew.

128. *Empires of the Sand*, pp. 308–312 and 317–320.

130. "Colonel Lawrence . . . dominating": Gilbert, *Churchill IV*, p. 545.

130. "*The Chairman* . . . Abdullah": *Ibid.*

131. "that Feisal . . . solution": Churchill to Lloyd George, 14 March 1921 (Chartwell 17/18).

131. Sayyid Talib: Karsh and Karsh, *Empires*, p. 312; Keay, *Sowing the Wind*, pp. 153–154 and 158–159.

132. "In response . . . their support": Churchill to Lloyd George, 14 March 1921 (Chartwell 17/18).

132. Strictly speaking, the two issues were not at all interrelated. But we can use a more recent analogy. For example, in the 1990s, Britain agreed to the German request for the European Union to recognize Bosnian independence in return for German backing that would allow the United Kingdom to opt out of the Social Chapter clauses of the latest EU treaty.

132. "On this . . . of April": Churchill to Lloyd George, 14 March 1921 (Chartwell 17/18).

132. "method . . . separate": *Ibid.*

133. "I have . . . formula": *Ibid.*

133. The cost-cutting . . . session: Gilbert, *Churchill IV,* pp. 546–547.

134. "emphasised . . . year": *Ibid.,* p. 547. If one can substitute "Presidential election" for "new financial year," the strong similarities between 1921 and 2003–2004 do become rather obvious.

134. "military commanders . . . as possible": *Ibid.*

134. Trenchard: *Ibid.,* pp. 547–548.

135. "Incredible waste . . . pure waste": Churchill to Lloyd George, 14 March 1921 (Chartwell 17/18).

135. *New York Times:* I am grateful to Philip Turner for telling me of *New York Times* articles on this subject.

135. London *Times:* for example, Simon Jenkins, 3 March 2004.

135. Kurdish people: Churchill to Lloyd George, 16 March 1921, "Policy in Kurdistan" (Chartwell, 17/18).

135–36. "that it might . . . interests": and other quotations, gilbert, *Churchill IV,* pp. 548–549.

137. telegraphed Lloyd George . . . "military": Churchill to Lloyd George, 16 March 1921, "Kurdistan" (Chartwell 17/18).

137. the vital necessity . . . to India: and quotations, Gilbert, *Churchill IV,* pp. 550–551.

138. "subsidies and commitments": *Ibid.,* pp. 551–552.

139. The truth . . . and Syria: Karsh and Karsh *Empires,* p. 311.

140. Lawrence had served . . . 1920: Cornwallis was to spend most of the next twenty-five years in Iraq, fourteen as the real power in the nominally independent Iraqi Ministry of the Interior, and then eleven years as Ambassador to Britain up until 1945.

140. The Sub-Committee . . . Ibn Saud: Their hope that the grant to Ibn Saud would deter the marauding Ikhwan troops was unfulfilled. Within three years, only Yemen was left independent, with the rest of the Arabian peninsula under British protection or Saudi rule. Hussein, meanwhile, would get his money, provided he did not allow Mecca "to become a focus for anti-British or pan-Islamic intrigue." Following its conquest three years later by Ibn Saud, it became the latter, as it has been ever since. See Churchill to Lloyd George, 20 March 1921 (Chartwell 17/13).

140. "Mr. Churchill . . . seen no more": Gilbert, *Churchill IV,* pp. 552–555, for an account of Sir Herbert Samuel's talks with Churchill in Cairo.

140. The Cartwell Papers . . . petitions: (Chartwell 17).

140–141. "arrived at" . . . "of Zionism": Gilert, *Churchill IV,* pp. 552–555, for a very helpful summary of the discussion.

141. It "would be" . . . in Transjordan: see Karsh and Karsh, *Empires,* pp. 314–325 and *Churchill IV,* pp. 558–575, for full and detailed descriptions.

141. "It was his view . . . other alternative": Gilbert, *Churchill IV,* p. 553.

141. Wyndham Deedes: Deedes's son, the journalist Bill, is famous for being the recipient of the famous and fictitious "Dear Bill" letters ostensibly from Sir Denis Thatcher. He is also the model of the naïve young journalist in Evelyn Waugh's well-known novel *Scoop.* The British Establishment continues from generation to generation. . . .

143. "three days . . . by default": Gilbert, *Churchill IV,* p. 555.

143. as Efraim and Inari Karsh: Karsh and Karsh, *Empires,* pp. 1–6.

143. Martin Gilbert: see *Churchill IV,* pp. 576–599, for a fascinating account.

143. David Fromkin: in Peace to End, pp. 15–20, which accords very much with my own view.

144. "expense . . . commitment": Wilson diary, 22 March 1921, in Gilbert, *IV/2,* p. 1406.

145. "One of . . . laughed at": T. E. Lawrence to Bob Lawrence, 20 March 1921, in *ibid.*, p. 1405.

146. This was . . . Churchill's detractors: for example, Wilson diary, 19 March 1921, in *ibid.*, p. 1404.

146. Churchill's telegram to Lloyd George: Churchill to Lloyd George, 19 March 1921 (Chartwell 17/18); 20 March 1921 (Chartwell 17/13).

146. "telegraph . . . Iraq": Churchill to Lloyd George, 19 March 1921 (Chartwell 17/15).

147. "We think" . . . in Iraq": all from *ibid.*

147. (The Naqib's . . . in 1920): From in *Peace to End,* pp. 507–508.

148. "It is anticipated" . . . "leaves Cairo": Churchill to Lloyd George, 16 March 1921 (Chartwell 17/15).

148. As David McDowall . . . argues: *A History,* pp. 137–139.

149–150. "Acting on . . . our territory": *Policy in Kurdistan,* Churchill to Lloyd George, 16 March 1921 (Chartwell 17/15).

150. as David McDowall points out: *A Brief History,* pp. 115–180, for what must be the definitive account of the subject.

150–151. "we have repeatedly . . . this matter" . . . "Should fighting . . . arm the Greeks": all quotations from Churchill to Lloyd George, 16 March 1921 (Chartwell 17/15).

151–152. "We are fully . . . will occur" . . . "As an instance . . . workable policy": all quotations from Churchill to Lloyd George, 18 March 1921, (Chartwell 17/19).

153. Talib was no saint: *Peace to End,* p. 508; Franklin, Karsh and Karsh, *Empires,* pp. 177–179 (for background) and pp. 312–313.

153–155. "Among Shereefians . . . system" . . . "Moreover . . . Transjordania" . . . "but this will . . . a community" . . . "I could not help . . . not sought": all quotations from Churchill to Lloyd George, 18 March 1921 (Chartwell 17/19).

155. "we have no doubt . . . own ends" . . . "Much intrigue . . . of candidature": all quotations from Churchill to Lloyd George, 21 March 1921 (Chartwell 17/18).

156. *empire lite:* a phrase that has been made known by the human rights writer and academic Michael Ignatieff, to whom I am grateful for it.

156–157. "devoted exhaustive consideration" . . . "They were much . . . attack the French" . . . "Your remark . . . act accordingly" . . . "Your proposals . . . Anatolian state": all from Lloyd George to Churchill, 22 March 1921 (Chartwell 17/18).

158. "an Arab rather than a Palestinian solution": Gilbert, *Churchill IV,* pp. 558–575 and 615–662 for a full and fascinating account.

158–159. Churchill . . . with Lloyd George . . . "not clear . . . to him quietly": all quotations from Churchill to Lloyd George, 23 March 1921 (Chartwell 17/1).

159. "things have gone . . . in the press": T. E. Lawrence to Feisal, 23 March 1921 (Chartwell 17/18).

Chapter 6: Winston's Bridge

Note: I am particularly grateful for the excellent work done by Sir Martin Gilbert for much of the material in this chapter, and to the excellent references in the books by Sluglett and Sachar, who have done invaluable work in the Colonial Office archives.

161. "cross like a bear": Austen Chamberlain to his sister Hilda, 8 May 1921 (Chamberlain Papers, Birmingham University).

161. Frances Stevenson: Frances Stevenson's diary, 25 April 1921, quoted in Gilbert, *IV/3,* p. 1451.

162–163. "fed up" . . . "He is . . . or three years" . . . "Churchill is not . . . as possible . . . ". . . "At lunch . . . possible point": Marlowe memorandum for Lord Northcliffe (*Times* Archives).

163. Sayyid Talib: karsh and Karsh, *Empires,* pp. 312–313.

163. "to await . . . elections": Churchill to Cox, 5 July 1921 (CO 730/3, National Archives).

164. "All this seems . . . result" . . . "There is also . . . their place" . . . "(1) To get . . . under Arabs": Churchill note to Shuckburgh, 9 July 1921, in CO 730/3. (Gilbert's biography says the recipient is Sir Archibald Sinclair, *Churchill IV,* p. 798.)

165. "main thing . . . Feisal": Churchill to Cox, 9 July 1921 (Chartwell 17/16).

165. "If our policy . . . garrison there": Churchill to Sir Laming Worthington-Evans, 15 July 1921 (Chartwell 17/7).

165. "sad case . . . poacher": Gilbert, *Churchill IV,* p. 800.

166. "Feisal . . . conditions": Haldane to Churchill, 23 July 1921, quoted in Gilbert, *Churchill IV,* p. 800.

166. "now really feared": *Ibid.*

166–167. "incredible figure" . . . "there was . . . my accepting" . . . "Desperately anxious . . . consent to do": Churchill to Cox, 2 August 1921 (Chartwell 17/16).

167. "wanted to go . . . Air Force": Churchill to Worthington-Evans, 2 August 1921 (Chartwell 17/8).

167. "I consider . . . estimate": Churchill to Cox, 2 August 1921, (Chartwell 17/16).

168–169. "Policy and Finance . . . 1922–23" . . . "The Emir . . . Exchequer" . . . "But this . . . are inviolate": Churchill Cabinet Memorandum, 4 August 1921 (Chartwell 17/16).

169–170. "I am sorry . . . the estimates": Churchill to Lloyd George, 7 August 1921, (Lloyd George Papers).

170. bad news: Cox to Churchill, 4 August 1921, in Gilbert, *IV/3,* p. 1581.

170. "rather disquieting" . . . "encourage . . . frontier" . . . "Cairo . . . wreck it": Churchill to Lloyd George, 9 August 1921 (Lloyd George Papers)

170. Very fortunately for Churchill, such a nightmare alliance never took place. The Greek successes, though, were to be short-lived, and Lloyd George's strategically disastrous policy of supporting Greece against Kemal's nationalist forces would soon be causing the British government very major trouble indeed. One could also say, therefore, that it was just as well for Britain that Kemal's forces did not launch a frontal attack on the British-ruled parts of Kurdistan, since they might have been far from "badly organized," and militarily very successful. Fortunately, too, the British military in Mesopotamia did not share Sir Percy's "alarmist" views, regarding the Turkish border movement as no more than "pinpricks." Thankfully, they were proved right, and Churchill's other nightmare never happened.

170. Much has been written . . . conducted: for example, Dodge, *Inventing Iraq*, pp. 17–21; Abdullah, *A Brief History of Iraq*, p. 120; Tripp, *History of Iraq*, p. 48; and Kedourie, *The Chatham House Version*, p. 242.

171–172. "I hope . . . by you" . . . "I told him . . . Iraq Assembly": Churchill to Cox (not sent), 15 August 1921 (Chartwell 17/16).

172. "Independence . . . 1922": Keary, *the Wind Sowing*, pp. 111–123 for a great summary.

172–174. "It seems . . . himself" . . . "But I have . . . opportunity" . . . "His proper . . . the tune" . . . "My friend . . . hold you": Churchill to Cox, 15 August 1921 (Chartwell 17/16).

174. *Empires of the Sand:* Karsh and Karsh, p. 311.

195. "General Gouraud . . . trust them": Churchill to Cox, 15 August 1921 (Chartwell 17/16).

175. a version . . . to Sir Percy: Churchill to Cox, 15 August 1921 in CO 730/4, (National Archive).

175–176. "I hope . . . you so' " . . . "I am quite . . . thick & thin": version in Lloyd George Papers, 15 August 1921.

176. "Generally speaking . . . recover it": Cox to Churchill, in Gilbert, *Churchill IV,* p. 806.

176. When the Cabinet . . . if possible: Cabinet meeting, 18 August 1921, CAB 23/25, National Archive.

177. Cabinet Committee [on Iraq]: "he had just . . . the future" . . . "The High . . . autonomy" . . . "Although the Mandate . . . by the League": 19 August 1921, in CAB 23/27.

178. "must proceed . . . procedure . . . object": Churchill to Cox, 20 August 1921 (Chartwell 17/16).

178. "anxious . . . child": Fisher diary, 19 August 1921, *IV/3,* p. 1609.

178. "Feisal's objections . . . the Mandate": 19 August 1921 CAB 23/27, (National Archive).

179. "You should tell Feisal . . . as possible": Churchill to Cox, 20 August 1921 (Chartwell 17/16).

179. "you seem . . . family losses": Sir Abe Bailey to Churchill, 26 August 1921 (Chartwell 1/140).

180. "Mustapha Kemal . . . failure": Churchill Cabinet Memorandum, 26 September 1921 CAB 24/128, (National Archive).

181. "tribes are quiet": Gilbert, *Churchill IV,* p. 807.

181. memorandum on unemployment: Churchill Cabinet Memorandum, 28 September 1921, (Chartwell 22/7.

181. Lloyd George perplexed and irritated: Lloyd George to Churchill, 1 October 1921 (Chartwell 22/7).

181. "opposed to . . . Feisal": Balfour to Churchill, 5 October 1921, quoted in Gilbert, *Churchill IV,* p. 807.

181–182. "We shall have . . . been contemplated": Churchill reply to Balfour, 10 October 1921 (Chartwell 17/10).

182. Irish independence in 1922: For a marvelous account of Churchill's involvement, see Gilbert, *Churchill IV,* pp. 663–749.

182. "are of course . . . altogether": Churchill Cabinet Memorandum, 26 October 1921 (Chartwell 17/13).

182. "subject to . . . negotiations": Churchill to Curzon, 8 November 1921, in Gilbert, *IV/3,* p. 1664.

182. "Feisal . . . Kemal": Churchill to Cox, 11 November 1921 (Chartwell 17/16).

183. "would enormously . . . of Iraq": Gilbert, Gilbert,*Churchill IV,* p. 808.

183. "independent . . . alone" "in the . . . responsibility": Gilbert, *Churchill IV,* p. 809.

183–184. "I am . . . foreign questions": Churchill minute, 24 November 1921, CO 730/16.

184. "What is . . . next year". . . "there is . . . cost": Churchill Minute, 25 November 1921 (Chartwell 17/11).

184–185. "has only just . . . against them": Churchill to Cox, 28 November 1921, (CO 730/16).

185. "simply ridiculous": Wilson diary, 5 December 1921, quoted in Gilbert, *IV/3,* p. 1684.

185–186. "Latest War . . . local labour": Churchill to Cox and Haldane, 13 December 1921 (Chartwell 17/16).

186. . . . quoted in many recent books: Clive Ponting and John Simpson have criticized Churchill on television, Simpson during the 2003 Gulf War. See also Simons, *Sumer to Saddam,* p. 213, where he also quotes the Churchill memo below.

186. "If the people . . . antidotes": Meinertzhagen memorandum, 14 December 1921, quoted in Gilbert, *Churchill IV,* p. 810.

186. "I am ready . . . be supplied": Churchill Minute, CO 730/7.

187. "I can't understand . . . sneeze": Churchill Minute, 24 November 1921, (CO 730/7).

187. "obstruction . . . character": Churchill to Lloyd George (not sent), 28 January 1922 (Chartwell 17/27).

187. The issue . . . on 9 February: All this while Churchill was bogged down in dealing with problems of Indians living in Kenya—an issue not resolved until the Kenyan government brutally expelled them all in the 1970s.

187–188. "A fierce economy . . . cleared out": Churchill to Cox, 1 February 1922 (Chartwell 17/22).

188. "I do not wish . . . good solution": Churchill to Cox, 4 February 1922 (Chartwell 17/26).

188. The Cabinet Committee . . . on the 9th: Gilbert, *Churchill IV,* p. 811.

188–189. "No. Not a penny . . . Treaty with Iraq": *Ibid.,* p. 812.

189. "I asked . . . govern anything": T. E. Lawrence to his brother Bob, 14 February 1922, quoted in Gilbert, *IV/3,* p. 1775.

189. "right of foreign representation" . . . " puppet monarch" . . . "abominate" . . . "a mere . . . of tribes" . . . "Cabinet . . . made good": all from CAB 23/29.

190. "The people . . . interpretations . . . "a definite . . . alliance": *Churchill IV,* pp. 812–813.

190. "kind of . . . to him": *Ibid.,* p. 813.

190. The Iraq Committee . . . on the 14th: Fisher Diary, 14 March 1921, *IV/3,* p. 1807.

190–191. "the signature" . . . "had been . . . world" . . . "He had always

... in Mesopotamia" ... "pointed out ... Mesopotamia" ... "would rather ... the Turks": Cabinet Meeting, 20 March 1922 (CAB 23/29).

191. threatened to resign: Lloyd George to Frances Stevenson, 22 March 1922, in Gilbert, *IV/3*, pp. 1815–1816; Sir Philip Sassoon to Lloyd George, 24 March 1922, *ibid.*, p. 1826.

191. "misunderstanding" ... "I consider ... great war" ... ". . . Lawrence's influence": Churchill Cabinet Memorandum, 31 March 1922 (Chartwell 17/27).

192. "in so far ... weakness to me": Cox to Churchill, 4 April 1922, in Gilbert *Churchill IV,* p. 813.

192. "cause us ... future": Curzon to Lloyd George, 5 April 1922 (CAB 23/30).

192–194. "The British Government ... towards Iraq" ... "The meaning ... altogethr" ... Of Course, ... maintain order" ... "We therefore ... requires our aid" ... "Does he ... Great War": all from Churchill to Cox, 19 April 1922 (Chartwell 17/26).

192–194. "Feisal is most ... ultimatum": Churchill to Curzon, 24 April 1922 (Chartwell 1/157). Sir Percy Cox had floated the idea of Feisal visiting London to help break the deadlock.

195. "I cannot understand ... our Mandate": Churchill Memorandum on Iraq for Major Young, 3 May 1922, CO 730/21.

195–196. "it seems to me ... stormy period" ... "Well that ... any kind" ... "While ... I am necessary": T. E. Lawrence to Shuckburgh, 4 July 1922, in Gilbert, *IV/3*, p. 1925.

196. "I very much regret ... Arab Affairs": Churchill to Lawrence, 8 July 1921 (Chartwell 17/26).

196. "get out ... by Winston's bridge": Lawrence to the journalist R. D. Blumenfeld, 11 November 1922, *IV/3*, p. 2122.

195–197. "serious defects ... revealed" ... "it was decided ... forlorn hope": for the Bullard note and Cox comment, see Gilbert, *Churchill IV,* pp. 815–816.

197. "within a specified . . . without it": *Ibid.,* p. 816.

197. "was Feisal's . . . our part": Churchill note to Shuckburgh, 17 August 1922 (CO 730/23).

197. "Playing a vey low . . . about him": Churchill to Lloyd George, 24 August 1922, in Gibert, *IV/3,* p. 1966.

197–198. "I have learned . . . have received. . . from what date?": Churchill to Feisal (not sent), 17 August 1922 (Chartwell 17/25).

199. "No argument . . . Iraq" . . . "the extremists" . . . "quite unfitted . . . bad administration": Cabinet meeting of 28 August 1922, CAB 23/31.

199. look at this differently. . . . : for example, Simons, *Sumer to Saddam,* pp. 211–217; Abdullah, *Brief History,* p. 130.

200–201. "I am deeply . . . revenue" . . . "I have to . . . anxiety to me" . . . "I do not . . . country". . . . "The enormous . . . my resources" . . . "I think we. . . special study": Churchill to Lloyd George, 1 September 1921 (Chartwell 17/27). Sadly, the Kurds would beg strongly to differ here, for had Britain pulled out of the bulk of Iraq but stayed in the Mosul *vilayet,* the Kurds might never have ended up a constituent part of the new Iraqi state, since their status in the mandate area was not finalized by the League of Nations. Of small sentences do major decisions come. . . .

201–202. "It is quite possible . . . misfortune" . . . "Surveying . . . worth having": Churchill to Lloyd George, 1 September 1921 (Chartwell 17/27).

203. "The Greeks . . . little sympathy": Churchill to Curzon, 5 September 1922, in Gilbert, *IV/3,* p. 1977.

203–204. "The whole problem . . . Mesopotamia" . . . "Strategically . . . chosen battle-ground" . . . "Whatever . . . been avoided". . . . "It was quite clear . . . Mohammedan world": Lloyd George to Churchill, 5 September 1922 (Chartwell 17/27). This was vital in light of the tens of millions of Muslims over whom Britain ruled in what is now India, Pakistan, and

Bangladesh, not to mention Islamic parts of Africa such as Zanzibar. As we have seen, this was also an issue of great importance to Churchill.

204–205. "Having beaten the Turks . . . govern them ourselves" . . . "Feisal has responded . . . courageously" . . . "If we have failed . . . put the alternatives": Lloyd George to Churchill, 5 September 1922 (Chartwell 17/27).

206–207. "Turkey was prostrate . . . the Turks". . . . "Such a peace . . . cope with them" . . . "At the same time . . . Baghdad itself" . . . "This crisis . . . important matters": Churchill to Lloyd George, 6 September 1922, *ibid.* It was, though, primarily the advice of the British that was to matter increasingly in Iraq, however "constitutional" Churchill intended the country to be. This was to be the worst of both worlds, since Britain was to get the blame, but did not actually rule the country itself. Indirect rule, always a British favorite, from the Raj in India through to countries such as Swaziland in Africa or the Malay States in Asia, was a high-risk strategy, especially if the local ruler turned out to be unsatisfactory.

207. Sir Martin Gilbert: in *Churchill IV,* pp. 818–819.

207. "Like you . . . to avoid it": Churchill to Lloyd George, 6 September 1922 (Chartwell 17/27).

207. on 7 September: Cabinet meeting (CAB 23/31).

207. "a bad hat": Curzon to Churchill, 12 September 1922 (Chartwell 17/27).

207–208. "Before bringing . . . anchor" . . . "wealth . . . at each stage": Churchill to Curzon, 14 September 1922 (Chartwell 17/27).

208. War was distinctly possible: Churchill had been wise not to risk war with Turkey. However, it was a failure to do precisely that at Chanak in the Dardanelles and Conservative refusal to contemplate a Turco–British war that were about to remove Lloyd George from for the rest of his life.

208. Major Hubert Young: in Gilbert, *Churchill IV,* p. 824.

208. "You must . . . Asia Minor horizon": *Ibid.,* p. 824.

209. "This draft Treaty . . . Treaty relations" . . . "The Arabs . . . League of Nations": Cabinet Minutes, 5 October 1922 (CAB 23/31).

209. Churchill did not . . . there wasn't one: Not until 1932 would Iraq get its full independence, and even then there were to be considerable numbers of strings attached.

209–210. "King Feisal . . . extremists" . . . "It had been . . . sign the Treaty" . . . "The moment . . . Turkish attack": Cabinet Minutes, 5 October 1922 (CAB 23/31).

211. "latest news . . . collision inevitable": Major Young to Churchill, 6 October 1922 (CO 730/34).

211–212. "The Treaty . . . two years ago" . . . "The view . . . right one to adopt": Cabinet Minutes, 5 October 1922 (CAB 23/31).

Chapter 7: From Feisal to Saddam

218. Thabit Abdullah: see *A Brief History of Iraq,* pp. x–xv for a superb chronology, and pp. xxi–xxii and 123–215.

218. Charles Tripp: see *A History of Iraq,* pp. x–xv for another superb chronology, and pp. 3–385 for the history of the British-created state.

218. Geoff Simons: see *Sumer to Post-Saddam,* pp. 181–399.

218. Elie Kedourie: see *The Chatham House Version,* pp. 236–285.

INDEX

ABOUT THE AUTHOR

Christopher Catherwood is an historian and writer based in Cambridge, England, and Richmond, Virginia. He is married to musicologist Paulette Moore Catherwood, from Virginia, and both he and his wife teach for the Institute of Continuing Education of Cambridge University. He also teaches history for the School of Continuing Studies at University of Richmond in Virginia and spends each summer there as a Writer in Residence for their History Department. In addition, Catherwood teaches twentieth century history for INSTEP, a Tulane University affiliated study abroad program in Cambridge. He is the author of several books, notably *Christians, Muslims and Islamic Rage; The Balkans in World War Two;* and *Why the Nations Rage.*

Christopher has also been a consultant to Tony Blair's former Strategy Unit's Strategic Futures Team, where he worked in the building used by Churchill as First Lord of the Admiralty in the First and Second World Wars. He holds degrees from Oxford and Cambridge Universities, and has been a Rockefeller Fellow at the University of Virginia's Virginia Foundation for the Humanities and Public Policy.